Essays in Contemporary Economics

George C. Bitros • Nicholas C. Kyriazis
Editors

Essays in Contemporary Economics

A Festschrift in Memory of A. D. Karayiannis

Springer

Editors
George C. Bitros
Department of Economics
Athens University of Economics
& Business
Athens
Greece

Nicholas C. Kyriazis
Department of Economics
University of Thessaly
Volos
Greece

ISBN 978-3-319-10042-5 ISBN 978-3-319-10043-2 (eBook)
DOI 10.1007/978-3-319-10043-2
Springer Cham Heidelberg New York Dordrecht London

Library of Congress Control Number: 2014956664

Printed on acid-free paper

Springer is part of Springer Science+Business Media (www.springer.com)

Preface

Our friend, colleague, trusted co-author and associate Anastasios D. Karayiannis, or Tassos as his friends called him, passed away in January 2012 and was buried in his beloved island of Aegina, where he was born, grew up and lived with his family. In the years leading to his death, almost every day we spent a lot of time discussing the big issues we researched and wrote about, and our discussions provided us with great comfort and intellectual stimulation. Contrary to the common saying that life is like a leaf in the wind and that death erases everything, Tassos sowed a lot of good seeds in his life, which, we are sure, bear sweet fruits for all the students he taught over the years and all those who read his papers in the various fields of economics that he enriched.

Taking the liberty of a personal note, I should like to point out that we had planned a lot of research and writing. Having retired and running well into my 70s, I was working hard. George, he used to tell me, slow down because I cannot follow your frantic pace. He understood that I was in a hurry, as the horizon of my productive life was catching up with me, and we had to complete our research agenda. On probabilistic grounds I expected that I would pass away first and he, like the firm believer in democracy and the free market economy that he was, would continue to fight for their revival in our own country and beyond. Unfortunately, the fate that controls the future of us all wished it differently. He passed away first and now I and all those who shared similar views with him have to shoulder this burden without his companionship. But the battle for these ideals continues and every contribution for their advancement should be welcome. At least this was our motivation when in 2009 we started to write our book about the raging crisis in democracy and the free market economy, all around the world and particularly in Greece. From the Greek edition of this book, nothing I think would reflect more accurately his convictions than the following excerpts:

> "Experience over the millennia suggests that democracy and free market economy are continuously reborn through an eternal sequence of crises. In the uncertain world we live, this is a painful process accompanied by significant advantages. In particular, democracy and free market economy receive disturbances from natural disasters, wars, government mistakes, technological revolutions, citizen weaknesses, etc., and transform them in a most

> creative manner, since in the countries where democracy and free market economy take roots individual rights are protected and per capita material prosperity increases.
>
> This conclusion holds also today. Due to the proximity and severity of the present crisis, we tend to think that it is unprecedented. Yet, when in a few years the disturbances subside, democracies will function more effectively, domestic and world markets will diffuse the goods and services of new technologies to more distant places, and above all individual liberties will be enjoyed by more people and in more countries than ever before in human history. In essence this is the message of hope that our book seeks to send to all those who agonise about the future."

Had he lived just 1 more year, he would have been extremely pleased to read the same above testament in the English edition of our book.

As an academic, Tassos focused his teaching and research in the history of economic theory. But his intellectual interests were much wider and spanned several other fields of economics. Among the latter, entrepreneurship, education, and the role of institutions in economic growth were the ones that became the mainstay of our cooperation. To the common effort, he contributed sparingly his vast knowledgeable of the ancient Greek literature and his knack for meticulous documentation, and he felt very happy when finally the letters of acceptance arrived from the publishers and journal editors. Tassos was not the typical Greek academic. He was devoted to teaching and research and none of the frivolous temptations of everyday life could distract his attention from the higher purposes he had set to accomplish in his life. That is why, for us and all his friends, his passing was a true loss.

The present volume consists of papers that were presented in a conference held late in 2013 in the facilities of the University of Thessaly in Volos. We have organized them into four parts under the headings "Greece and European integration," "Issues in the methodology of economics," "Institutions and the free market economy," and "Insights for today from ancient Greece." In the first part, George C. Bitros and Jurgen G. Backhaus look at the structural as well as international financial and monetary issues that have emerged from the recent economic crisis in Greece. In particular, the former author raises and attempts to answer the following question: Given that the Greek economy was structurally unprepared to withstand the shocks from entering into the European Union (EU) in 1981 and into the Eurozone in 2001, how can we explain the failure of EU authorities to hold Greece accountable long before it went bankrupt in 2009? As for the latter author, after drawing attention to the huge public debt in the USA, which prevents raising the nominal interest rates much above their present levels, he goes on to describe a proposal for handling the problem of Greece that may be Pareto optimal in the sense of minimizing the consequences from its bankruptcy to both the USA and the EU.

Part II includes five papers with main focus in the methodology of economics. In the first paper, Stavros A. Drakopoulos argues that, apart from establishing the physics scientific ideal in economics, Edgeworth and Fisher influenced the formation of many key components of current mainstream economics such as use of mathematics, aversion to methodological issues, and anti-psychologism. The next two papers by Michael S. Zouboulakis and Sarah D. Dodd highlight the theoretical and historical underpinnings of the notion of the firm and its emergence in the form of modern enterprises. The context in the former paper is the writings of Adam Smith and John Stuart Mill, whereas the inquiry in the latter paper is set in Protestant England during the three centuries from 1600 to 1900. In the following paper Cosimo Perrotta looks at the conceptual weaknesses but also the fresh insights that can be gained from the analysis of the stationary sate. He concludes that on the way to that state inequality may be reduced and other forms of production, aside from those based on profit and competition, may emerge. This explains also why to us as editors it appeared very natural to close this part with the paper by Panagiotis G. Korliras, which focuses on the issues of inequality and social justice in the writings of Leon Walras.

Part III contains three papers which address aspects of institutions either from an analytical-functional perspective or from the perspective of the evolutionary-historical process through which they emerged. In the first paper Carl H. Lyttkens reports on his experiences to defend his ownership rights on a piece of land in front of a regional court in Sweden. In the heart of his story lies bounded rationality and he establishes that, even in the courts of a very advance society, decision making under imperfect and limited information may lead to surprising results. The second paper by Elias Katsoulis is extremely well-timed because it comes in the middle of an international debate regarding Piketty's recent book on the distribution of the wealth in the world. His is a totally different conclusion, by submitting that the institutions of free world markets may hurt temporarily middle classes in advanced societies, but they favor middles classes in emerging countries. In the last paper in this part, Ioanna-Sapfo Pepelasis and Angeliki Tzavara trace the path from rags to great riches of a Greek moneylender in Venice in the first half of the nineteenth century. Costantino Bogdano from Patras made it big, we learn, by acting as credit facilitator, and hence economic growth promoter, in the tradition of the famous Venetian bankers, but with a human face towards his associates, clients, and the society in general.

Finally, in Part IV we placed four papers, all of which have a common thread. Namely, they describe the functioning and assess the performance of various institutions in ancient Greece with an eye toward the problems faced by cotemporary democracies. In the first paper Paschalis A. Arvanitidis and Nicholas C. Kyriazis make a strong case for the optimal properties of direct democracy in the form of "...equitable distribution of political powers, credible protection of property rights, innovative creation and dissemination of knowledge (i.e. fairly symmetric information), expediency in interaction and cooperation (i.e. low transaction costs), and effective coordination and alignment of interests, all of which are essential for collective action towards growth and prosperity." The following paper by Nicholas C. Kyriazis, Xenophon Paparrigopoulos, and Emmanouil-Marios L. Economou explains the values which are necessary for direct democracy to take roots and yield its wonderful results. The authors are able to trace the origins of these values in the settings of the Phalanx and Triremes and they attribute much of the success of ancient Athens to their optimal adaptation in the governance of the city-state of Athens. Supportive of this argument is also the next paper, where Constantine Collmer highlights why and how the same values were adapted in the establishment of a free market economy as a necessary but not sufficient condition of direct democracy. Lastly, Part IV closes with the paper by Christos Baloglou. In it the author turns his attention to the evolution of the ancient institution of "Syssitia" up to early Christian times and assesses their role as a potent mechanism in the fair distribution of wealth.

The group of distinguished scholars who took part in the conference knew Tassos in person and joined us to mark his passing and to contribute with their papers to his lasting memory. We thank them all and hope that the quality of the volume meets their expectations.

We are particularly thankful to the authors who traveled from abroad and gave us the pleasure to enjoy their company and inspirational discussions.

Finally, we extend our thanks and sincere appreciation to the faculty and the secretarial staff of the University of Thessaly, Department of Economics, in Volos, for hosting the conference and contributing significantly to its success, as well as to the Society for Economic Research and the Kyriazis Foundation for making the conference possible through two small grants.

Athens, Greece
Volos, Greece
2014

George C. Bitros
Nicholas C. Kyriazis

Contents

Part I Greece and European Integration

1 **European Union Failures in Greece and Some Possible Explanations** 3
George C. Bitros

2 **Some Thoughts on Greece from a European Perspective** 23
Jürgen G. Backhaus

Part II Issues in the Methodology of Economics

3 **The Physics Scientific Ideal in the Works of Edgeworth and Fisher** 31
Stavros A. Drakopoulos

4 **Elements of a Theory of the Firm in Adam Smith and John Stuart Mill** 45
Michel S. Zouboulakis

5 **The Birth of Modern Enterprise Theology: Protestant England: 1600–1900** 53
Sarah Drakopoulou Dodd

6 **The Stationary State: Deadlocks and New Perspectives** 75
Cosimo Perrotta

7 **Leon Walras on Social Justice** 91
Panagiotis G. Korliras

Part III Institutions and the Free Market System

8 Surprising Institutions 103
Carl Hampus Lyttkens

9 The Middle Class and the Market 117
Elias Katsoulis

10 A Moneylender in Venice: Costantino Bogdano 'da Patrasso', c. 1800–1844 127
Ioanna-Sapfo Pepelasis and Angeliki Tzavara

Part IV Insights for Today from Ancient Greece

11 The Qualities and Workings of Direct Democracy: Lessons from Classical Athens 161
Paschalis A. Arvanitidis and Nicholas C. Kyriazis

12 The Glue of Democracy: Economics, Warfare and Values in Classical Greece 175
Nicholas C. Kyriazis, Xenophon Paparrigopoulos, and Emmanouil-Marios L. Economou

13 Civic Market and Sortition Democracy 191
Constantine Collmer

14 Fair Distribution of Wealth: From the Greek Syssitia to the Dinners of Love 199
Christos P. Baloglou

Author Index 221

Subject Index 227

About the Authors

Paschalis A. Arvanitidis Currently Assistant Professor of Institutional Economics at the Department of Economics (University of Thessaly) and a visiting professor of Urban Economics and Development at the Department of Planning and Regional Development (of the same institution). He is an engineer and an economist with specialization in institutional economics, spatial economics, and economic development. His research interests include institutional economics with an emphasis on methodology and economic development at a local, regional, and national level. He holds membership in seven professional organizations and since 2004 he has participated in many EU and nationally funded research projects related to regional and local development. He has published on similar matters in international and national refereed journals.

Jürgen G. Backhaus Jürgen G. Backhaus (1950), JSD 1976, PhD (Econ) 1985, holds the Krupp Chair in Public Finance and Fiscal Sociology at Erfurt University since November 2000. Between 1986 and 2000, he held the chair in Public Economics at Maastricht University. In 2006 he received the Cross of the Order of Merit of the Federal Republic of Germany (Knight's Cross); in September 2004 he was awarded an honorary doctorate by the University of Thessaly (Greece). He has published more than 70 books and monographs, about 200 articles in refereed journals and book chapters, and more than 30 scholarly notes and 70 reviews. His research interests span economics, but also neighboring disciplines such as law, fiscal sociology, and environmental sciences. In 1994 he founded (with Frank H. Stephen) the European Journal of Law and Economics, of which he is now the only editor. He is also the editor of the book series *The European Heritage in Economics and the Social Sciences* (Springer), *Essays on Fiscal Sociology* (Lang), and, since 1978, *Frankfurt Contributions to the Sciences of State* (Haag+Herchen).

His five most important book publications are:

Handbook of the History of Economic Thought: Insights on the Founders of Modern Economics, New York: Springer, 2010 (in print); *Elgar Companion to Law and Economics*, Cheltenham: Edward Elgar, 1999, 2002 (2nd); *Modern Applications of Austrian Thought*, Oxon: Routledge, 2005; with Richard E. Wagner: *The*

Handbook of Public Finance, Boston: Kluwer, 2004; and—in the works—*Dictionary of Law and Economics*, to be published by Edward Elgar.

Christos P. Baloglou Christos P. Baloglou (13.7.1962) studied Economics (B.Sc., M.A. in Econ., Ph.D.) and Pedagogics (B.Sc.). He is a prominent author with a long list of respected publications in international scholarly journals in Greece and abroad. He has specialized in Economic History and History of Economic Thought and his main fields of research are Ancient Greek and Byzantine Economic History and Thought, Mathematical Economics in the Nineteenth Century, and Economic Thought in the Nineteenth Century Greece, especially the influences of Liberalism and Saint-Simonism on the Greek intellectuals. He is working in recent years on the Economics of the New Testament. His books have been praised by the Academy of Athens.

George C. Bitros He obtained his Ph.D. in economics from New York University in 1972 and he stayed on for teaching and research until 1976. In that year he returned to Greece in the position of Senior Research Associate in the Bank of Greece and 3 years later he moved on to the Athens University of Economics and Business where he served as Professor of Economics until his retirement in 2007. He has published extensively in major scholarly journals. He has served as research associate in the National Bureau of Economic Research (USA). He has held advisory posts in government, government commissions, and major business concerns, and he referees for several international journals.

Constantine Collmer He serves as editorial journalist for the weekly EPIKAIRA and monthly NEA POLITIKI, both political and financial journals. At the undergraduate level, he studied law, politics, and economics in the National and Kapodistrian University of Athens, whereas at the graduate level he studied economics at UCLA. Over the years he has worked for almost every Athenian newspaper, covering primarily financial issues. In the last 14 years he has written extensively regarding the folly of Greece joining the EMU and in each of the last 10 years he has authored a book on economic and political subjects pertaining to Greece, which have been published by Livanis publishers of Athens.

Sarah Drakopoulou Dodd She is Professor of Enterprise and Small Business at Middlesex University, Associate Professor of Entrepreneurship at ALBA Graduate School of Business (Athens, Greece), and Academic Director of AHEAD, the ALBA Hub for Enterprise and Development. Her research focuses on the impact of sociocultural factors on the quality and quantity of entrepreneurship, especially the processes and structures of entrepreneurial networks. Dr Dodd has also studied alternative entrepreneurship, growth strategies, family business, and cross-cultural conceptualizations of the entrepreneur. An additional research stream includes the relationships between theology, religion and entrepreneurship, with special emphasis on the history of entrepreneurship thought within religious movements. Dr. Dodd's research has been published in leading entrepreneurship and management journals, including the Journal of Business Venturing, Entrepreneurship Theory and Practice, Management Decision, the Scandinavian Journal of Management, Entrepreneurship and Regional Development, the International Small Business Journal, the Family Business Review, and the International Journal of Entrepreneurship and Innovation.

Stavros A. Drakopoulos Professor Drakopoulos obtained a B.A. in economics from The Economics University of Athens and an M.Sc. and Ph.D. in economics from the University of Stirling, UK. He was a Teaching Assistant (1986–1988) at the University of Stirling, Lecturer A (1988–1989) at the University of Glasgow, Lecturer B (1990–1996) at the University of Aberdeen, Assistant Professor (1996–2000), and Associate Professor (2000–2005) at the University of Athens. He is currently a full Professor of Economics in the Department of Philosophy and History of Science of the University of Athens (since September 2005). His research interests include Economic Methodology and History of Economic Thought, Labour Economics and Subjective Well-being, and Alternative Theories of Choice. He has 44 scientific publications in refereed journals, 2 books, 11 articles in edited books and encyclopedias including books published by Routledge, Edward Elgar, and Springer, and 14 Book Reviews.

Emmanouil Marios L. Economou At present he is a graduate of the Department of Economics, University of Thessaly in Greece (2004). In 2010 he took his M.Sc. on *Applied Economics* at the same university. He is currently a Ph.D. candidate at the Department of Economics, University of Thessaly in Greece. His research focuses on the relationship between Economics, Institutions, and Warfare. His research areas also include Economic History and Defence Economics. He has already published five papers in international academic journals and a handbook and he has participated in many conferences.

Elias Katsoulis He studied Political Science in Otto-Suhr Institute at the Free University of Berlin. He holds his Ph.D. from the same university. In 1980 fulfilled his habitation at the Panteion University of Social and Political Science/Athens, where he was elected Professor by the Department of Political Science. Until 2004 he was Professor of Political Sociology at the Panteion University. He was also a visiting professor in FU-Berlin and the National and Kapodistrian University of Athens. He is the author, among others, of "Socialism and the State" (1975, in German) and "The Return of Politics. Financial Market Capitalism and 'New Globalization'" (2012, in Greek). He was the director of the National Centre of Social Research in Greece (1990–1993). He is the editor of the scientific Journal "Science and Society."

Panagiotis G. Korliras He was born in Athens in 1946. He earned his Ph.D. from the University of Rochester in the USA and was professor at the Department of Economics of the Athens University of Economics and Business from 1978 until 2013. His areas of expertise are macroeconomics and monetary theory and policy.

For the previous 15 years he was also teaching the "History of Economic Thought" course. He has published many articles in journals as well as books, including "Modern Macroeconomics" (co-edited with R. Thorn, New York 1979) and (in Greek) the "Theories of Unemployment and Inflation" (1979), "Economic Justice" (1982), "Philosophy of Political Economy" (1991), "The Quest of Economic Order-Essays in the History and Philosophy of Political Economy" (2003), and "Monetary Theory and Policy" (third enlarged edition 2006). In the period 2010–2013 he served as Chairman and Scientific Director of the Centre of Planning and Economic Research (KEPE) in Athens.

Nicholas C. Kyriazis combines academic and business experience. He took his diploma and Ph.D. in Economics in Bonn University Germany and has been a visiting Professor at Harvard and Trier Universities. He is currently Professor and Chairman at the Economics Department, University of Thessaly, Greece. Previous business positions he has held include Directorate General for Research of the European Parliament, advisor to the government of the National Bank of Greece, and advisor to the Minister of Finance and secretary General of Public Administration. He was also an advisor of the Hellenic Minister of Defence since 1998 and one of the major consultants for the Greek Command, Control, Communications, Computers and Military intelligence (C4I). He is currently chairman of the board, Alpha-Trust-Andromeda Investment Fund (listed in the Athens Stock Exchange), Vice President of Ergoman Telecommunications (a service providing company), Vice President of "Black Orange" (a movie producing company), and the President of the "Kostas Kyriazis" foundation. He has published about 30 papers in international academic journals (15 on institutional issues and on various aspects of direct democracy) and 5 books on economics and strategy. He is also one of Greece's well-known novelists with 16 novels published in Greece and 3 also in English. In 2005 the President of the French Republic honored him with France's highest decoration, the Knight of the Legion of Honour (Chevalier de la Legion d' Honneur), for his contribution to the European integration of the EMU. He is currently Chairman of the Economics Department, University of Thessaly, Greece.

Carl Hampus Lyttkens He is Professor of Economics at Lund University, Sweden, since 2000. Lyttkens was born in 1955, received his Ph.D. in Economics in 1985, and became Docent in 1992. Most of the 1990s he was Senior research fellow at the Swedish Medical Research Council. Lyttkens' main research interests are: 1) New institutional economics applied to the ancient Greek economy; 2) Health economics, including income differences and health, globalization and health, education and health, and behavior and incentives in public health care. He is currently responsible for three major externally financed research projects. He has organized several international conferences and teaches and supervises students regularly both at the undergraduate and Ph.D. levels. His publications include more than 40 articles in international peer-reviewed journals, and he recently published *An Economic Analysis of Institutional Change in Ancient Greece* on Routledge.

Xenophon Paparrigopoulos He was born in Athens and he studied law at the Law School of the University of Athens (1980); he subsequently obtained an LL.M. (1981) and an S.J.D. (1984) degree from Harvard Law School, specializing in jurisprudence and the philosophy of law. Between the years 1987 and 1991 he taught at the Panteion University (Athens) an introductory course in law, a course on theories of justice, as well as political anthropology and philosophy. In 1995 he joined the faculty of the University of Thessaly as Assistant Professor of philosophy, history, methodology, and general theory of law. He now teaches introduction to law, commercial law, and law and economics. He also teaches medical ethics at the Medical School of the University of Thessaly. In the past he has taught in several Departments of the University of Thessaly a number of courses, covering topics of law, ethics, and legal philosophy. His doctoral thesis, entitled "Family, Law and Society," was published in 1993. He is the author of one more book on the "Rule of Law" (1988) and a number of articles. His current research focuses on the theory of human rights and the economic analysis of law. Since 1989 he is a member of the Scientific Service of the Hellenic Parliament.

Ioanna-Sapfo Pepelasis (BA Harvard University, Ph.D., London School of Economics) is Associate Professor of Economic History at the Department of Economics at Athens University of Economics and Business. She has co-edited Diaspora Entrepreneurial Networks: Four Centuries of History (Berg, 2005), Entrepreneurship in Theory and History (Palgrave, Macmillan 2005), Country Studies in Entrepreneurship. A Historical Perspective (Palgrave Macmillan, 2006), and European Banking Historiography: Past and Present (Alpha Bank, 2009). She has published articles in international edited volumes and refereed journals. She has received a prize from the Ottoman Bank Archive in 2003. She heads the "History of entrepreneurship and the Greek corporate sector" project at the Athens University of Economics and Business. She has served on the Councils of the European Business History Association and the European Association of Evolutionary Political Economy. She has also served as a member of the board of the directors of the Greek Centre for Planning and Economic Research.

Cosimo Perrotta Former professor of History of Economic Thought. He has served as Council Chair of the European Society for the History of Economic Thought (2002–2006). He has published articles in *History of Political Economy*, *European Journal History of Economic Thought*, *History of Economic Ideas*, *History of Economic Thought and Policy*, *History of Economics Review*, *Moneta e Credito*, *Banca Nazionale Lavoro Quarterly Review*, *Rivista italiana economisti*, *Journal of Economic Asymmetries*, etc. He was a referee/invited reviewer of the above journals and others, and of Italian Ministry of Research (CINECA). He has published with Routledge, Elgar, Kluwer, Wirtschaft und Finanzen, il Mulino, Biblioteca Complutense, Bruno Mondadori, etc. Among his books are *Consumption as an Investment*, Routledge; *L'arretratezza del Mezzogiorno*, with Claudia Sunna and others, Bruno Mondadori. He was an invited/key speaker, in the last 5 years, at

Coimbra, Athens, Tokyo (Sophia University), Mexico City (UNAM; Eshet Conference; Colegio de México), Rome (Ecole française; Accademia dei Lincei), Milan, Tokyo, Waseda University.

Angeliki Tzavara She studied in Greece and then in France, where, in 2004, she obtained her Ph.D. at the University of Paris I Panthéon—Sorbonne. The thesis subject was "Clarentza: a Medieval City of the Latin Morea (second half of the XIIIth-first half of the XVth centuries" (in French), published in 2008. She carried out research at the Venetian State Archives and also at those of Florence and Turin. She now lives near Venice and collaborates with the Hellenic Institute of Venice in various editorial and research projects. She is also an associated member of the French Research Centre (CNRS). Her scientific interests are related mainly to the Latin Orient. She has published two books and various articles concerning the history of the Principality of Achaia, the Venetian colonies in Greece, the Venetian trade in the Orient, and the Greeks in Venice. She has participated in various international congresses on these subjects in Europe and the USA.

Michel Zouboulakis Ph.D. (Economics) and M.Sc. (DEA in History and Philosophy of Economics), University of Paris 1, B.Sc. (Economics) University of Thessaloniki. Currently he is Professor in the History and Methodology of Economics, in the Department of Economics at the University of Thessaly, Greece. He is the author of *La science économique à la recherche de ses fondements. La tradition épistémologique ricardienne, 1826–1891* (Paris: Presses Universitaires de France, 1993), of a textbook on Economic Methodology (University of Thessaly Press, 2007) and of a recent book *The varieties of economic rationality: from Adam Smith to contemporary behavioural and evolutionary economics* (London: Routledge 2014). He has also published articles in international peer-reviewed journals such as *European Journal of the History of Economic Thought, Journal of the History of Economic Thought, Journal of Economic Methodology, Economies et Sociétés, History of Economic Ideas, cahiers d'economie politique, Revue Economique, Journal of Institutional Economics, Forum for Social Economics, Communist and Post-communist Economic Studies*, and *European Journal of Law and Economics.*

Part I
Greece and European Integration

Chapter 1
European Union Failures in Greece and Some Possible Explanations

George C. Bitros

1.1 Introduction

Prior to 1974 Greece achieved: high economic growth rates ($\approx$7 %); remarkable price stability (<2.5 %), which enhanced the international competitiveness of Greek products and services and maintained the balance of payments under manageable control; enviable reduction of unemployment (<2.5 %); significant improvement and expansion of social services; and it achieved all these results by incurring a very limited public debt (<12.5 % of GDP in 1974). After 1974, economic growth fell to about one third ($\approx$2.4 %) and the unemployment rate more than doubled in the period 1980 ($\approx$6 %), while in the decade of 2000 it nearly quadrupled ($\approx$9 %). The explosive deficits in the Balance of Payments were contained only thanks to large EU aid, and the budget deficits carried public debt to unsustainable heights ($\approx$150 % of GDP in 2011). So now Greece is under the supervision and tutelage of her creditors.

Some economists may think that the setback happened because, before 1974, the Greek economy was nearly "closed", whereas after its accession to EU membership in 1981 it opened to international competition.[1] But the setback was mostly due to three groups of other factors. The first and most significant has to do with the

In arriving at the present version of this paper I benefited significantly from the insightful comments and editorial suggestions of D. Katsoudas P. Vourloumis and A. Volbert, as well as discussions with S. Manos, P. Mihas and M. Pelt. To all of them I should like to extend my sincere appreciation. However, all responsibility for errors of fact of interpretation rests with me.

[1] The European Union (EU) has evolved in many directions. Two of them are the number of participating countries (e.g., EU6 refers to the six founding member-countries) and the nature of the union from an economic point view (e.g., the European Economic Community (EEC) was a

G.C. Bitros
Department of Economics, Athens University of Economics and Business, 76 Patision Street, Athens 10434, Greece
e-mail: bitros@aueb.gr

G.C. Bitros, N.C. Kyriazis (eds.), *Essays in Contemporary Economics*,
DOI 10.1007/978-3-319-10043-2_1

resistance of Greek governments in introducing structural reforms in line with the "economic constitution" of the EU, i.e. the Treaty of Rome, particularly after 1975. The second is associated with the inefficiencies that took hold in the domain of public administration and the wider public sector; and, lastly, the third group of negative factors relates to the specific economic policies that were implemented.[2]

This paper addresses the following issue: Greece signed an Association Agreement with the EEC in 1961; this aimed at full membership within 22 years.[3] The agreement was partially frozen for 7 years (1967–1974) at the initiative of the EEC Commission as a reaction to the military regime that assumed power in Greece in 1967. It was re-entered into force upon the restoration of parliamentary democracy in 1974. Subsequently, Greece became a full member of the EEC in 1979 and of the European Monetary Union (EMU) in 2000.[4] As noted above, in the course of these years Greece went from riches to rags. Most certainly the major share of the blame should be attributed to the failures of the authorities in Greece herself. But should the EU be absolved of all responsibility for what has happened? The objective here is to search for an answer.

Section 1.2 pursues two tasks: First, it explains the challenges Greece faced at the time the Association Agreement was concluded in 1961; and, second, it assesses the effectiveness with which Greek governments dealt with these challenges, as well as the initiatives the EU authorities took to assist Greece in preparing for full membership in the 22 years that this agreement allowed. Sections 1.3 and 1.4 take up the same tasks as above for the periods of full membership and since 2000 when Greece acceded to the EMU. Then, in view the calamities that befell Greece in recent years, Sect. 1.5 poses and attempts to shed light on the following questions: If Greece was unprepared in 1981, and the evidence shows overwhelmingly that it was, why did the EU grant Greece a full membership status? Given that, from a structural point of view, the economy of Greece in the period 1981–2001 was even worse than in the period 1961–1981,[5] why did the EU give Greece the green light

---

custom union). Henceforth I shall refer generally to EU and to particular abbreviations like EEC only when needed for reasons of emphasis.

[2] For reasons that have become subject of very intensive research, during the 1970s and 1980s western economies experienced a significant productivity slowdown. I have been advised that this may have contributed to the slowdown of economic growth in Greece. If it did, in all probability its influence should have been minimal.

[3] In the preamble to the Agreement of Association the contracting parties recognize that "The support given by the EEC to the Greek nation's efforts to improve its standard of living will eventually facilitate the accession of Greece to the Community." Furthermore, the contracting parties agreed to consider the possibility of accession: "when the operation of the Association Agreement makes it possible to envisage the integral acceptance by Greece of the obligations under the Treaty establishing the European Economic Community [GB: they meant the Treaty of Rome]." (Article 72)

[4] The treaties of Greece's accession to the EEC and to the Eurozone were ratified in 1979 and 2000, and came into force in 1981 and 2002.

[5] After 1974 Greece progressed further into a statist country. Gwartney and Lawson (2006) find, for example, that from 1980 to 2008 Greece with respect to: (a) property rights protection, fell the

for the EMU? Since EU experts knew fully well after 2001 what was coming in view of the procrastination of Greek governments to adopt the necessary structural reforms, why did they not react on time but waited, instead, until after the crisis erupted? Finally, Sect. 1.6 summarises the findings and draws some conclusions.

1.2 1961–1981: What Went Wrong That the EU Authorities Ignored

The tariff regime that the Association Agreement established was favourable for Greece. In particular, the Agreement created a declining tariff advantage over a period of 12 years, which was designed to bring about two results: First, to give the Greek economy time to start growing through increased exports to the Community, and hence with lesser constraints to her Balance of Payments, and, second, to adjust to the more competitive countries of the EU, thus enabling it to stand on its own in the face of the demanding conditions within the Community. Eichengreen (2007), Georgakopoulos (2002) and many other researchers have found that the agreement yielded favourable effects for Greece, since it helped the products of her traditional industrial sectors gain shares in the EU markets and perhaps it contributed also to her rapid economic growth over this period. However, when the usefulness of the Association was debated in the late 1950s, the issues regarding exports were neither the only issue nor the most important. The main focus of the debate was on the structural reforms that Greece would have to adopt in order to integrate smoothly into the Community within the 22 years of adjustment that were provided for in the agreement. To ascertain beyond any doubt that this was the case, here is how Papandreou (1962) summed up the challenge that Greece confronted at the time:

> Greece has recently concluded an Association Agreement with the European Common Market with the prospect of full membership some 22 years hence. It is fair to say that, given the terms of the association, Greece has a small margin of time in which to achieve the structural transformations needed for survival in the European Common Market. (p. 25)

Moreover, regarding the nature and range of the "structural transformations" that were needed, Papandreou (1962) was certain that these ought to be oriented towards the social and economic envisaged by the Treaty of Rome. Below is a sample of the reforms he considered urgent for Greece's survival, not just in the Custom Union of EEC, but in the expected economic union, the "European Common Market":

> There is a pressing need to streamlining the presently cumbersome "system" of government regulation of economic activity. In some sense there is "too much" government on the

50th position from the 25th; (b) the conditions for commerce, mainly towards third countries, tumbled to the 80th position from the 39th; and (c) state regulations in credit markets, labour markets, and enterprises, slipped to the 90th position from the 72nd. It is also noteworthy that on the basis of price controls and barriers to entry, Mylonas and Papaconstantinou (2001) find that in 1998 Greece ranked as the most illiberal country in the European Union.

> Greek economic scene, while there is too little research and too little planning, and the organizational apparatus for the execution of various plans is practically absent. The mosaic of fiscal credit and market regulations which are subject to abrupt changes without notice can hardly be expected to encourage private investment activity of the right kind. (p. 103)
>
> Where the market mechanism, the competitive process is allowed to perform the resource-allocation task, it ought to be allowed to work. The rewards for success should be high—but so should be the penalties for failure. The barriers to entry—which in Greece reach unusual heights—ought to be lower if not removed. "Saturated" lines of endeavour and "closed" professions ought to be exposed to the rigors of the competitive process. (p. 104)
>
> The overwhelming emphasis which is presently given to large and spectacular but narrow-scope projects must give way to a systematic exploration of the developmental possibilities of small industry (including agriculture-based small industry)… (p. 104)
>
> …It is essential to come to understand that an efficient export sector cannot be grafted upon an inefficient economy. Greece's low capacity to export is a symptom of structural weakness, of resource misallocation, of missing links in the distribution chain—and should be handled as such. Special measures, such as preferential credit and fiscal treatment for export-oriented firms, while of doubtful effectiveness in the short-run, are often distinctly harmful in the long-run. (p. 105)

So, given that what had to be done was well-known to all parties who decided to place Greece on a path of full EU membership, the question is: Did they rise to the challenge their responsibilities entailed?

In Bitros (2013) I explain in considerable detail why and how Greek institutions failed miserably to deliver on this historic opportunity. The passing of the new Constitution in 1975, which gravely eroded property rights and set the stage for the expansion of the state and the destruction of private markets; the backtracking of A. Papandreou, who as leader of the Pan-Hellenic Socialist Movement (PASOK) in the 1970s proposed reforms opposite to the ones he recommended in his 1962 monograph; and the wide nationalizations of banks and industries that a supposedly conservative government introduced and the Confederation of Greek Industries swallowed passively, are only a few examples of ill-conceived reforms that pushed the social and economic structures towards an organisation based on central direction and control. If one finds this assessment subjective and prejudiced, one may be reminded of, say, the following assessment to which Georgakopoulos (2002) arrived upon examining the factors responsible for the bad performance of the Greek economy after 1981:

> …besides, of course, the inappropriate economic policies, which do not seem to have initiated the troubles but which certainly led to a deterioration in the situation, a number of external and internal factors could be mentioned, including the 1978 and the 1985 oil price increases, the rise of the South Eastern Asia countries, which were producing a similar range of manufactured products at lower cost, the inappropriate model of Greece's development in the post-war years etc. However, the most important factor seems to have been full membership of the European Community, something for which the economy was totally unprepared. This sounds strange for a country that has been an associate member of the European Economic Community for 20 years and was supposed to gradually align tariffs and prepare itself for the final accession as full member, while receiving substantial amounts of resources from the EU budget. Although the country was simply supposed to prepare itself to become a full member of the European Communities it was, in reality, totally unprepared.

Moreover, if these assessments are not convincing enough, one may be reminded that the "structural transformations" Papandreou (1962) called for 50 years ago are only now being introduced as an integral part of the multiple austerity programmes which have been imposed on Greece by her Creditors.

Drawing on the above, the responsibility of Greek governments and their advisors who promoted publicly the advantages of Greece within the European family of nations, but, at the institutional level, did everything in their power to turn Greece into a quasi-collectivist state, is a fact, and it will not escape the ire of historians in the future. However, what is of interest here is the question if, and to what extent, responsibility lies also with the EU. When the European Commission "froze" the Association Agreement in 1967 reacting to the imposition of military rule in Greece, the message was clear and loud: It stressed the commitment of the EU to democracy, and, by doing so, it created a precedent for all European nations with aspirations similar to those of Greece. Yet, after the restoration of Democracy in 1974 and the re-activation of the Association Agreement, the European authorities failed to notice that the institutional changes in Greece were inconsistent with the main pillars of the Treaty of Rome. Let me explain: Bitros and Karayiannis (2013) establish that Democracy is impossible to take root and flourish without a free market economy. Quite expectedly this finding explains why the founding fathers of the EU constructed the Treaty of Rome on the twin pillars of democracy and the free market economy. However, as mentioned in the preceding paragraph, the institutional changes in Greece, particularly after 1974, worsened its structural imbalances even further than in 1961. The barriers to entry into markets became higher and more widespread. The shielding" of professions became universal. Individual labour contracts were replaced by collective ones. With the acquiescence and support of governments Labour Unions, particularly in the public sector, grew gigantic and interlocked with the political parties in a way rendering them uncontrollable, and so on. In view of these changes Greece not only became oblivious of her obligations under the Treaty of Rome, but also distanced herself from them by moving in the opposite direction. Therefore, the European authorities, as guardians of the Treaty, ought to have warned Greece on the provisions highlighted in footnote 2 above. Perhaps they did express their displeasure through official channels; but nothing openly enough for Greek citizens to hear and nothing in the nature of a friendly but candid reminder that Greece was going astray.[6]

This implies that the relevant European authorities experienced a notable failure. It was a failure by omission which could have been mitigated only if Greece had not

[6] This criticism applies mainly to EU's leaders, since from official documents we know that the technocrats in the European Commission expressed strong reservations about the preparedness of Greece to enter as a full member into the EEC. For example, According to the opinion that the European Commission presented to the Council in January (1976):

> The Greek economy at its present stage of development contains a number of structural features which limits its ability to combine homogeneously with the economies of the present member states. (p. 8)

been granted full membership status in 1979.[7] Was their decision justified? On account of all available evidence it was not, since from a structural point of view Greece's economy in 1981 was in a worse state than in 1961, and further away from the imperatives of the Treaty of Rome. During the period 1961–1981, per capita income in Greece converged significantly to that of the EEC average. Yet, even though improvement in living standards might have created optimism among European politicians and technocrats regarding Greece's ability to survive within the European common market, the EU authorities ought to have disallowed Greece from entering into the EEC totally unprepared as she was. Why did they do so is an issue to which I will return later, in Sect. 1.5.

1.3 1981–2001: Divergence Instead of Convergence

The Agreement of Accession of Greece to the EEC came into effect in 1981. In that year, PASOK won the elections and Papandreou[8] as its leader became Prime Minister. While serving as head of the main opposition party after 1974, Papandreou had taken a highly anti-American and anti-European stance. Actually he won the elections claiming that the EEC and NATO "represented the same evil syndicate", and upon his proclamations to take Greece down to a Third-World socialist path. In this political climate, and being as astute as he was, it did not take him long to conclude that: (a) Greece commanded certain geopolitical advantages that he could leverage in return for EU accommodation with his policies; (b) since the EU had condoned the strongly interventionist policies of previous Greek governments, no issues regarding convergence along the lines mandated by the Treaty of Rome would be raised, and (c) given the wide gap in living standards that existed at the time, and the cost Greece would absorb by opening her markets to European competition, a strong case could be made for renegotiating the terms of the Accession Agreement as well as asking for generous financial assistance. The EU refused to renegotiate the Accession Agreement but, pretty much, gave in to all other demands made by Papandreou's governments in the 1980s. It thus established a precedent of ill-conceived concessions that contributed significantly to the inertia that lead to the present calamities of Greece. The following examples suffice to

[7] Whatever the failings and derelictions were on the part of the EU during the period of association, certainly they do not absolve the Greek side of its responsibilities. However, failure to act early on by the EU might have been interpreted by Greeks as encouragement to continue. The time element is important because, the deeper one slips into a bad situation, the harder it becomes for one to adopt the necessary remedies to get out of it.

[8] By then he had forgotten what he wrote in Papandreou (1962) and many other books as a research economist with top notch international reputation. In retrospect, it now seems that once he turned to politics, nothing was more useful for him than the means and the slogans to stay in power.

Table 1.1 Net[a] inflows of financial aid from the European Union as a percentage of GDP

1981	0.003	1991	0.046	2001	0.031
1982	0.012	1992	0.039	2002	0.027
1983	0.016	1993	0.044	2003	0.020
1984	0.016	1994	0.041	2004	0.022
1985	0.017	1995	0.035	2005	0.016
1986	0.024	1996	0.048	2006	0.021
1987	0.029	1997	0.039	2007	0.018
1988	0.025	1998	0.039	2008	0.020
1989	0.029	1999	0.043	2009	0.009
1990	0.032	2000	0.043	2010	0.013

Sources: 1. Ministry of Finance, Introductory Report of the Budget, Athens, various issues; 2. GDP from the AMECO data base

[a]This term implies that the amounts of funds used to compute the percentages in this table are net of the annual contributions of Greece to the EU budget

highlight the nature and extent of EU responsibility in the face of the behaviour and practices of Greek governments regarding Greece's obligations vis-a-vis of the Treaty of Rome.

1.3.1 The Debacle of Financial Assistance

A central policy objective of the EU has been to promote the convergence of the economies of the member-states at the national and regional levels. The implementation of this policy is pursued by various means, including the provision of financial assistance. Table 1.1 below shows the net assistance Greece received annually over the period 1981–2010 as a percentage of the Gross Domestic Product (GDP). From these figures it turns out that the assistance averaged 2.7 % of GDP per annum, a very generous percentage by any comparison. Were the objectives of these policies and generous financing achieved in Greece? Or, to put it differently, did this huge transfer of resources help Greece converge at the national or regional level? Let me work out the answer, first with respect to convergence at the national level.

Suppose that the trend growth rate of Total Factor Productivity (TFP) in Greece was nil throughout the 1981–2001 period. Then, from the growth accounting point of view, her GDP would be expected to grow at the trend rate at which the above EU assistance flowed into Greece. This implies that GDP would be increasing at the trend rate of 2.7 %, and, given that the population did not increase much, per capita income would be growing roughly at the same rate. Hence, if the trend rate of growth in the EU during the same period fell, say, in the neighbourhood of 2 %, Greece would have converged to EU average living standards, albeit at a slower rate than in the period 1961–1981, when the trend growth rate in Greece was much higher than in the EU. Did this expectation come true? No; definitely not. According to the European Commission (2003, 7) Greece converged by 5.94 % and 2.34 % in the periods 1960–1970 and 1970–1980, respectively; diverged by 6.13 in the period 1981–1990; converged by 1.14 % in the period 1990–2003; and most certainly it must have diverged greatly since 2003 due the deep recession in recent years. Therefore, on account of this analysis it is reasonable to conclude that the EU failed to steer Greek governments into channelling the financial assistance into growth promoting investments, instead of using it mostly for consumption purposes.

Turning next to the presumed convergence among various regions of Greece, the evidence from the available literature is in favour of the view that the divergence actually widened. For example, Siriopoulos and Asteriou (1998) and Petrakos and Rodriguez-Pose (2003) find divergence among Greek regions for the periods 1970–1996 and 1981–1997, respectively, and the same trend is reported by Petrakos and Psycharis (2006) using improved data and more sophisticated econometric techniques. Thus, given that a large share of the EU assistance was earmarked for projects that sought to promote convergence of the less to the more affluent regions of Greece, these findings indicate that the policy failed at this level as well, and indeed not without EU responsibility, for three reasons: First, because the EU designed and put in place the allocation mechanisms of the assistance. Second, because EU had final authority for approving the projects and monitoring their implementation; and third, because the EU failed to prevent the widespread abuses that accompanied the administration of the assistance by successive Greek governments.

Furthermore, with regard to the last point, it is important to note that, even worse than the failure of the financial assistance to boost convergence, were its unintended effects on the attitude of citizens and on the integrity of the relatively feeble institutions that existed in Greece. Today it is customary for foreigners to refer to Greece as a highly corrupt and inefficient country. But few wander what the easy money of financial assistance would do to their countries and institutions, if the donors trusted that governments would abstain from the temptation to use the assistance unscrupulously in order to perpetuate their presence in government. The astonishing realisation though is that, in the case of Greece, the EU Authorities failed badly, because had they read the report that Porter (1947) submitted to the USA administration, they would have concluded that Greek governments could not be trusted to put in place the necessary mechanisms for utilising the assistance effectively and without compromising its intended purposes.

1.3.2 Structural Reforms in Reverse

In the late 1970s, the few domestic economists who were openly supporters of the free market economy reckoned that, despite the high adjustment costs that would be involved, full membership in the EEC was valuable and useful because, at least,

Greek governments would be forced to introduce structural reforms in the directions foreseen by the Treaty of Rome. They were badly disappointed. Soon after the Pan-Hellenic Socialist Movement (PASOK) took over in 1981, Papandreou's government started to replace competition by administrative controls in every market that had escaped the "socialmania"[9] after 1974. They introduced direct price controls in a wide range of markets. They expanded the range of the so-called "closed" professions and promoted—with taxpayer money—the formation of labour unions. They nationalised Skaramanga Shipyards and named them "Peoples' Shipyards". They established state enterprises to promote barter trading and to control the prices of imported goods like coffee. They attempted unsuccessfully to abolish intermediation in farm produce; and in general with their policies they showed their disdain for the fundamental market principles the EU stands for.

I did not mention above the indirect nationalisation in 1983 of 67 by then problematic business concerns, with the presumptuous intention to return them to the private sector after restructuring.[10] I did it intentionally because I wished to stress that, even though this policy was profoundly in violation of the Treaty of Rome, the relevant EU Authorities looked the other way and they did nothing to prevent it. For, here you had a state organisation saving private enterprises from bankruptcy, thus diluting competition and promoting a policy which benefited the politicians, the shareholders and the workers involved, and sent the bill to the taxpayers.[11]

At the end of the 1980s the structural divergence of Greece peaked and mainstream politicians, who worried about the continuing stagnation of economic growth and the huge public deficits that pushed public debt to unsustainable levels, started to talk about market-oriented structural reforms. The first government that embraced liberalisation, deregulation and privatisation was the one under Prime Minister Constantine Mitsotakis, which governed from 1990 to 1993. However, as it was burdened with the mess left over by Papandreou's governments and ministers from the old statist guard, it didn't accomplish much in the above fronts;[12] nor were

[9] This term was used to describe the extensive nationalisations that were undertaken by the supposedly conservative government of New Democracy (ND) under prime minister Constantine Caramanlis.

[10] Through the so-called Organization for the Restructuring of Enterprises (ORE), besides nationalizing healthy companies such as the Heracles Cement Company, PASOK used the control of the National Bank of Greece and other big banks to nationalize nearly bankrupt groups of companies such as Piraiki-Patraiki, which were kept alive by loans not justified on "business" terms. This was done in order to avoid unemployment in politically sensitive areas. From the 67 enterprises that were taken over by ORE, all but 3, which are still running with government supports, have shut down. Unfortunately, this policy, i.e. of not allowing the natural death of moribund enterprises for reasons of political expediency, has been followed by all subsequent governments and as a result, to some extent, we are faced with the same problem today.

[11] Modest estimations show that the cost to taxpayers from the operations of the so-called Organisation for the Reconstruction of Enterprises reached 3 billion Euros.

[12] Mitsotakis's government had only a one seat majority in the parliament. As a result, it was politically weak and it could not control the powerful unions in the wider public sector, and most

any meaningful structural reforms undertaken by the governments that followed, even though Prime Minister Costas Simitis, as head of subsequent PASOK governments, committed very frequently to act. Thus, with the full acquiescence of the EU Authorities, the structure of the Greek economy became exceedingly unfit for survival in the competitive environment of world and EU markets.[13]

1.3.3 Scary Imbalances

In recent years there has been a lot of talk about the so-called "Greek statistics". In Bitros (2013) several economists take a look at the statistics that are available to domestic and international researchers and find no irregularities, with the exception of a few times series which are politically sensitive. In this category falls the time series of public deficits, because Greece is suspected of having met the limit set by the Treaty of Maastricht untruthfully, i.e. by understating the size of the deficit in the budget of the central government in the observation year 1999. However, even though the doubts expressed by Eurostat in this respect are legitimate under the light of the available evidence, this debate is beside the point, because there were plenty of data out there which showed that Greece was diverging, and hence its admission into the Eurozone ought to have been delayed or even abandoned.

For a solid example, consider the time paths of the main components of the external balance, which are exhibited in Fig. 1.1. From this it turns out that after 1985 Greece lost competitiveness to such an extent that by 2001 its deficit in the Balance of Payments was close to 15 % of Gross National Product (GNP). By virtue of this all-inclusive index of performance, any economist would have concluded that the economy of Greece was marred by wide imbalances, structural and otherwise, that the country was marginalised by European and global competition, and that her governments worsened the situation because of their hard core statism and their ideological abhorrence of free markets. Yet, against all warnings, the EU in 2000 gave Greece the green light.

1.4 2002 to Date: Greece in the EMU

Concerned from the continuous postponement of structural reforms, a few economists and business leaders broke their criticism in the open. I myself started already from the second half of the 1990s to warn with repeated essays in the Sunday newspaper "TO BHMA" about the undesirable economic and social consequences,

---

particularly in the electricity, telephone and transportation state-owned enterprises. This experience should have given ample warning to the EU authorities regarding the structural deformities that dominated labor and other markets in Greece.

[13] In the late 1990s numerous researchers stressed that even before entering the European Monetary Union (EMU) Greece had more regulations of markets for goods and services and more of labour markets than any country in the EU. On this, see for example Nicoletti et al. (1999).

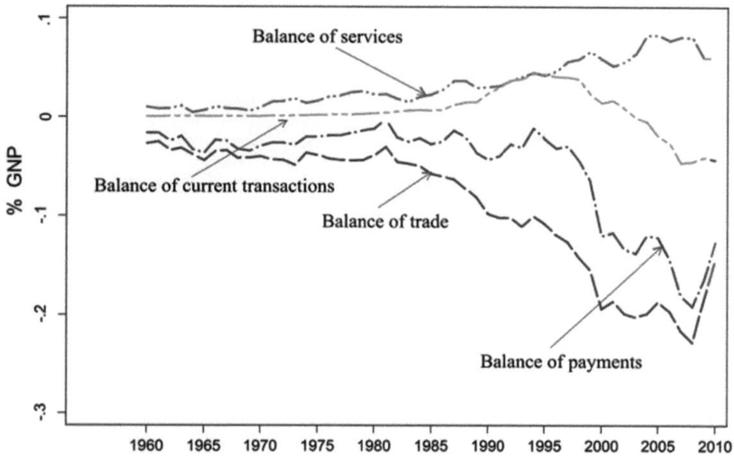

Fig. 1.1 The balance of payments

if Greece entered into the Eurozone unprepared.[14] While I was supportive of the government's efforts to achieve fiscal adjustment, the lack of any progress in the front of structural reforms stirred my worst fears about the disinflation that would erupt sometime in the next few years. Unfortunately, not only the EU Authorities failed to exert pressure on Greek governments to introduce the necessary structural reforms, but, on the contrary, encouraged by various short-sighted technocrats they made reassuring proclamations that relieved Greek governments from the urgency to act. In support of this assertion, here is a quotation from the introduction of Jacques Delors, President of the European Commission, to the paper by Pagoulatos (2002):

> From now on, we must forget the stereotypes of Greece's marginalization in the Union because they are obsolete. I share the author's assessment of the current position of Greece in Europe as a success story, whether this be in items of to its political, economic or administrative evolution, its integration into the EMU and the single market or its international stance. I also know the huge role Prime Minister Kostas Simitis has played in this success, which I feel should be emphasized in this brief forward.

After this ebullient view of the prospects of Greece in the Eurozone, there can be no surprise that fiscal aggregates derailed again for good. For those who still doubt that the EU bears a good measure of responsibility, Fig. 1.2 shows how the current tragedy of Greece started to evolve right after 2002. In particular, starting from 1993, in the years of observation 1998–1999, governments managed to shrink public deficits (in Fig. 1.2 it is shown as declining negative public savings, i.e. borrowing) well enough to achieve the admission of Greece into the Eurozone.

[14] In addition to my essays in the popular press, in Bitros (1992) and again in Bitros and Korres (2002) I spared no effort to warn about what would be the awful predicament, if Greek governments failed to introduce the necessary structural reforms.

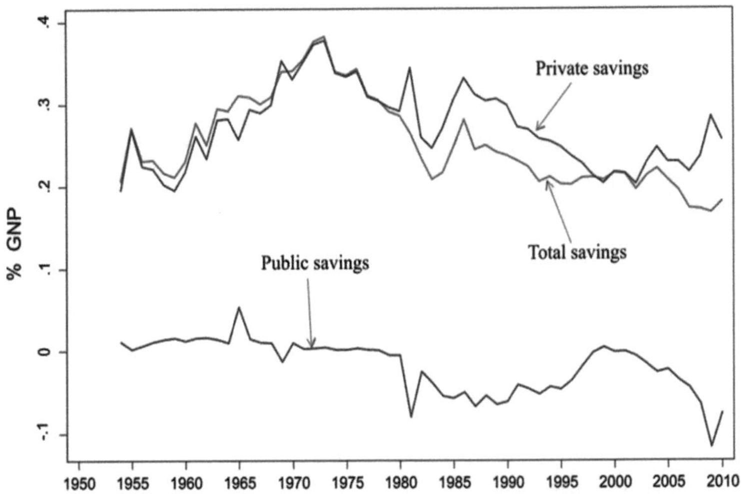

Fig. 1.2 National savings and its components

But, subsequently, public deficits accelerated until in recent years they exploded and brought Greece to the brink of open bankruptcy. To corroborate further that this assessment is based on solid evidence rather than on casual observation, here is one of the many sharp verdicts Katsimi and Moutos (2010, 569) arrive at in their very meticulous study:

> The Greek economy entered the second phase of the pre-EMU accession period in 1994 with both a large public debt and a large budget deficit, and went through a reduction of 9 percentage points (of GDP) in its budget deficit between 1993 and 1999 in order to be admitted to the euro area. Unfortunately, these efforts were to a large extent abandoned in subsequent years. This was because, in the pre-EMU accession phase, the threat of exclusion acted as a hard budget constraint that forced the Greek government to redress its fiscal imbalances. In contrast to the output-driven, "hard-conditionality" of the pre-accession period, the EMU period was characterized by the "soft-conditionality" of the Stability and Growth Pact (SGP), which allowed Greece even more than other governments to breach both the letter and the spirit of the Pact.

In other words, as Greece had done in the past with the Treaty of Rome (1957), it violated repeatedly the letter and the spirit of the Stability and Growth Pact (1997) and yet EU leaders looked the other way.

1.5 Possible Explanations for EU's Approach to Greece

The presentation in the preceding three sections leaves no doubt that the EU Authorities failed repeatedly to hold Greek governments accountable for violations of the Treaties Greece signed with the EU over the past five decades. In particular, not only they did not express reservations in the face of these violations, but, in two crucial occasions, in 1981 and 2000, they even rewarded Greece with concessionary decisions. In this light the question that comes to mind is this: How can one explain these failures of the EU in the case of Greece? The objective below is to describe briefly the rudiments of certain possible explanations.[15]

1.5.1 Tying Greece to the West

History books suggest that on the basis of the agreement reached by the great powers that won the Second World War, i.e. The United States of America (USA), the United Kingdom (UK) and the Union of Soviet Socialist Republics (USSR), Greece came under the influence of the USA and UK. From the relevant literature it is also known that the USA took the lead in the reconstruction of Greece by providing substantial financial assistance through the Truman Doctrine and the Marshall Plan up to 1952 and with lesser amounts of aid in the following years. Finally, from Pelt (2003) we learn that sometime in the second half of the 1950s the USA relinquished much of its influence in Greece to West Germany and the North Atlantic Treaty Organization (NATO) with the understanding that they would exercise responsibility for keeping Greece tied to the West. According to Pelt (2003), the admission by West Germany of nearly 300,000 Greek immigrants, the considerable investments German firms started to undertake in Greece and the Agreement of Association with the EEC in 1961, were policies which affirmed the influence West Germany gained in Greece for itself and on behalf of NATO and the EEC.

In 1974 the invasion of Cyprus by Turkey provoked the downfall of the military regime, which ruled in Greece since 1967, and the return to democracy under a provisional government headed by Karamanlis. Due to the anti-American climate that prevailed at the time, Karamanlis withdrew Greece from the military wing of NATO. However, shortly afterward he declared publicly and forcefully that "Greece belonged to the West", he asked for reactivation of the 1961 Agreement of Association with the EEC, and, simultaneously, he petitioned the starting of negotiations for full membership. These moves could be interpreted as a reaffirmation of the status quo in the region and as a warning to the leaders of the EU in general, and West Germany in particular, as to what might happen, if they failed to admit Greece to the EEC. Most likely, therefore, the Agreement of Accession in 1981 was concluded on the same geopolitical imperatives with those that led to the Agreement of Association in 1961.[16]

[15] Aside of the explanations referred to below, one could think of several others. For example, non-German countries might have an interest to keep Greece in the EU in order not to weaken the weight of the "rest of Europe" in the light of the massive political and economic power of unified Germany. In the text I did not occupy myself with such scenarios because I construed them as highly unlikely.

[16] Perhaps it is of some importance to note that Greece re-entered into the military branch of NATO on October 22, 1980.

In short, despite the errors of USA foreign policy in Greece and Cyprus, and despite the gross violations of the Treaty of Rome by Karamanlis's post-1974 governments, with their decision in 1981 EU leaders sought to keep Greece tied to the West.

1.5.2 Giving in to Papandreou's Blackmail and Simitis' Charm

When, in the elections of 1974, Papandreou introduced his slogan against EEC and NATO, as well as his other proclamations about turning Greece into a third world socialist state, actually he was posturing to secure that EU and NATO: (a) would not interfere in the electoral process; (b) would not raise objections to the statist economic policies he intended to apply, and (c) would continue to provide financial and other assistance. Since the cold war continued and the plans of USSR for expansion in this region did not show signs of abatement, EU leaders gave in to Papandreou's blackmail and Karamanlis' warnings.[17]

The above scenario explains rather convincingly the EU decision regarding the 1981 Agreement of Accession and the generous financial assistance that followed. But it is less illuminating regarding the EU decision in 2000 to admit Greece into the EMU because, by the early 1990s, Papandreou's threats had waned and Greece's geopolitical significance had started to decline under the new trends precipitated by the dissolution of the USSR in 1991. Regarding these trends, remember that in the 1990s Russia lost its superpower status and became entangled in serious economic problems. The USA became dominant in the world and, with the cooperation of the EU, it started upgrading Turkey into a regional power. The stance of Greece in various Balkan issues rendered its friends in the West nervous, etc. So how can we explain the EU decision in the year 2000? I can think of two possible explanations: The first is that EU leaders gave in to the charms of Simitis, who, in 1996 took over as Prime Minister of the PASOK government, replacing Papandreou who was seriously ill. Since within a few years Simitis managed to bring about successfully the required macroeconomic adjustment and Greece met the Maastricht criteria, why doubt that he would deliver also in due course on the structural reforms? Simitis needed encouragement to continue with these reforms and with their positive decision they showed full confidence in his leadership. The second explanation is the following.

---

[17] A reader has suggested that the EU decision in 1981 may have been influenced also by two additional factors: Namely, the interest of certain key European leaders in the purchases of military equipment by Greece, and the solidarity among socialist parties which were coming to power at the time. Perhaps they did play some role. But there is no way of knowing and in any case, with the major challenges that Greece presented, their influence could not be more than marginal.

1.5.3 A Latent Strategy for Greece's Europeanization

From a structural point of view Greece was unprepared to enter into the Eurozone. After it entered, economists knew that, if Greek governments procrastinated in adopting the necessary structural reforms, eventually the consequences would be domestic deflation in the form of significant undesirable adjustments in the real wages and in the rate of unemployment. In addition economists knew that domestic deflation would become necessary sooner than later depending on the size of public deficits and debt. Hence, EU leaders guessed that, if Greek governments failed in the front of structural reforms and went over a fiscal cliff, there was a real possibility that their countries might be called upon at some point to bail Greece out. Still they decided to let Greece enter into the Eurozone. My hunch is that they did so because, if the case came down to bailing Greece from bankruptcy, they believed that the cost would be well worth it. Why would that be so? An answer is that, it would give them the opportunity to control the terms of Greece's true Europeanization once and for all.

1.5.4 Natural Resources and Markets

The going for Greeks is tough now because, in addition to the economic sacrifices and the suffering from unemployment, the structural reforms underway demand of them to change their habits and thinking. In this unsettled climate, politicians, opinion makers and media with adversarial views, genuine or contrived, regarding the Europeanization of Greece, attempt to gain followers by claiming that the EU is after our "natural resources" and "markets". Their arguments regarding "markets" are baseless in the prevailing globalised environment of open economies and can be ignored, but not their claims regarding "natural resources".

Europe has few natural resources of its own compared to other parts of the world. As a result, since minerals and fossil fuels play a central role in the economy, securing such resources in adequate and uninterrupted supply has been a very high priority in the EU. Depending on the changes in production technologies and goods produced, the list of minerals which are considered critical from one period to the other changes. From the Molinares report of Buijs and Sievers (2011) it turns out that the list of critical minerals in the last 40 years included gold, bauxite, chromium, platinum, cobalt, manganese, tungsten, phosphate, lithium, etc. The question then is: Has Greece deposits of fuels and critical minerals in such quantities that might motivate the EU to overlook Greece's violation of its membership obligations?

The key resources in Greece include iron ore, lignite, zinc, lead, bauxite, nickel, petroleum and magnesite. In 2010, Greece was the world's fourth largest producer of pumice and a leading producer of perlite; it produced about 1 % of the world's bauxite and 9 % of the world's bentonite, whereas it held a leading position in

Europe in the production of Nickel. But from these only bauxite and nickel have surfaced systematically in the lists of critical minerals.

A feasibility study in 2006 established that Greece can become the top producer of gold in the EU. Also, various reports in the last few years have foreshadowed good prospects for the discovery of petroleum and gas deposits. But these possibilities are still in the exploratory phase. Therefore, based on the above, it is unlikely that the availability of fossil fuels and minerals played any significant role in the EU decisions with regard to Greece.

1.5.5 History and Civilisation

In Bitros and Karayiannis (2010, 2013) we established that the wealth and the marvels of ancient Athens that we admire so much today resulted from the ingenious combination ancient Athenians achieved of democratic institutions with an outward looking economy based on free markets. By implication, Greeks knew and practiced the principles of democracy and of free market economy on which the EU is founded long before any other European nation. To be sure, in the decades since the uprising and the liberation from the Ottoman Empire in 1821, Greeks failed to set up a well-organised state. But, time and again, when major world conflicts in the twentieth century threatened the foundations of democracy and individual freedoms, Greeks were there on the side of the nations that defended these values, appearing in the European eyes in the battlefields to be true descendants of ancient Greeks. Thus, based on the way cultured people in the West think about Greece when it comes to defending democracy, one cannot preclude that Greece's history swayed some most critical EU decisions in her favour.

Nor is it likely that Greece's contribution to civilisation could leave European leaders and intelligentsia unmoved; and I do not mean only the place in their hearts of the Titans of Greece's ancient philosophers, tragedians, physicists, mathematicians, etc. For, contemporary Greece has a vivid cultural presence, which is amply evidenced by her world-renowned : poets, like Kavafy and the two Nobel laureates Seferis and Elytis; authors, like Kazantzakis, whose books have been translated widely all over the world; symphony orchestra conductors and opera singers Mitropoulos and Callas; composers like Skalkotas, Theodorakis and Hatzidakis, etc. In short, Greece is a small country which has made a disproportionately large contribution to Western civilization, not only in ancient but also in modern times. Therefore, EU leaders, most of whom have been raised on the "classics", may have a tendency to treat Greece as a special case because of her overall presence in the world, downplaying the problems of her economy.

1.5.6 Greece Is "Too Small to Matter"

The argument outlined above, according to which EU Authorities took a bet when they decided in 2000 to admit Greece into the Eurozone, gains support from still another consideration. This emanates from the realisation that, since Greece has very small weight relative to the mass of the EU, whatever social and economic shocks might arise from her side they would be utterly unlikely to cause any problem for the EU as a whole. Expressing the same thought differently, if an expert stood in 2000 and looked into the future of the common currency, no matter how smart and knowledgeable, he could not have imagined a situation where the mismanagement of Greece's economy would have created the possibility of bringing down the European, and through it the international financial system.[18] However, in the last 4 years, experience has shown that, from the mismanagement of big banks in the USA, which were thought to be "too big to fail", to the mismanagement in the EU of a small economy like that of Greece, which was thought to be ' too small to matter", such possibilities do exist and, if they are allowed to materialize, their consequences might be catastrophic for the democratic way of living.

To conclude, in 2000 EU experts and leaders could not have been aware of the risks that the failure of a small economy like Greece might cause a cascading failure, which could potentially bring down the entire European monetary system. No one knew of the existence of such "systemic risks", so most likely they took the bet by underestimating the cost of bailing out Greece in case she went bankrupt. Hence, in this light, it is not surprising that the leaders of Germany and France find it hard to explain to their citizens why they will have to share in the costs for preventing the open bankruptcy of Greece.

1.5.7 Massive EU Institutional Failure

The presentation in Sect. 1.4 established beyond reasonable doubt that Greece violated systematically the letter and the spirit of all treaties she signed with EU in the last five decades. In the preceding sub-sections I commented on several conceptualisations which have been advanced in the literature in order to explain the crucial decisions of EU leaders to admit Greece to the EEC in 1979 and to the Eurozone in 2000. However, nothing that has been said so far precludes the likelihood that the EU responsibility for what happened in Greece may lie with

[18] To be sure, the possibility of a so-called "butterfly effect", according to which a small and insignificant disturbance somewhere in the world might cumulate under certain circumstances into a catastrophic event, was long known to experts. But at the time there was no precedent of such an occurrence happening in actuality, so it would be quite farfetched to hold European leaders and technocrats responsible for not allowing for it in advance.

the implementation and monitoring mechanisms which have been setup to make sure that country-members abide by their obligations.

In this respect, one should be reminded that much ink has been wasted as to whether Greece provided her partners with the correct data regarding public deficit and debt prior to entering the Eurozone. But these issues are secondary to the violations that the Greek political class committed in failing to advance the agenda of the Treaty of Rome and the necessary structural reforms, which would have made Greece a viable member of the Eurozone. Didn't the administration in Brussels see what was happening in the 1980s and 1990s with the mess Greek governments made of the Greek economy? Didn't they see the massive frauds in the usage of the Community assistance and the wasteful projects to which it was directed? How could they cooperate in the destruction of the Greek agriculture without insisting in its timely restructuring? These and numerous other questions need to be addressed soon by the European Commission in the spirit of democratic accountability. For, until they do so, European citizens living in Greece will be entitled to suspect that they are victims of a massive EU institutional failure, since a country as ill prepared as Greece was admitted into the monetary union.[19]

Summary of Findings and Conclusions

In 2000 the structure of the Greek economy was further away from what was envisioned in the Treaty of Rome than it was in 1961. Markets were regulated centrally by administrative controls, stifling competition and reducing the flexibility of the economy to adjust to domestic and external shocks. Professions were "closed" to protect the incomes of privileged minorities. The public sector in the narrow sense was oversized and operated extremely inefficiently, whereas the broader public sector was dominated by powerful labour unions, often holding the government and the citizens hostage, etc. Thus, in view of Greece's demonstrable unpreparedness to join the Eurozone, only partly geopolitical but mostly reasons that can be traced in significant EU institutional failures and underestimation of systemic risks may explain why EU leaders decided to let it proceed.

With their decision EU leaders took a bet. If Greek governments did introduce the required structural reforms, Greece would transform herself into a true European country and all would be fine. If they didn't, the time would come for domestic deflation and then they would have to bail out Greece in order to avert an open bankruptcy. But, in that eventuality, they would have the ability to dictate the terms and the speed of structural reforms.

(continued)

[19] In other words, in the absence of such an assessment, Greek citizens are entitled to suspect that the overwhelming emphasis placed on the view that Greece was admitted in the Eurozone on the basis of falsified statistics is a cheap excuse to avoid discussion of the substantive issues raised above.

This is exactly what is happening now and the major likelihood is that, within a few years, Greece will turn into a truly European country. Unfortunately, the cost to the Greek people is much-much higher than if structural reforms had been introduced in smooth and timely fashion. But, in a democracy, the sovereignty of the people comes with a cost; the Greek people ought to have watched out for the integrity and the character of the leaders they elected all these years. In my view this explanation highlights exceptionally well the behaviour of EU leaders, as well as my predictions all along that they would foot whatever bill for bailing out Greece.

References

Bitros GC (1992) Structural policies to unwind the Greek fiscal tangle. In: Skouras TS (ed) Issues in contemporary economics, vol 5, The Greek economy: economic policies for the 1990s. Macmillan, London, pp 23–29

Bitros GC (2013) "From riches to rags or what went wrong in Greece", in G. C. Bitros (guest editor) on Greece and Greek statistics. J Econ Soc Meas 38:3–39

Bitros GC, Karayiannis AD (2010) Morality, institutions and the wealth of nations: some lessons from ancient Greece. Eur J Polit Econ 26:68–81

Bitros GC, Karayiannis AD (2013) Creative crisis in democracy and economy. Springer, Berlin

Bitros GC, Korres GM (2002) Economic integration: limits and prospects. Palgrave Macmillan, New York, NY

Buijs B, Sievers H (2011) Critical thinking about critical minerals: assessing risks related to resource security. www.polinares.eu

Eichengreen B (2007) The European economy since 1945. Princeton University Press, Princeton, NJ

European Commission (1976) Opinion on the Greece's application for accession. Brussels, p 8

European Commission (2003) Catching-up, growth, and convergence of the new member states. Publication 7718

Georgakopoulos T (2002) Overprotected and underprepared: EU-Accession, the Greek way, Friedrich Ebert Stiftung, Digitale Bibliothek

Gwartney JD, Lawson RA (2006) The impact of tax policy on economic growth, income distribution, and allocation of time. In: Paul FE, Miller FD, Paul J (eds) Taxation, economic prosperity, and distributive justice. Cambridge University Press, Cambridge, pp 28–52

Katsimi M, Moutos T (2010) EMU and the Greek crisis: the political-economy perspective. Eur J Polit Econ 26:568–576

Mylonas P, Papaconstantinou G (2001) Product market reform in Greece: policy priorities and prospects. In: Bryant R, Garganas N, Tavlas G (eds) Greece's economic performance and prospects. Bank of Greece/The Brookings Institute, Athens, pp 499–543

Nicoletti G, Scarpetta S, Boylaud O (1999) Summary indicators of product market regulation with an extension to employment protection legislation. OECD ECO Working Paper, 226

Pagoulatos G (2002) Greece the European Union and the 2003 Presidency. Groupment D' Etudes et de Recherches, Notre Europe, Research and European Issues No 21

Papandreou AG (1962) A strategy for Greek economic development. Center of Economic Research, Research Monograph 1, Athens

Pelt M (2003) Tying Greece to the West: US-West German-Greek relations 1949–1974 (Studies in 20th and 21st Century European History). Museum Tusculanum Press, Copenhagen

Petrakos G, Psycharis Y (2006) Regional policy in Greece: an overview and the recent policy change. ideas.repec.org/p/wiw/wiwrsa/ersa06p948.html
Petrakos G, Rodriguez-Pose A (2003) Regional inequality in the EU. Topos 20(21):51–76 (in Greek)
Porter PA (1947) Tentative Report of the American Mission to Greece, 868.50/4-347, NA
Siriopoulos C, Asteriou D (1998) Testing for convergence across the Greek regions. Region Stud 32:537–546

Chapter 2
Some Thoughts on Greece from a European Perspective

Jürgen G. Backhaus

2.1 Introduction

It has frequently been suggested that the Greek debt should be shaved, and at issue was simply the size of the haircut. In this short paper, I suggest that such a haircut should indeed happen, but in a way that is very different from the previous suggestions and rather beneficial from the Greek point of view.

2.2 The Greek Option

In recent decades, several countries have come to face surging public debts and needs to restructure. Specialized banks have emerged that bought seemingly valueless public debt, for instance the Argentine public debt, and presented the respective governments with the titles, once these had come to fruition. The governments were forced to pay the 100 % of the full credit, although they had often only received a fraction thereof as the paid out credit, since these credits often were valued below par already when they were granted. This plan would introduce a Greek option.

Currently, these titles go for about 30 % of the par value. My program suggests to institute by law an option for the Greek government to enter any trade of Greek bonds at the terms negotiated by the respective parties. When, for instance, one of these large banking institutions buys up Greek loans for let's say 27 % of par value, the Greek government could step in and buy back its own bonds at these 27 %. This

J.G. Backhaus (✉)
Staatswissenschaftliche Fakultät, Krupp-Stiftungslehrstuhl für Finanzwissenschaft und Finanzsoziologie, Universität Erfurt, Nordhäuser Straße 63, 99089 Erfurt, Germany
e-mail: juergen.backhaus@uni-erfurt.de

G.C. Bitros, N.C. Kyriazis (eds.), *Essays in Contemporary Economics*,
DOI 10.1007/978-3-319-10043-2_2

would amount to a substantial saving for the Greek state, essentially a haircut at more than two-thirds of the par value.

This proposal also has an interesting twist for the banks that hold Greek titles. Discreetly, they could start unloading these titles in small portions, thus improving their balance sheets. To the extent that the international banks actually pick up the ball, the Greek government could step in and buy back its bonds at sharply reduced prices. Again, this would be in the interest of all parties involved, the bond holders, the Greek government and ultimately also those international banks who certainly carry no loss by offering to buy bonds on which sale a third party exercises its option.[1]

2.3 The Context Between the European Bank Policy on Interest Rates and the Greek Dilemma

The natural interest rate according to Wicksell is what can be earned in real investments in countries, where such investments are warranted. When money is readily available, as it is made available through low interest rates by the banks, banks will look for investments that are very secure, as the low interest rates cover no margin for uncertainties, uncertainties that every interesting investment project will have. Akin to the labour market, the credit market does not only operate via the interest rate, as the labour market cannot be relied upon only by letting the wage flow freely. Employing a slew for three Euros an hour may not be worth your while, as he needs more supervision than his output warrants. If interest rates are unnaturally low, this does not feed investment projects everywhere, as the banks have no risk margin and will then rather prefer to park the money with the central bank overnight. Greece is a country with lots of investment opportunities, many of which could bear returns above 10 %, however with a risk. As Frank Knight has taught, there is not only the risk, but there is also uncertainty. For this reason, investments need to be such that they can yield, under plausible assumptions and given possibilities for totally unforeseen events returns that require much higher interest rates than the low interest rate policies allow. Originally, potential private investors would have stepped in, taking the chance of risk and uncertainty and have invested in Greek projects, many Greek investors included. The stern low interest rate policy

[1] An option is a security whose owner has a right to buy (sell) it at a specified price on a specified date (or, with an American-type option, on or before the specified date). Trading of options on common stock began in 1973 and has since spread to other commodities. Option pricing theory provides a unified theory for the pricing of corporate liabilities. Of its more recent extensions, perhaps the most significant is its application in the evaluation of operating or 'real' options in the capital budgeting decision problem. From: Merton, Robert C., "options", "The New Palgrave Dictionary of Economics", Eds. Steven N. Durlauf and Lawrence E. Blume, Palgrave Macmillan, 2008, The New Palgrave Dictionary of Economics Online, Palgrave Macmillan. 13 November 2013, doi:10.1057/9780230226203.1229.

by the European central bank, which has no Greek cause, but is only caused by the overburdening debt of the United States, leaves Greece bereft of the necessary investment funds. In addition, the Greek government has practically disowned the most likely investors at home. When by way of the utility bill you have to pay, the assessed value of your home -in parts, this has happened twice- it is no wonder that Greek capital has fled overseas, where it desperately seeks for investments instead of at home.

A solution here offered is different from those that are currently available. The root of the problem is the US debt. The United States of America have such an enormous debt, that it cannot be calculated. It cannot even be said, how many public entities are able to incur public debt in the United States. On this basis, an estimate of the total debt is obviously impossible. The root of the problem is the United States' public debt, which in turn requires an interest rate policy by the board of governors so low that even an increase by a percentage point would render the federal government insolvent. One interest point, however, would by no means be sufficient. The natural rate of interest according to Wicksell is what at the margin a reasonable investment project will yield, that may be about 6 %. Think about raising the discount rate to about 5 %. This would starve the federal US government, the states, the local governments, the counties, and so forth of refinancing opportunities and potentially set forth a wave of public bankruptcies. Obviously, the US government could not tolerate such a course by the European central bank. Pressure would be put on the board of governors of the European central bank to change its mind. Imagine the impossible, that they do not give in. They just are unavailable for a time. The European central bank can help out by buying their gold.

The solution for the Greek dilemma lies in investments in Greece, and these are hindered by the current low interest policy. Sensible investment projects, sleeping beauties, should be kissed awake with 7 % interest loans guaranteed by the Greek central bank, and the European help should consist in providing lent collateral for these loans by buying up the American gold.

2.4 Saving Greece, the EMU and Ultimately the US

The proposal contained in this paper is straightforward and strictly in the Paretian tradition. Each move is Pareto superior, but after all the moves have been completed, the world will look rather different from what it is now.

Since the proposal is developed from a European point of view and in particular takes the Greek position into account, the paper superficially looks almost anti-American; yet, the proposals developed here ultimately also benefit the United States of America.

If you look at the balance sheet of the German central bank and the European central bank, it is immediately obvious, that it reveals the holdings of a lot of US-dollars and US-dollars denominated assets. It is a matter of prudent central bank policy and prudent bank policy in general to unload these assets as quickly and discreetly as possible and exchanges them for something stable, for better or worse, this may be gold. The German gold reserves have already been repatriated, and the United States do not only have an enormous debt, but they also have substantial gold reserves which can be bought. Since announcing these policies would result in a surge of the price of gold, the policy should be implemented discreetly and calmly on the long term. It is urgent, however, to unload the US-dollar denominated assets, in the meantime instead of gold also common stock could be bought by the central banks, as Karl Brunner had suggested in the seventies of the last century.

As far as the US debt is concerned, it should be noted, that not only the debt itself is beyond proportion, but measurable in principle. This is at least true for the debt of the nation, the 50 states and the about 10,000 municipalities. In addition, there are counties, but each county also tends to have a development board which also can issue debt. Furthermore, the school districts can issue public debt, as can many other institutions, for instance those that run a stadium, a park or the like. The number of these debt issuing bodies is not known, and for this reason, the extent of the outstanding debt is equally unknown. In addition, in the 1970s, when I travelled in Chile, you could earn a premium when you exchanged German marks for escudos, as it was then well known that about half of the circulating US bills were fakes. Although new bills have been introduced, the situation has certainly not changed, hence what cannot even be controlled by the US Federal Reserve Bank can certainly not be controlled by other bodies.

Once the US denominated assets and the greenbacks themselves have been unloaded, my proposal is to transfer these amounts to the Kreditanstalt für Wiederaufbau and set up a fund in which these assets serve as collateral for a credit policy aimed at Greece.

The policy of very low interest rates pursued by the US Federal Reserve Bank also under its new leadership of Dr. Yellen from the American point of view is a matter of necessity. Otherwise the service of the enormous debt would balloon in such a way that US federal bankruptcy would be a necessity. These low interest rates, however, imply that credit cannot be extended. Any reasonable credit has a margin of risk, as no sensible investment project is conceivable that carries no risk whatsoever. For this reason, debt should be extended at an interest rate roughly equal to the natural rate of interest, that is reflecting the yield of investment opportunities, something like 6 or 7 %. Any visitor to Greece will not fail to notice that the country is abundant with interesting investment opportunities, which the German Agency for Reconstruction, Kreditanstalt für Wiederaufbau, could address with the money gotten through the sale of the US-dollar denominated assets. In this case of a Greece assistance package, there is no doubt that Greece would pay back the loans. First of all, it is not the state of Greece that is incurring the credit, rather the various investors, Greek and international, would be the debtors, and the investment projects would provide enough collateral for the credits to be secured.

Does this plan have any chance of being adopted? As I pointed out in the beginning, the plan consists of a series of steps, each of which makes ample business sense. Where the plan appears to have an anti-American sting, this is not an un-American feature of the plan. The tea party movement would certainly concur with addressing the American dilemma in this way, as would many Americans, whether they are politically organized or just private citizens who think patriotically.

When I presented my ideas in Athens, my Greek colleagues were primarily concerned that buying up American gold and repatriating the German gold would inflate the gold price beyond proportion. As it happens, my suggestions and proposal could not have been more timely, as currently the price of gold is at an all-time low. This is another good reason to think carefully about translating the proposal into practice.

Reference

Karl Brunner made this point in various publications and also in his lectures at the University of Konstanz in the seventies

Part II
Issues in the Methodology of Economics

Chapter 3
The Physics Scientific Ideal in the Works of Edgeworth and Fisher

Stavros A. Drakopoulos

3.1 Introduction

The desire to elevate the scientific status of economics to that of the physical sciences has a long presence in the history of economic analysis (e.g. Mirowski 1984). A number of key figures in the classical school such as A. Smith, J.B. Say and J.S. Mill viewed physical sciences as the ideal scientific model for economics. Thus, examples of the analogy between economics and physical sciences can be found in Smith (astronomy), Cairnes (chemistry), Say (chemistry and physics) and Mill (1874) (geometry) (Smith 1980ed; Cairnes 1875; Say 1803; Mill 1874). The strive to imitate the methods of physics became much more apparent with the emergence of the marginalist school. Jevons' assertion that the theory of economy presents a close analogy to the science of statical mechanics (Jevons 1871, viii), and Walras' prediction that mathematical economics will rank with the mathematical sciences of astronomy and mechanics (Walras 1965, 47, 48), are indicative examples in this respect. However, the work of second generation marginalist F.Y. Edgeworth, represents the highest point of physics and in particular of classical physics methodological influence. Edgeworth not only carried the analogy to its extreme, but also provided a thorough methodological justification. Similarly, the work of I. Fisher, the populariser of marginalism and neoclassical economics in the US, also exhibits the same tendency. Fisher took terms and concepts from classical physics and transferred them directly to economics, also providing the

An earlier version of the paper was presented to the Conference in memory of Anastassios D. Karayiannis at the University of Thessaly, Volos, October 18–19, 2013. Special thanks for comments are due to the conference participants.

S.A. Drakopoulos (✉)
Department of Philosophy and History of Science, University of Athens, University Campus, 15771, Athens, Greece
e-mail: sdrakop@phs.uoa.gr

G.C. Bitros, N.C. Kyriazis (eds.), *Essays in Contemporary Economics*,
DOI 10.1007/978-3-319-10043-2_3

appropriate methodological basis for their use. Thus, the writings of those two influential economists were paramount for the general acceptance of "economics being parallel to physics" methodological paradigm.

The physical science ideal has played, and still plays a key role in the formation of orthodox economic methodology (see also Drakopoulos 1994). The paper discusses the development of this ideal in the works of Edgeworth and Fisher, also demonstrating that these authors provided the methodological justification for its adoption in economics. It also examines the most important consequences of this methodological stance for contemporary mainstream economics. In particular, the paper argues that the high degree of formalism of current mainstream economic theory, the established tradition of anti-psychologism, and the relegation of methodological critique, are the most important consequences of the physics methodological ideal. The paper starts with a discussion of the methodological approach of Edgeworth. The following section concentrates on Fisher's methodological ideas. Section 3.4 examines the most important repercussions of their influence for contemporary mainstream economics. The final section concludes.

3.2 Edgeworth: Physics and Psychics

For most historians of economic thought, Edgeworth is considered to be one of the most influential figures of marginalism and of the early neoclassical economics. Edgeworth made extremely significant contributions to numerous subfields of economics including contract and exchange theory, the theory of monopoly and duopoly and taxation theory. However, the impact of his methodological approach for the subsequent development of mainstream economic methodology has not been adequately appreciated by most economic methodologists. More specifically, Edgeworth's most important work "*Mathematical Psychics*: *An Essay of the Application of Mathematics to Moral Sciences*" (1881) sets the basis for the methodological justification of formalism in social sciences and particularly in economics. Methodological arguments supporting the use of mathematics in economics can be found in the works of previous theorists such as Cournot, Jevons, and Walras (Turk 2012). However, Edgeworth provides a very systematic methodological grounding for the use of mathematics in the study of social phenomena and more importantly, of the methodological ideal of physics. In this sense, Edgeworth's work represents the height of the physics emulation in the history of economic discourse. The opening page of his main work is indicative:

> An Analogy is suggested between the Principles of Greatest Happiness, Utilitarian or Egoistic, which constitute the first Principles of Ethics and Economics, and those Principles of Maximum Energy which are among the highest generalizations of Physics and in virtue of which mathematical reasoning is applicable to physical phenomena quite as complex as human life. (Edgeworth 1881, v)

His next step is to provide a detailed methodological justification for the close analogy between physics and social sciences and particularly, economics. The first argument supporting the employment of the methods of mathematical physics to social science, is based on the assumption that every social phenomenon is the concomitant of a physical phenomenon. As he states:

> The application of mathematics to the world of soul is countenanced by the hypothesis (agreeable to the general hypothesis that every psychical phenomenon is the concomitant, and in some sense the other side of a physical phenomenon), the particular hypothesis adopted in these pages, that Pleasure is the concomitant of Energy. *Energy* may be regarded as the central idea of Mathematical Physics; *maximum energy* the object of principal investigations in that science. By aid of this conception we reduce into scientific order physical phenomena, the complexity of which may be compared with the complexity which appears so formidable in Social Science. (Edgeworth 1881, 9, italics in original).

Given the close connection of Energy and Pleasure, the maximization principle in the social sciences mentioned in the opening quotation, is easier to be accepted as a fundamental concept in economics.

The second important reason for the application of mathematics to economics is the quantitative nature of the discipline. In Edgeworth's words:

> Quantity of labour, quantity of pleasure, quantity of sacrifice and enjoyment, greatest average happiness, these are no dreams of German metaphysics, but the leading thought of leading Englishmen and corner-stone conceptions, upon which rest the whole systems of Adam Smith, of Jeremy Bentham, of John Mill, and of Henrey Sidgwick. (Edgeworth 1881, 97, 98)

In order to respond to the plausible point that data in physics is much more sophisticated than data in economics, Edgeworth argues that the lack of precise numerical data and exact functional relations in economics is not an obstacle to the application of mathematical methods. He even cites the example of hydrodynamics where the available data is similar to economic data and where relations among variables are central (Edgeworth 1881, 4, 5).

The application of mathematics and tools from physics is greatly facilitated by the combination of Utilitarianism with economics under the methodology of "mathematical psychics" (see also Creedy 1980; Mirowski 1984, 1994). Therefore, the central idea of the 'Hedonic Calculus' is the maximization of utility which naturally facilitates the application of optimization methods from physics to economics. The following statement is indicative:

> Now, it is remarkable that the principal inquires in Social Science may be viewed as *maximum-problems*. For Economics investigates the arrangements between agents each tending to his own *maximum* utility; and Politics and (Utilitarian) Ethics investigate the arrangements which conclude to the *maximum* sum total of utility. Since, then, Social Science, as compared with the Calculus of Variations, starts from similar data *-loose quantitative relations*-and travels to a similar conclusion –determination of *maximum*- why should it not pursue the same method, Mathematics? (Edgeworth 1881, 6, 7 italics in original).

Given the above, Edgeworth provides many specific examples demonstrating specific applications of mathematical reasoning appropriate to economics. The case of the calculus of variations is central:

> It is the first principle of the calculus of variations that a varying quantity attains a maximum when the first term of variation vanishes, while the second term is negative (mutatis mutandis, for a minimum)... In the simple cases which in the infancy of Mathematical Psychics are along presented in these pages, we know by observation not what the second term is, but that it is continually negative. (Edgeworth 1881, 91).

The aim of a unified science of physical and mental phenomena can be found in his notion of 'psychophysics'. Edgeworth often cites contemporary works in psychology and especially the work of psychophysicists such as Weber, Fechner, and Wundt. One can note here the contrast with the subsequent aversion by most orthodox theorists of incorporating research from psychology into economics. In particular, Edgeworth states:

> This 'moral arithmetic' is perhaps to be supplemented by moral differential calculus, the Fechnerian method applied to pleasures in general. For Wundt has shown that sensuous pleasures may thereby be measured, and, as utilitarians hold, all pleasures are commensurable. (Edgeworth 1881, 60)

He was extremely enthusiastic about incorporating the findings of psychophysics into the economic and utilitarian calculus. A good example in this respect, is Fechner's Law which relates the quantity of sensation to the quantity of stimulus (intensity of stimulus), and the stimulus threshold. In his previous work (1877), Edgeworth modified this "Law" in view of his subsequent hedonic calculus as follows:

$$\pi = \mathrm{k}[(\mathrm{y}) - \mathrm{f}(\beta)]$$

where the symbols π, k, f, y and β respectively denote, 'the pleasure of a sentient element', 'capacity for pleasure', a function which the first differential is positive and the second is negative, the quantity of pleasure for stimulus and 'the "threshold", the lowest value of stimulus for which there is sense of pleasure at all', while β and k are co-efficients' (Edgeworth 1877, 42). He will employ this relationship in order to set a basis for his utilitarian calculus where he ultimately links it to the Bentham's Greatest Happiness Principle and even to the Malthusian relationship between the quantity of food and the level of population (see also Newman 1987, 90–91). Furthermore, Edgeworth contributed to the spread of statistical methods in economics. His works "Methods of Statistics" (1885) and 'Observation and Statistics' (1887) became extremely influential for the theory and application of statistical techniques to social and economic data (see also Stigler 1986; Baccini 2007).

Edgeworth's work and especially his *Mathematical Psychics*, represents the peak of the combination of the application of mathematical and physics tools to economics. His identification of maximum energy of physics with that of the maximum pleasure in economic calculus is Edgeworth's central idea. Moreover, his conception of man as a pleasure machine clearly implies the legitimacy of incorporating psychophysics into economic theory. Therefore, Edgeworth's work represents the quintessence of the strive to transform economics into exact science on a par with physical sciences.

3.3 Fisher: Hydraulics and Economics

Edgeworth's methodological stance gained momentum among subsequent main figures in the history of mainstream economics. Thus, after Edgeworth, there was further incorporation of mathematics and methods from mathematical physics in economic theory. The next figure who contributed to the formation of current ideas about method in economics was Irwin Fisher who is considered to be one of the most important promoters of marginalism in America. According to many specialists, Irving Fisher, accomplished the most thoroughgoing mathematization of marginalist theory (e.g. Breslau 2003; Zouboulakis 2003). In line with Edgeworth, his methodological viewpoint is focused on the direct analogy between economics and physics. The approval of Edgeworth to Fishers' approach can be seen by Edgeworth's book review of *Mathematical Investigations* in the *Economic Journal* (1893). Edgeworth speaks highly of this work and especially Fisher's use of analogies from physics. He praises Fisher's analogy of economic and mechanical phenomena and especially the illustration of pure economics with hydrodynamics (Edgeworth 1893).

One of Fisher's doctoral supervisors was the influential theoretical physicist Willard. Gibbs. Fisher was much affected and probably impressed by Gibbs' physics methods. Thus, in order to complement the arguments in his doctoral thesis, he built an eLabourate hydraulic machine with pumps and levers, allowing him to demonstrate visually how the equilibrium prices in the market adjusted in response to changes in supply or demand. More specifically, he devised a liquid dynamic model of the behaviour of prices in general equilibrium. In this model, there are tubes connecting the various vessels of water that represent the interrelations between supply and demand for different commodities. The equilibrium water level represents economic equilibrium (Tobin 1987; Breslau 2003). It is extremely interesting, that Fisher, did not think of this devise as an illustration, but believed in its direct relation to economic phenomena. As Breslau writes "There is nothing in either of these texts to indicate that the role of these mechanical models is any different from that of mathematical models, in making, and not simply illustrating, theoretical arguments" (Breslau 2003, 397). The close analogy is repeated in Fisher's *The Purchasing Power of Money*, where there is also another liquid dynamic model describing the monetary system. The model is used to demonstrate the economic principle that the value of the bullion and the currency will tend to equilibrium (Fisher 1911, 112–148).

The vector mathematics of Fisher's professor Willard Gibbs, allowed for the commensuration of all demand, or indifference curves, in terms of homogeneous units of utility (Breslau 2003, 397). The following quotation provides the core of his methodological viewpoint.

> The introduction of mathematical method marks a stage of growth—perhaps it is not too extravagant to say, the entrance of political economy on a scientific era. (Fisher 1892, 85 or 1965, 109)

Apart from the above general position, Fisher, promoted the specific mathematical methodology of optimization under constraints that was to become standard in economic modelling. As J. Tobin states: "On a remarkable range of topics, modern theorists adopt and build upon Fisherian ideas, sometimes unknowingly. Fisher's methodologies, not just his use of mathematics but his explicit formulations of problems as constrained optimizations, is the accepted style of present-day theorizing" (Tobin 1985, 34). This method was widely applied to problems in classical physics and especially classical mechanics.

Furthermore, a substantial number of pages in his most important work are devoted to demonstrate the direct analogies between economics and physics and especially mechanics. Fisher was convinced that terms from physics correspond to terms in economics thus supporting explicitly the analogy between economics and classical mechanics. He presents a list of terms that economists use and which have been employed from physics. Examples are: equilibrium, stability, elasticity, expansion, inflation, reaction, distribution (price), levels, movement, friction (Fisher 1892, 24). His next logical step is to construct a table of correspondence of terms and concepts between classical mechanics and economics.

In mechanics		In economics
A particle	Corresponds to	An individual
Space	"	Commodity
Force	"	Marginal utility or disutility
Work		Disutility
Energy	"	Utility
Work or energy = Force × space	"	Disutility or utility = MU × commodity
Force is a vector (dir. in space)	"	MU is a vector (dir. in commodity)
Forces are added by vector addition.	"	MUs are added by vector addition
Work and energy are scalars	"	Disutility and utility are scalars
Equilibrium will be where net energy is maximum	"	Equilibrium will be where gain is maximum

Fisher (1892, 85–86)

The above table of correspondence between economics and physics does not serve as a mere indication of similarities. For Fisher, the fundamental approach towards the analysis of economic phenomena should be based on these concepts. As Breslau points out: "In all of these areas (price formation, the monetary system, interest) Fisher proceeded by translating problems that had been understood in terms of differentiated social actors and goods, into terms of a mechanical system equilibrating a homogeneous substance (Breslau 2003, 399). For instance, in his discussion of the relationship between price, quantity and marginal utility, he uses the example of a cistern where the amount of liquid represents commodity and the distance of its surface from the top, its marginal utility (Fisher 1892, 26).

The direct analogies between economics and classical physics are not confined to Fisher's most important work. In his subsequent *The Purchasing Power of Money*, he assigns the quantity theory of money the status of a an exact physical law. As he writes:

> Practically, this proposition [the quantity theory of money] is an exact law of proportion, as exact and as fundamental in economic science as the exact law of proportion between pressure and density of gases in physics, assuming temperature to remain the same. (Fisher 1911, 320)

In the same manner, he repeats his conviction about the status of 'laws in economics in his subsequent and probably, his most well-known work *The Theory of Interest*. He states:

> I) Rational and empirical laws in economics are thus analogous to rational and empirical laws of physics or astronomy. Just as we may consider the actual behaviour of the tides as a composite result of the rational Newtonian law of attraction of the moon and the empirical disturbances of continents, islands, inlets, and so forth, so we may consider the actual behaviour of the rates of interest in New York City as a composite of the rational laws of our second approximation and the empirical disturbances of Federal Reserve policy together with numberless other institutional, historical, legal, and practical factors. (Fisher 1930, 107).

In a discussion among prominent American economic theorists of the period, Fisher presented his views regarding the nature of the disciplines with such figures as H.J. Davenport, W.H. Hamilton, Richard T. Ely, and B.M. Anderson, Jr. This discussion which was published in the *American Economic Review*, the physics ideal is present and clear. As he writes:

> II) One of the speakers has said that economics is not physics. No, but its method is the method of physics, and I believe a study of physics to be one of the best preparations for a young man intending to enter economic theory. The trouble with economic theory is that economists have entered the field, either from the a priori side of philosophy and metaphysics where the proper importance of cold facts has not been recognized, or on the other hand, from the side of history where only facts and not principles have been studied. (Davenport et al. 1916, 167).

Thus, in line with Edgeworth, Fisher's work established a close connection between physics and economic concepts and furthermore, he introduced specific mathematical methods from classical physics to economics. These methods are widely used in contemporary economic theorizing. More importantly, he provided an extensive methodological justification for the physics analogy in economics. In this respect, his approach had a major influence to the development of orthodox economic methodological viewpoint.

3.4 The Methodological Influence of Edgeworth and Fisher

The explicit references to the physics methodological ideal are not present in current economics. It seems that most orthodox economists are confident regarding the scientific status of the discipline in spite of the widespread criticism. Thus they do not feel the need to refer to the analogies from physics for methodological justification. However, the physics methodological ideal heavily promoted by Edgeworth and Fisher has exerted considerable influence on many crucial aspects of the discipline (see also Mirowski 1989). In our view, there are three important features of current mainstream economics which are heavily connected with the adoption of the physics ideal. These three are: the mathematization of economics, the hostility towards methodological discussion and the negative attitude towards incorporating findings from other social sciences and especially from the related field of psychology.

3.5 The Mathematization of Economics

The close methodological analogies between economics and classical physics advocated by both Edgeworth and Fisher clearly facilitated the extensive use of mathematics in economic analysis. As was observed, the systematic use of mathematics was justified by both authors in terms of making economics more scientific in the manner of physics (see also Turk 2012).

Edgeworth's introduction and most importantly his methodological justification, of the calculus of variation (finding the maximum by using the signs of first second derivatives) is an indicative example in this respect. The use of Lagrange equations is another example of a mathematical method borrowed directly from classical mechanics. Furthermore, Fisher's doctoral thesis operated in the framework of Walrasian general equilibrium where he was able to apply the methods of vector calculus of his mentor, the physicist W. Gibbs. Fisher also explored in great detail, the mathematics of utility functions maximization (see also Tobin 1985).

The subsequent use of these methods became standard especially after the publication of Samuelson's *Foundations.* Samuelson himself admits to this influence in an essay dealing with the intellectual development of his seminal work:

> III) I was vaccinated early on to understand that economics and physics could share the same formal theorems (Euler's theorem on homogeneous functions, Weierstras's theorems on constrained maxima, Jacobi determinant identities underlying Le Chatelier reactions, etc.), while still not resting on the same empirical foundations and certainties. (Samuelson 1998, 1376)

With above in mind, one can explain the widespread use of the specific mathematical tools found in most contemporary mainstream economics texts. In particular, the main analytical technique of constraint optimization (taken directly from classical mechanics) is preferred over other analytical mathematical methods such as input-output matrices or Markov chains (see also Mirowski 1984). The almost universally used nowadays concept of utility, which for Edgeworth and Fisher corresponds to the classical notion of energy, can be viewed in the same framework, although a number of authors have shown that the concept is not necessary for most contemporary formulations (e.g. Wong 1978). In general, the high degree of mathematization of contemporary mainstream economics has been the subject of much debate which focuses on the nature and method of the discipline (see for instance, Beed and Kane 1991; Dow 2012).

3.6 The Anti-methodology Stand

One can notice the contemporary view popular among many mainstream theorists that questions concerning the method of economics are not worthy. For instance in a series of well-known writings, Frank Hahn argued that the study of economic methodology is irrelevant (e.g. Hahn 1992). Caldwell (1993), Lawson (1994) and Backhouse (2010) among many others, have addressed this issue pointing out the anti-methodology stance of mainstream economics is widely accepted without serious arguments (see also Hoover 1995). However, this hostility to economic methodology is not novel but goes back to Fisher:

> IV) It has long seemed to me that students of the social sciences, especially sociology and economics, have spent too much time in discussing what they call methodology. I have usually felt that the man who essays to tell the rest of us how to solve knotty problems would be more convincing if first he proved out his alleged method by solving a few himself. Apparently those would-be authorities who are forever telling others how to get results do not get any important results themselves. (Fisher 1932, 1).

A number of explanations regarding this negative attitude towards the study of economic methodology have been suggested. Ideological concerns, psychological motives, merely defensive responses through fear, or dislike, of criticism, the lack of any philosophical training, and sheer ignorance, are some of the reasons mentioned in the literature (see for instance, Lawson 1994). The physics scientific ideal is also relevant in explaining the general hostility towards the study of economic methodology. The scientific prestige of physics and thus of the economics of Edgeworth and Fisher, makes methodological discussion and critique obsolete, in the sense that it shields economics from methodological attacks. Most mainstream economists are content with the methodological outline provided by Friedman's (1953) essay which effectively dismisses any methodological discourse concerning the role of assumptions in economics. It is indicative that in this essay, Friedman also uses the analogy of physical sciences in his effort to construct the methodological basis of positive economics:

> V) In short, positive economics is, or can be, an "objective" science, in precisely the same sense as any of the physical sciences. (Friedman 1953, 4)

Thus, the high scientific status of economics, deriving from its close analogies to physics, renders any methodological discussion obsolete.

3.7 Anti-psychologism

Another consequence of the classical physics methodological ideal was the rejection of findings from other social sciences and especially from psychology. As was discussed, Edgeworth was in favour of incorporating psychological findings, but this stance should be seen in the context of his overall methodological perspective. More specifically, Edgeworth viewed psychological phenomena as a legitimate field for the application of mathematical tools. Thus, his willingness to link 'hedonic calculus' from psychophysics to utilitarian calculus in economics. On the contrary however, Fisher was clearly against the inclusion of psychological concepts in economics. As he writes in the beginning of his *Investigations*:

> VI) "To fix the idea of utility the economist should go no farther than is serviceable in explaining economic facts. It is not his province to build a theory of psychology." (Fisher 1892, 11)

The differences in attitudes are due to the fact that Fisher thought of psychology as a 'soft' subject not worthy for consideration by the hard science of economics. In this sense, the following statement is indicative:

> VII) But the economist need not envelope his own science in the hazes of ethics, psychology, biology and metaphysics. (Fisher 1892, 23)

In the same conceptual tradition, Pareto believed that the construction of the fictional model of economic man was adequate for the needs of economic theory, thus clearly implying that psychological findings are not necessary (Pareto 1971; see also Bruni and Guala 2001; McLure 2010). In more modern times, one of the main aims of Samuelson's revealed preference theory was to dismiss the alleged psychological concepts of utility theory (Samuelson 1938, 61–62; Samuelson 1947). This clearly indicates that a psychology-free economics was a very important methodological goal (see also Wong 1978; Drakopoulos 1997).

The dismissal of psychological findings was linked to the aim of the scientific character of economics. The rejection of all "metaphysical and psychological elements" was one of the main requirements for the establishment of the 'scientific' status of economics. An additional reason for the tendency to separate economics from other social sciences, including psychology, has to do with the perception of economics as the most advanced of the social sciences, and hence the one that is closest to the physical sciences (Seligman 1969; Dow 2002, 170–175). The anti-psychologism bias of mainstream economics is also closely linked to the irrelevance of the assumptions thesis expressed in M. Friedman's (1953) well-known paper. The central idea here is that the realism of behavioural assumptions in economics does not matter as long as aggregate data behaves as if these assumptions were accurate (Friedman 1953). This clearly implies that findings from psychology are not nor relevant for economics given that assumptions do not matter for the validity of the theory.

Thus, anti-psychologism as a widely accepted methodological position provided a strong shield from criticism targeting the behavioural foundations of mainstream economics. Furthermore, it provided support for the pure 'economic' approach to human behaviour, which is seen as extremely successful and superior compared to other social sciences (for a detailed account of the uneasy relationship between mainstream economics and psychology, see Lewin 1996; Rabin 2002).

Concluding Comments

Although analogies between economics and physics can be found in a number of classical and marginalist authors, Edgeworth's and Fisher's works represent the highest point of classical physics imitation. These two influential economists transferred important terms and concepts from classical physics to economics. In addition, they provided the methodological grounding for the adoption of the physics scientific ideal in mainstream economics. This scientific ideal was extremely influential for the formation of current mainstream economics thinking as was seen through the works of Samuelson, Friedman and others. It was also seen that there were important consequences of this methodological stance which are the following: (1) the physics ideal meant that economics should adopt the established mathematical methods from physics. This was one of the most important reasons for the increased mathematization of economic theory. (2) The status of mainstream economics as a 'hard' science led to the relegation of the methodological discussion concerning the status of orthodox theory. Furthermore, the anti-methodology stance shields mainstream economics from heterodox attacks. (3) The 'hard' science status also implies that economics does not need to adopt findings, concepts, or generally ideas from other 'soft' social fields like psychology.

In general, the arguments presented in the paper might contribute to the better understanding of the role of the physics scientific ideal in shaping important elements of contemporary mainstream economic theorizing. The discussion might also contribute to the methodological debate concerning the role of the scientific ideal in mainstream economics.

References

Baccini B (2007) Edgeworth on the foundations of ethics and probability. Eur J Hist Econ Thought 14:79–96

Backhouse R (2010) Methodology in action. J Econ Methodol 17:3–15

Beed C, Kane O (1991) What is the critique of the mathematization of economics? Kyklos 44:581–612

Breslau D (2003) Economics invents the economy: mathematics, statistics, and models in the work of Irving Fisher and Wesley Mitchell. Theory Soc 32:379–411

Bruni L, Guala F (2001) Vilfredo Pareto and the epistemological foundations of choice theory. Hist Polit Econ 33:21–49

Cairnes J (1875) The character and logical method of political economy. Macmillan, London

Caldwell B (1993) Economic methodology: rationale, foundations, prospects. In: Mäki U, Gustafsson B, Knudsen C (eds) Rationality, institutions and economic methodology. Routledge, London, pp 45–60

Creedy J (1980) Some recent interpretations of mathematical psychics. Hist Polit Econ 12:267–276

Davenport H, Hamilton W, Ely R, Fisher I, Anderson B (1916) Tendencies in economic theory—discussion. Am Econ Rev 6:62–169

Dow S (2002) Economic methodology: an inquiry. Oxford University Press, Oxford

Dow S (2012) Foundations for new economic thinking: a collection of essays. Palgrave Macmillan, Basingstoke, Hampshire

Drakopoulos SA (1994) Some implications of the new physics for economic methodology. S Afr J Econ 62:198–209

Drakopoulos SA (1997) Origins and development of the trend towards value-free economics. J Hist Econ Thought 19:286–300

Edgeworth FY (1877) New and old methods of ethics or "Physical ethics and methods of ethics". James Parker and Co., Oxford, Also in Newman (ed.) (2003)

Edgeworth FY (1881) Mathematical psychics: an essay of the application of mathematics to moral sciences. Kegan Paul, London

Edgeworth FY (1885) Methods of statistics. J R Stat Soc, Jubilee volume, pp 181–217

Edgeworth FY (1887) Observations and statistics: an essay on the theory of errors of observation and the first principles of statistics (read 25 May 1885), Transactions of the Cambridge Philosophical Society, XIV, pp 138–69

Edgeworth FY (1893) Review of Fisher's Mathematical investigations. Econ J 3:108–112

Fisher I (1892) [1965] Mathematical investigations in the theory of value and prices. Yale University Press, New Haven

Fisher I (1911) The purchasing power of money: its determination and relation to credit, interest and crises. Macmillan, New York

Fisher I (1930) The theory of interest, as determined by impatience to spend income and opportunity to invest it. Macmillan, New York

Fisher I (1932) Statistics in the service of economics. J Am Stat Assoc 28:181

Friedman M (1953) The methodology of positive economics, in Essays in positive economics. University of Chicago Press, Chicago

Hahn F (1992) Reflections. Royal Economic Society Newsletter, 77

Hoover K (1995) Why does methodology matter for economics? Econ J 105:715–734

Jevons WS (1871) The theory of political economy. Macmillan, London

Lawson T (1994) Why are so many economists opposed to methodology? J Econ Methodol 1:105–134

Lewin S (1996) Economics and psychology: lessons for our own day from the early Twentieth Century. J Econ Lit XXXIV:1293–1323

McLure M (2010) Pareto, Pigou and third-party consumption: divergent approaches to welfare theory with implications for the study of public finance. Eur J Hist Econ Thought 17:635–657

Mill JS (1874) Essays on some unsettled questions of political economy. Longmans, Green, Reader and Oyer, London

Mirowski P (1984) Physics and the 'marginalist revolution'. Camb J Econ 8:361–379

Mirowski P (1989) More heat than light: economics as social physics, physics as nature's economics. Cambridge University Press, Cambridge

Mirowski P (1994) Marshalling the unruly atoms: understanding Edgeworth's career. In: P. Mirowski (ed), Edgeworth on chance, economic hazard and statistics. Rowman & Littlefield, Lanham

Newman P (1987) Edgeworth, Francis Ysidro. In: Eatwell J, Milgate M, Newman P (eds) The New Palgrave: a dictionary of economics, vol II. Macmillan, London, pp 84–98

Pareto V (1971) [1907] Manual of political economy (transl. by A. Schwier). MacMillan, London

Rabin M (2002) A perspective on psychology and economics. Eur Econ Rev 46:657–685

Samuelson P (1938) A note on the pure theory of consumer's behaviour. Economica 5:61–71

Samuelson P (1947) Foundations of economic analysis. Harvard University Press, Cambridge, MA

Samuelson P (1998) How foundations came to be. J Econ Lit 36:1375–1386
Say JB (1803) Treatise on political economy, English edition. A.M. Kelley, New York, 1964
Seligman B (1969) The impact of positivism on economic thought. Hist Polit Econ 1:256–278
Smith A (1980 ed.) Essays on philosophical subjects, edited by WPD Wightman. Clarendon Press, Oxford
Stigler S (1986) The History of Statistics, Cambridge, MA: Harvard University Press
Tobin J (1985) Neoclassical theory in America: J. B. Clark and Fisher. Am Econ Rev 75:28–38
Tobin J (1987) Fisher, Irwin. In: Eatwell J, Milgate M, Newman P (eds) The New Palgrave: a dictionary of economics, vol II. Macmillan, London, pp 369–276
Turk M (2012) The mathematical turn in economics: Walras, the French mathematicians, and the road not taken. J Hist Econ Thought 34:149–167
Walras L (1871) [1965] Elements of pure economics, transl. by W. Jaffe. Allen and Unwin, London
Wong S (1978) The foundations of Paul Samuelson's revealed preference theory. Routledge and Kegan Paul, London
Zouboulakis M (2003) L' équation des échanges de Fisher et la loi de Boyle. Les limites de l'analogie physique en économie. Econ Soc 33:2191–2206

Chapter 4
Elements of a Theory of the Firm in Adam Smith and John Stuart Mill

Michel S. Zouboulakis

4.1 Introduction

Although the notion of the firm was officially introduced by Ronald Coase in his seminal paper of 1937, the concept itself was not strange to Classical Political Economists despite a well received view. To explain the "strange disappearance of the entrepreneur from the centre of the stage of economic debate", Blaug (1986 78) has stated that "English classical economists, regarded production and the investment of capital as a more or less automatic process, involving no critical decision making and certainly no risky judgment or imagination of any kind". As against this view, it is suggested here that theoretical considerations on the nature of the firm were present in the work of at least two classical economists namely Adam Smith and John Stuart Mill. After presenting very briefly Coase's contribution, an attempt will be made to reveal that internal organization of industrial firms and their organization were thoroughly discussed in Classical Political Economy. Smith and Mill have provided two distinct elementary explanations for the existence of firms, related to the advantages of the division of Labour and the needs for larger capital accumulation respectively.

An earlier version of this paper was presented at the 2007 ICABE at the University of Piraeus and the 13th Annual ESHET conference at the University of Macedonia in 2009. I am grateful to the attendants of both sessions as well to Prof. T. Lianos and G. Bitros for their useful remarks and comments.

M.S. Zouboulakis (✉)
University of Thessaly, Department of Economics, 43, Korai Str. 38333, Volos, Greece
e-mail: mzoub@econ.uth.gr

G.C. Bitros, N.C. Kyriazis (eds.), *Essays in Contemporary Economics*,
DOI 10.1007/978-3-319-10043-2_4

4.2 The Absence of a Neoclassical Firm and Coase's Critique

In standard microeconomics—the General Equilibrium model—resources are allocated by means of the price mechanism to produce commodities that are also distributed through the very same mechanism. This is how Henderson and Quandt (1958) describe the firm in their famous textbook:

> A firm is a technical unit in which commodities are produced. Its entrepreneur (owner and manager) decides how much of and how one or more commodities will be produced, and gains the profit or bears the loss which results from his decision. An entrepreneur transforms inputs into outputs, subject to the technical rules specified by his production function. (p. 42)

In that sense, no business firms—i.e. durable rent seeking organizations—are needed. Whenever a businessman foresees a profit in a particular industry, he/she gathers instantaneously and without any transaction cost the best available resources to produce or provide what the consumer needs. Moreover, in the former sense producers are supposed to have unlimited cognitive capacities not only about the present quality and price of inputs but as well about the future of consumer preferences and market characteristics. Only then it is possible to reach optimal decisions, by eliminating the sources of future uncertainties. Thus, business decision making is trivialized to the application of simple rules of maximization. As Baumol correctly concluded, "there is no room for enterprise or initiative" (1968, 6) and the neoclassical firm is "entrepreneurless".

Ronald Coase, in his seminal paper of 1937, criticized the unrealisticness of this view and pointed out that in the real world there are important costs of participating in a market such as costs for "discovering what the relevant prices are", "costs of negotiating and concluding a separate contract for each exchange transaction", costs for directing and "obey the directions of an entrepreneur" and finally costs of making long term contracts to minimize the risks of the future (Coase 1937, 390–391). These costs have come to be known, after Arrow, as "transaction costs"[1] and because they form an important part of the real business world, durable profit oriented organizations do exist to minimize their burden: "The main reason why it is profitable to establish a firm would seem to be that there is a cost of using the price mechanism" (Coase 1937, 390).

In a broader perspective, a comprehensive definition of the firm is the following:

> A firm is defined as an integrated and durable organization involving two or more people, acting openly or tacitly as a 'legal person', capable of owning assets, set up for the purpose of producing goods or services, with the capacity to sell or hire these goods or services to customers. (Hodgson 2001, 317).

[1] Although the concept is introduced by J.R. Commons in 1931 and definitely established by Coase, the term 'TC' was coined by Arrow in a US Congress committee paper in 1969, as Williamson (1985, 18) reports. For a detailed analysis of the concept see Furubotn and Richter (1998, 47–76).

Starting from this broader definition our task will next be focused on stressing out the presence of the concept of the firm in Classical Political Economy.

4.3 The Idea of the Firm in Smith's *Wealth of Nations*

Not accidentally, in his 'Nobel Lecture' Coase refers to Adam Smith to point out that the main theme of the *Wealth of Nations*, was that "the economy could be coordinated by a system of prices (the 'invisible hand') and furthermore with beneficial results" (Coase 1992, 713). In his view, Smith was the father of the idea of an economic system working by itself, and therefore he is the one to be blamed of the lack of interest of economists about what happens in between the entrepreneurial idea, the acquisition of the factors of production and the sale of the goods that are produced by these factors. Coase's view is still accepted by New Institutionalists such as Furubotn and Richter (1998, 457) who bravely conclude that "Classical theory proper had no theory of the firm"! This is not the place to discuss how simplistic is this description of Adam Smith's self-regulated economic system (cf. Sen 2011). Only the latter view, about the lack of any theory explaining the existence of firms in Classical Political Economy will be challenged here.

To begin with, every student in Economics is aware of the positive effects on productivity resulting from the "Division of Labour". In the very first chapter of his book Smith studies precisely how the effective organization of labour inside a firm (his famous pin-making manufacture) increases its productive power. Following William Petty and Denis Diderot, Smith developed a full account of the effects of the division of labour considering it as the main factor of productivity and subsequent economic progress: "improvement of the dexterity of the workman", "saving the time lost in passing from one sort of work to another", "invention of machines. . .in order to facilitate and quicken" the task of the workman (Smith 1776, 11–13).[2] The organization of labour gets more effective as capital accumulation grows: "labour can be more and more subdivided in proportion only as stock is previously more and more accumulated" (Smith 1776, 291–292). Although he makes no clear statement of the idea of returns to scale, Smith is definitely conscious of the fact that the size of the firm determines the degree of division of labour and its level of organization. In that sense, the very existence of firms is explained through the division of Labour dynamics: as the market grows, firms are created and get larger employing more Labour and capital, and the division and specialization of Labour increases, pushing productivity to grow as well as

[2] Beraud (1992, 318) traces the influence of Diderot and makes full account of the effects of the division of labour according to Smith. As known, Plato and Xenophon have already analyzed both ideas of the social and technical division of labor. See Schumpeter (1954, 56) and Karayiannis (1990a). Smith has also recognised the alienating effects of the over-extended division of labour on workers' character and intellectual ability (1776 II, 302–3). Cf. West (1996).

"universal opulence".[3] As Schumpeter has emphasized, "nobody, either before or after A. Smith, ever thought of putting such a burden upon division of labour" (1954, 187). The overall economic prosperity was in fact based upon specialization in production and division of Labour (Sen 2011, 259).

Because of his attention into the organization of the firm, Smith is able to recognize the multiple functions of entrepreneurship and to distinguish clearly three components of profit in his theory of value (a) "the profits of the undertaker of the work who hazards his stock"; (b) the proper returns of capital "regulated altogether by the value of the stock employed" and (c) the remuneration of management or, "the wages of a particular sort of labour, the labour of inspection and direction" (Smith 1776, 54). To explain the nature of profits, he underlines the fact that managing a firm is often the work of a different person than the owner of the capital:

> In many great works, almost the whole labour of this kind is committed to some *principal clerk*. His wages properly express the value of his labour of inspection and direction. Though in settling them some regard is had commonly, not only to his labour and skill, but to the trust which is reposed in him, yet they never bear any regular proportion to the capital of which he oversees the *management* (Smith 1776, 55, emphasis added)

This early reference to the principles of management is extremely relevant for our purposes here, for it shows not only that the size of the firm really matters both for the amount of profit as well for the cost of management.

For that same reason Smith never leaves out of his sight the nature of the firm even in the more policy oriented second part of the *Wealth of Nations*. So, in the Book V, Smith studies meticulously two kinds of foreign trade firms, the "regulated companies" and the "joint-stock companies". In the former, individual merchants join the Company having the monopoly of trade with certain geographical regions, after paying a contribution to it and accepting its regulations, run their firm upon their own stock and at their own risk. In the latter, many merchants join their stock together and "each member shares in the common profit or loss in proportion to his share in this stock" (Smith 1776, 256). Smith compares the incentives, the risks and the insecurity problems of the "directors" of the two kinds of foreign trade companies through detailed case studies of specific British firms which dominated the international commerce in eighteenth century. He furthermore examines the organisation, asset specificity and running expenses of these firms. To give an example of the accuracy and depth of his analysis, an early description of the principal-agent problem is given bellow:

> The directors of [joint stock] companies, however, being the managers rather of other people's money than of their own, it cannot be expected, than they should watch over it with the same anxious vigilance with which the partners in a private copartnery frequently watch over their own. (1776, 264)

[3] Pitelis (1998, 1012) explains the emergence of firms as "the result of the merchants' desire to further their interests by effecting a more efficient division of labor", without mentioning Smith.

Far from ignoring the role and necessity of firms as coordinating mechanisms, Smith proved himself to be an accurate observer of the institutional specificities of big business organisations and of the principal-agent problem.

4.4 The Idea of the Firm in Mill's *Principles*

David Ricardo's Political Economy focused on the capitalist owner of the factors of production, rather than on its economic and managerial functions. For that reason no theoretical insight into the capitalist firm was ever made by Ricardo. On the contrary, J.B. Say contributed significantly to understand the process of decision making inside a firm by re-discovering Richard Cantillon's genuine concept of 'entrepreneur'. Say defined the entrepreneur as the person which takes the decisions about production, who "combines the factors of production into a producing organism", and who finally introduces the technological innovations into the productive unit, to face the competition and uncertainties of the market.[4]

According to Schumpeter (1954, 556), Mill was the first major economist who recognized this analytic progress:

> The decisive step was taken by J.S. Mill, who brought the term *entrepreneur* into general use among English economists and, in analysing the entrepreneurial function, went from 'superintendence' to 'control' and even to 'direction', which, he admitted, required 'often no ordinary skills'.

Say's contribution helped Mill to go beyond the Ricardian capitalist owner of the factor of production and to focus on the role of the entrepreneur and the internal organization of the firm. Industrial firms result from the historical tendency of the growth of capital and Mill tries to comprehend the details of this movement.

First, following Smith, Mill clearly distinguishes the functions of the capital owner from those of the capitalist investor and those of the manager, while introducing explicitly the term 'entrepreneur' into his analysis. This is why, in his distribution theory (Book II, Chap. XV), he defines three distinct components of profit: the "return for abstinence", the "indemnity for risk" and the "remuneration for the labour and skill required for superintendence" (1848, 406). He calls attention to the fact that "these different compensations may be either paid to the same, or to different persons". Speaking of the remuneration of superintendence, Mill seems to be aware of the requirements of effective industrial firm management:

> The control of the operations of industry usually belongs to the person who supplies the whole or the greatest part of the funds by which they are carried on... To exercise this control with efficiency, if the concern is large and complicated, requires great assiduity, and often, no ordinary skill. (idem)

---

[4] For a careful study of the entrepreneurial functions according to Say, see Fontaine (1999) and Hébert and Link (1982, 17–20) who also evaluate Cantillon's contribution. Cf. Karayiannis (1990b).

Second, Mill devotes a whole chapter (Book I, Chap. IX) on the distinct internal organizational problems of large scale industrial firms. Among the advantages of production on a large scale, he mentions the more advanced division of labour, the less than proportionate increase of "the expenses of a business", the greater possibility of investment to "expensive machinery" and "the saving in the labour of the capitalists themselves" (1848, 132–136). By the latter he meant that the effort of management increases to a lesser degree than the size of the firm. In Mill's words, "there is undoubtedly much more labour expended in the superintendence of many small capitals than in that one of one large capital" (1848, 136). As a modern economist would say, the size of the firm interacts with the process of internal decision-making (Arrow 1983, 229). Mill knew that and insisted on the advantages and the disadvantages of "joint stock companies". On the one hand, only such a company can afford the amount of capital necessary to build important projects such as a railway, and to guarantee the continuity of such costly and risky business operations such as banking and insurance. On the other hand, he recognizes that "joint stock or *associated management*" has some disadvantages over "individual management". As he emphasizes, "the chief of these is the much keener interest of the managers in the success of the undertaking" (1848, 138). Like Smith, Mill was aware of the principal-agent problem, believing that the "quality of the hired servants" is inferior to "the ministration of those personally interested in the work" (ib. 139). He even made accurate suggestions on how to increase the "fidelity and zeal of hired managers"; by keeping "the directing mind incessantly occupied with the subject" and giving them additional motives by connecting "their pecuniary interest with the interest of their employers, by giving them part of their remuneration in the form of a percentage on the profits" (1848, 141). The reason is that "management by hired servants, who have no interest for the result but that of preserving their salaries, is proverbially inefficient" (1848, 407). To enhance the efficiency of the hired managers Mill recommends that their remuneration should partly depend on the profits of the firm, "unless—he adds—they act under the inspecting eye, if not the controlling hand, of the person chiefly interested" (idem).

Finally, realizing that "industrial occupation should be carried on by larger and larger capitals" Mill offers a thorough study of the different legal forms of business associations or "partnerships".[5] Hence he compares the status of companies of unlimited and of limited partnership and the subsequent distribution of property rights inside these companies, with the contractual obligations arising from each legal form for each partner. Mill defends strongly the position that "complete freedom in the conditions of partnerships is indispensable" to take advantage of every legal form in different industries (1848, 906). He points out, for example, that "joint-stock companies with limited responsibility" because they are enforced by the law to give public information on the assets and accounts of the company, they

[5] Mill speaks about the legal forms of firms when he discusses the "ordinary functions of Government" in the last Book of the *Principles* (Chaps VIII & IX), in order to suggest the need for modernizing business law regulations.

offer sufficient warranties to their creditors. Full publicity and obligation to keep sincere accounts, counterbalance the lack of unlimited responsibility to secure both the capital and the transactions: "with proper securities for publicity, the capital of an association with limited liability could not be engaged in hazards beyond those ordinarily incident to the business it carries on" (1848, 901).

To sum up, Mill believed that industrial firms are the result of the progress of growth:

> as wealth increases and business capacity improves, we may look forward to a great extension of establishments, both for industrial and other purposes, formed by the collective contributions of large numbers (1848, 699).

Conclusions

New Institutional Economics, during the last three decades, has established that allocation of scarce resources is not made exclusively in the market between consumers and producers through the price mechanism in an institutional vacuum. Long-lasting hierarchical productive units are needed to collect, organize, coordinate and then distribute their products and services through the market, inside a particular and historically evolving institutional environment that contains formal regulations and organizations (Williamson 1985, 1992, 1994; Ménard 1994, 1995; Furubotn and Richter 1998; Henrekson 2007) and informal rules and institutions including social norms and values (North 1990; Hodgson 2006).

Classical Political Economists originally introduced the idea of the market as a self- adjusting mechanism, both as an analytical device and as a policy objective. Their macroeconomic, long-run perspective induced them to concentrate their attention to the conditions of distribution of the economic surplus through the market in a way that guarantees the reproduction of the economic system as a whole. Nevertheless, they did not neglect the problems related to the organization of production at the microeconomic level of the firm. As seen above, Smith explained the existence of firms as a means to increase productivity through more advanced technical division of Labour, inaugurating the competence-based theory of the firm (Hodgson 1998, 180). Mill explained that firms exist to face the needs for larger and larger capitals to produce more under the influence of the general progress of population and aggregate demand. Both Smith and Mill had a clear perception of the problems of internal organization of the industrial firms and how it affects their productivity, of the managerial functions of the entrepreneur as well as of the specificities related to the formal institutional structure of the industrial production units. Thus, the allegation of having no classical theory about the firm is simply not founded. Classical Political economists definitely believed that the market was not the exclusive coordinating mechanism of individual economic goals.

References

Arrow K (1983) Innovation in large and small firms. In: Swedberg R (ed) Entrepreneurship. The social science view. Oxford University Press, Oxford, 2000, pp 229–243

Baumol W (1968) Entrepreneurship in economic theory. Am Econ Rev 58:64–71

Beraud A (1992) La contribution fondatrice. Origine et développement de la pensée économique d'Adam Smith. In: Beraud A, Faccarello G (eds) Nouvelle histoire de la pensée économique. La Découverte, Paris

Blaug M (1986) Entrepreneurship before and after Schumpeter. In Swedberg R (ed) Entrepreneurship. The social science view. Oxford University Press, Oxford, 2000, pp 76–88

Coase R (1937) The nature of the firm. Economica 4:386–405

Coase R (1992) The institutional structure of production. Am Econ Rev 82:713–719

Fontaine P (1999) Classical political economy between two fires: Jean-Baptiste Say and Frank Knight on the enterprise economy. Hist Polit Econ 31:1–28

Furubotn E, Richter R (1998) Institutions and economic theory (2nd edn). University of Michigan Press, Ann Arbor, 2005

Hebert R, Link A (1982) The entrepreneur: mainstream views and radical critiques. Praeger, New York

Henderson HM, Quandt RE (1958) Microeconomic theory. MacGraw-Hill, New York, 1980

Henrekson M (2007) Entrepreneurship and institutions. Comp Labour Law Policy J 28:717–742

Hodgson GM (1998) Competence and contract in the theory of the firm. J Econ Behav Organ 35:19–201

Hodgson GM (2001) How economics forgot history. Routledge, London

Hodgson GM (2006) What are institutions? J Econ Issues 40:1–25

Karayiannis A (1990a) The Platonic ethico-economic structure of society. Quaderni di Storia dell'Economia Politica 8:3–45

Karayiannis A (1990b) The entrepreneurial function in economic literature: a synoptic review. Rivista Internazionale di Scienze Economiche e Commerciali 37:245–268

Ménard C (1994) Organizations as coordinating devices. Metroeconomica 45:224–247

Ménard C (1995) Markets as institutions versus organizations as markets. Disentangling some fundamental concepts. J Econ Behav Organ 28:161–182

Mill JS (1848) Principles of political economy with some of their applications to social philosophy, 7th edn 1873, re-edited by William J. Ashley 1909. A. Kelley, New York reprint, 1973

North DC (1990) Institutions, institutional change and economic performance. Cambridge University Press, Cambridge

Pitelis C (1998) Transaction costs and the historical evolution of the capitalist firm. J Econ Issues 32:999–1017

Schumpeter JA (1954) History of economic analysis. Allen & Unwin, London

Sen A (2011) Uses and abuses of Adam Smith. Hist Polit Econ 43:257–271

Smith A (1776) An inquiry into the nature and causes of the Wealth of Nations. The University of Chicago Press, Chicago, 1976

West EG (1996) Adam Smith on the cultural effects of specialization: splenetics versus economics. Hist Polit Econ 28:83–106

Williamson OE (1985) The economic institutions of capitalism: firms, markets, relational contracting. The Free Press, New York

Williamson OE (1992) Markets, hierarchies and the modern corporation: an unfolding perspective. J Econ Behav Organ 17:335–352

Williamson OE (1994) Transaction cost economics and organization theory. In: Smelser NJ, Swedberg R (eds) Handbook of economic sociology. Princeton University Press, Princeton

Chapter 5
The Birth of Modern Enterprise Theology: Protestant England: 1600–1900

Sarah Drakopoulou Dodd

5.1 Introduction

Drakopoulou Dodd and Gotsis (2007, 2009) and Anderson et al. (2000) have deployed the generic heading "enterprise values" to explore ancient and modern (theological and philosophical) reflection on entrepreneurship ethics. Their work focuses on areas such as "wealth creation and its use, labour, self-responsibility, relationships between family and economic activity, the pursuit of profit-bearing opportunities, price-setting and the raising, accumulation and use of capital" (Drakopoulou Dodd and Gotsis 2009, 101). Anderson et al. (2000, 12) claim that "the Thatcherite enterprise culture was probably the most entrepreneurial spirit of capitalism ever to blow across the face of modern Britain". They demonstrate that "many of its chief protagonists sought to validate and legitimate their work by reference to traditional (Protestant) religion .... in many cases, explicit statements are made to the effect that theological and moral beliefs were driving the Thatcherites to "create" the enterprise culture" (Anderson et al. 2000, 12). Anderson et al. (2000, 12) also set out an ideal type of Thatcherite Enterprise Culture Theology, as shown in the list below:

- Promotion of freedom of choice and "opportunity".
- Adherence to free market economics.
- Promotion of self-responsibility.
- Diminution of social for individual and familial setting and duties.
- Idealisation of the entrepreneur and enterprise.
- Rediscovery of "Victorian values", such as thrift and hard work.

S.D. Dodd (✉)
ALBA Graduate Business School, Xenias 6-8, Athens 115 28, Greece

University of Strathclyde, Hunter Centre for Entrepreneurship, Sir William Duncan Building, Glasgow G4 0GE
e-mail: dodsarah@alba.edu.gr; sarah.drakopoulou-dodd@strath.ac.uk

G.C. Bitros, N.C. Kyriazis (eds.), *Essays in Contemporary Economics*,
DOI 10.1007/978-3-319-10043-2_5

- Anti-collectivism.
- Reduction of government involvement in the economic and industrial spheres.
- Strong state as concerns law and order.
- The insistence on a moral and theological justification for all of the above.

The aim of this chapter is to follow the development of these ideas from their nascent forms in Protestant England, until they reach an advanced cultural expression by 1900. As the precursors, the progenitors, of modern enterprise ideology—and especially that with a religious overtone—it is instructive to follow the unfolding and evolution of these concepts through time. It is also an opportunity to bring together three areas of special interest to the late Professor Anastasios Karayiannis: entrepreneurship, religion, and the history of economic thought. I was honoured to have collaborated with Tassos Karayiannis on studies in these areas, and—although he and I disagreed firmly about Margaret Thatcher and her legacy—I am sure we would have enjoyed discussing the details of my argument, and I miss greatly Tassos' combination of erudite scholarship, humour, and analytic thought. This paper then, is written in memory of my friend and colleague Anastasios Karayiannis, and it sets out to explore the developing roots of modern Enterprise Theology, in England, between 1600 and 1900.

Protestant England, between 1600 and 1900, witnessed many events and agents that have been linked with the development of enterprise principles and values: the Puritans, the Dissenters, the Glorious Revolution; the England of Cromwell and Victoria; of Hobbes, Adam Smith and Samuel Smiles. This paper explores key historical, theological, economic, industrial, ideological and philosophical developments of these three centuries in England, identifying and analysing the process by which a holistic and powerful enterprise ethic came into being.

5.2 Setting the Scene: England in the Sixteenth Century

Whilst Europe had been engaged in the tumults of the sixteenth century, England had followed a unique path through these troubled years. At the same time as Calvin was imprisoned in France (1534), Henry VIII's Act of Supremacy was passed in England, and with it separation from Rome. The dissolution of the monasteries began two years later, and shortly after Luther's death Edward VI succeeded his father (1547), sponsoring Cranmer's two great Books of Common Prayer. As the religious wars broke out in France (1562), the 39 articles were published in England (1563–1571) under Elisabeth. During Elisabeth's reign there was: "... a steady growth of capitalism in textiles and mining, a great increase of foreign trade and an outburst of joint-stock enterprise in connection with it, the beginnings of something like deposit-banking" (Tawney 1936, 176). By linking the church and state together, the Church of England became a key tool in the reinforcement of the monarchy's policies, and was increasingly used to legitimate state actions (Tawney 1936, 165). In particular, the state religion was used to sanction an adherence to traditional values and order. As on the continent, however, Puritanism in England appealed to:

"... those classes in society which combined economic independence, education, and a certain decent pride in their status" (Tawney 1936, 202), i.e., the bourgeoisie. That the new commercial classes were also the theological radicals led to a polarisation between the traditional Church of England Royalists on the one hand, and the industrial Puritans on another. Tawney notes that it is in the rise of Puritanism that the true English Reformation occurred, and not in the establishment of the Church of England (Tawney 1936, 198). During the brief reign of Mary Tudor (1553–1559), the Puritan Radicals were driven from England, and were influenced on the continent by Calvin and Bucer. They returned to England during Elisabeth's reign, and disputed strongly with the High-Church elements of Anglicanism. This disputation continued under James I and Charles 1, leading eventually to the Civil War, and the Commonwealth, when new religious liberties encouraged increased debate between moderate Anglicans, Presbyterians, Independents and Separatists (Congregationalists).

In the sixteenth century, churchmen still looked to canon law, church councils and the Schoolmen to decide on the morality of usury, the just price, and commerce (Tawney 1936, 158). The general wariness towards all such activity remained in place. Early seventeenth century Puritan writers, like Baxter, continued to be firmly opposed to the pursuit of riches, ostentatiousness, and free-competition unfettered by ethical considerations (Sombart, 1959, 34; Hudson 1959, 58; Weber 1930, 157). However, as with the ascetic sects of the fourteenth and fifteenth centuries, an emphasis on hard work, thrift and quiet living, as well as exclusion from mainstream life, led to economic success for English Puritans (Hudson 1959, 58). This in turn led to political ambition and influence, exemplified in its most powerful form in the Civil War and the Interregnum Commonwealth.

5.3 The Revolutionary Seventeenth Century

5.3.1 The Puritan Revolution

The Puritan movement in England in the early seventeenth century was resistant to the continued secular and religious power of the Church of England. With its seats in the Lords, its cannon courts, and its support of the Stuart monarchy, the established church was challenged on political as well as theological grounds by the Puritans: "Puritanism provided an ideological discipline that transcended older loyalties and stimulated criticism of accepted standards and institutions; it gave men confidence, courage and a feverish enthusiasm; it stirred up notions of equality" (Shaw 1968, 8).

Not least among the bones of contention, then, was the tacit support of equality which this genre of Puritanism gave, very much in contrast with the Church of England's place as upholder of the monarchy and the land-owning aristocracy. Perhaps it is not surprising that a movement composed in the main of bourgeois merchants should come eventually to challenge the status quo, nonetheless their message is indeed revolutionary: "Their preachers taught a doctrine of spiritual equality: one good man was as good as another, and better than a bad peer or bishop or king" (Hill 1966, 8l). As corollaries to this spiritual equality, religious liberty, individualism, discipline, and self-responsibility were also hallmarks of the English Puritans of the early Seventeenth Century. The Independents, whose number included Thomas Cromwell, believed that: "the Church should be independent from the government, and that each local congregation should be free to govern itself in matters of worship" (Thomson 1976, 62). Individualism was introduced to Protestantism in terms of the relationship of each layman with God and of the emphasis on personal election and calling. Here it has become a Congregationalist vehicle used to undermine the mainstream' church discipline and worship. Both these types of religious individualism were eventually joined by economic individualism.

Christian ascetic groups dedicated to hard work have shown a tendency to succeed economically. Such success almost inevitably comes to be seen as a reward from God for one's labour. One's calling then no longer requires that one respects the station to which God has assigned one, but rather that one strives to better oneself socially via labour and quiet living. Thus does economic individualism enter into Puritan thought (Hill 1966, 92). "Individualism, as a doctrine, sees in the individual and his psychological aptitudes the necessary basis of society's economic organisation, . . .by allowing him all the scope for self-development which is possible . . . if is entirely opposed to the medieval scheme of life" (Robertson 1959, 77).

Religious and economic liberty were also demanded increasingly vociferously by Puritans, from a state which had become ever more involved in managing the development of capitalism through legislation and sale or grant of franchises to courtiers. The selection of individual liberty as a battle-cry by the seventeenth century Puritans was to have consequences for their descendants down the centuries, yet was profoundly spiritual and egalitarian on the lips of these men: "To justify themselves they must appeal to eternal principles - and the great principle they discovered was that of liberty, or, of the liberties of Englishmen. The right of the individual to live his life and to enjoy his property within the limits fixed by known law was by them for ever rendered secure" (Smith 1962, 203).

A combination of economic, industrial and religious factors eventually led to the Puritans taking up arms for liberty in Civil War, and seizing control of England (and the rest of the United Kingdom) for the 20 years between 1640 and 1660. The tenor of this revolution is well expressed by Hill, who notes: "When the men of the Long Parliament wanted a shorthand phrase to sum up their cause they said they were defending religion, liberty and property" (Hill 1966, 105). The Long Parliament (1640) abolished all clerical courts, substantially reducing the influence of church upon state administration. The belief in economic freedom also encouraged a belief in the right to property, such a significant feature of later English thought (as in the work of Locke).

The Puritans' strong commitment to liberty, independence, fairness in state administration, and equality of all (property-owning) people is highly idealistic.

The theological underpinning of the Puritan movement is perhaps the most revolutionary of all their aspects, however, and is some distance from Calvin and Luther's theology of the Predestination of the elect: "The essence of Puritanism as a revolutionary creed lay in the belief that God intended the betterment of man's life on earth, that men could understand God's purposes and co-operate with Him to bring them to fruition" (Hill 1966, 168).

Yet the emphasis on equality and liberty in Puritanism did not result in positive benefits for the very poor. The gradual sanctification of economic success, the adherence to older doctrines on the value of hard work, and the ascetic discipline administered by the Puritans naturally facilitated alterations in perceptions of the poor and destitute. Provision for the poor, which had gone hand-in-hand with Church and State control in Calvin's Geneva, fell by the wayside as the increasing importance of individual labour and will made poverty seem a self-imposed sin based in idleness. In the early seventeenth century, care for the poor was implemented through the Poor Laws, the building of alms houses and hospitals and employment generation schemes. Over the later half of the seventeenth century this paternalistic care for God's poor was to change dramatically, so that a moral imperative to save the poor and destitute by forcing them to work, as slaves if necessary, was promulgated. This was accompanied with low wages and short holidays to keep them from idleness and sin. This is not an insignificant alteration in a religious ethic which had, since the first Judaic writings, given the poor a special place in religious mythology, and had a strong tradition of charitable acts (see Tawney 1936, 263–270; Smith 1962, 436–437).

The Restoration denied the Puritans any further attempts at national implementation of their theocratic principles, and instead their diminished enthusiasm was internalised into pursuit for individual salvation, as perhaps best exemplified in Bunyan's Pilgrim's Progress (Hill 1966, 253; Bunyan 1969). The Act of Toleration, passed in the wake of the "Glorious Revolution" of 1689, permitted the Puritans and other Dissenters freedom of worship, whilst still prohibiting them from holding public office, or attending University. Denied national influence or scholarship, the business activities of the late seventeenth century Puritans became a key outlet for expression of their calling, so that: "After 1689 dissenters had to face the, perils of worldly prosperity, to which their higher code, of business ethics and their more, single-minded application both contributed... but as men prospered they lost some of their earlier enthusiasm" (Hill 1966, 294; see also Hudson 1959, 61).

It is from this period, at the turn of the eighteenth century, that we see most clearly the outline of the Thatcherite Enterprise culture take shape, as economic endeavours become of ever more importance to Dissenting Protestants, and as such are progressively given increasing religious justification: "Discarding the suspicion of economic motives, which had been as characteristic of the reformers as of medieval theologians, Puritanism in its later phases added a halo of ethical sanctification to the appeal of economic expediency, and offered a moral creed, in which the duties of religion and the calls of business ended their estrangement in an unanticipated reconciliation" (Tawney 1936, 239).

5.3.2 The Revolution in Science

Religious revolution in England, however, cannot be understood in isolation. The seventeenth century was a period when new departures were made in a whole range of areas which challenged the traditional, the established. Among these was the explosion in science. Throughout the whole of the period of the Reformation and growth of Protestantism, science had gone through the most rapid development in its history. From the heliocentric writings of Copernicus in the mid-sixteenth century, to the Newton in the mid-seventeenth, man's view of the Universe was transformed, and especially his view of the place of God and man within the new cosmos: "There has never been a greater revolution in the history of thought than that marked by the establishment of the Copernican astronomy. The abandonment of a geocentric universe of matter was logically followed by the relinquishment of an anthropocentric universe of thought" (Smith 1962, 67).

Luther and Calvin (Commentary on Genesis 1847–1850 edition) both attacked the writings of Copernicus, which challenged belief in the literal truth of the Bible. Throughout the sixteenth and seventeenth centuries, in spite of the early opposition of the churches, other sciences than astronomy made leaps forward. Researchers in physics discovered magnetism, optics (Kepler), mechanics, statics, hydrostatics (Galileo, Descartes), the, barometer, the thermometer, and chemistry. Euclid was translated into Latin for the first time in 1505, leading to huge advances in reckoning, decimals, logarithms, algebra, calculus of probabilities, mathematical method, theory of numbers, trigonometry, cyclametry, conics and analytical geometry. Exploration and the invention of the, microscope, led to the collection and tabulation of data in geography, biology, zoology, botany and anatomy. Among thinkers and scientists working in this period were Descartes, Boyle, Huygens, Newton, Leibniz, Galileo, Pascal, Copernicus, Erasmus, Kepler, Locke, Hobbes, Spinoza and Bacon (Smith 1962, 2, 67–111). In addition to the revolution in the practice of science, and understanding of nature, these developments engendered a paradigm shift in the scholar's perception of the universe: "The material world was disassociated from the world of God and assumed to be rational, so that if could be apprehended and mastered by observation and measurement" (Nussbaum 1953, 1).

Descartes in particular led the way for the rationalists, by developing a reasoned approach to metaphysics quite, different to the Bibliocentric thought which had preceded him: "That the order of nature is invariable, that the scientific method if the proper approach to philosophy, that the life of reason is the chief hope of and the chief glory of man—these are the truths inculcated by Descartes" (Smith 1962, 186). Although a Christian himself, Descartes opened the way for the removal of theology for science, since his "Christian orthodoxy was tacked onto systems of thought as logically viable without it" (Hampson 1968, 28; see, also Descartes 1968, 1984).

If Descartes was the genius behind rationalism, then Bacon (1561–1627) gave birth to modern empiricism, Bacon attacked the Schoolmen for their inability to separate theology and superstition from science, and set out a strongly empirical methodology which gave emphasis to observation and "objective" interpretation of the natural world, free from the constraints of biblical or magisterial teaching (see, for example, Hampson 1968, 36, Smith 1962, 151, Bacon 1975). The implication—the revolution—of Bacon and Descartes' thought was to disengage God and theology from whole areas of human enquiry, including philosophy, science, and politics.

Newton extended the scientific revolution, and gave shape to later thought by articulating the laws of gravity. This set in place a deterministic paradigm of interpretation which understood all things to operate in a mechanistic way, following precise laws (see, for example Nussbaum 1953, 27): "The beautiful simplicity of a single law which appeared to explain the operation of every kind of earthly and celestial movement was a triumphant example of the possibilities of the new learning" (Smith 1962, 37; see also Newton 1952). Contemporary writers agree that the importance of Newton in promoting the notion of a deterministic Universe with—at the very least—a first benevolent cause, gave momentum to the development of new theologies which managed to accommodate Christianity within the revolutionary scientific paradigm. In particular, the Providentialism of the eighteenth century (and thereafter) can be shown to have its roots in Newtonian concepts of divinity. This has not always been viewed as a wholly positive contribution to the development of scientific enquiry: "For two centuries, then, the effort of Europeans to master their world was caged within the limiting framework of a deterministic system" (Nussbaum 1953, 27)

This whole scientific movement lead for the search for answers to age-old questions in rational analysis, experimentation and observation, and not in appeal to scripture or the scholastics. Economic questions began to be submitted to the nascent political arithmetic, rather than to canon law or the schoolmen. By the late seventeenth century the church's teachings on socioeconomic matters were no longer the paramount legitimating resource for politicians or groups of lobbying industrialists. Instead, appeals were made to reason, empirical analysis and a rudimentary mechanistic understanding of market operations. Yet the Puritan and Calvinistic virtues which had been the hallmark of post-Reformation Protestant Entrepreneurs left a legacy of belief in thrift, hard-work and independent individualism behind, which formed a strange cultural syncretism with the growth of both rationalism and empiricism.

5.3.3 The Revolution in Political Thought

The discoveries, inventions and theories of the thinkers and scientists, then, did not encourage a belief in a mysterious cosmos ordered according to the whims of an unfathomable God. Philosophy too began to fashion world-views based on mathematical and mechanical, rather than religious models, glorifying reason and natural order. Political philosophy, building on the individualism of the new commerce, and the reason of the new sciences, developed theories of liberty constrained only by those laws needed, rationally, to protect itself. Particularly in England, this thinking become a basic tenet promulgated by Hobbes, the Levellers, Locke and Milton alike. Thomas Hobbes' (1946) sought to identify and examine the locus of a state's power over its members. Legitimation of (usually) monarchical or imperial states had traditionally made appeal to the so-called divine right of Kings. Hobbes instead maintained that citizens and subjects owed loyalty to the state because it provided a much needed mechanism to protect them from each other. Individuals were "self-moving, appetitive, possessive" (Macpherson 1962, 265), and rightly so in Hobbes' view. He postulated that they interacted with each other via market-based exchanges, and that these exchanges, as well as the property and person of each individual, required a stable and autocratic society to protect them. No recourse to arguments of divine-right was required to legitimate power and authority under Hobbes' schema, and a god-less political and societal structure could be envisioned. Hobbes' atheism did not assist the spread of his theories during his lifetime, but his work is indeed revolutionary, since for the first time in the Christian West he: "... eliminated religion altogether as a source of moral values, and based ethics, as well as political theory, on the purely human urge towards self-preservation" (Hampson 1968, 29).

Hobbes moves beyond the religious and mild economic individualism of the Puritans, to set the motive for man's actions wholly in self-interest. Since this is inimical with the Christian tradition to date, small wonder perhaps that only a non-believer could articulate such thoughts. As Drakopoulos has pointed out, Hobbes' moral frame of reference is essentially egoistic and hedonistic. Although Drakopoulos demonstrates that Gassendi (1592–1655) had somewhat earlier rediscovered the philosophy of Epicurus and Aristippus, Gassendi retained a providentialist God in his scheme of thought. Hobbes dispenses with the deity, however, and introduces a strongly materialist and psychological interpretation of man's 'moral' behaviour (see Gassendi 1972; Drakopoulos 1991, 19–24) on Hobbes and Gassendi, and in general for a thorough presentation of the place of hedonism in the development of modern economics): "The concepts of pleasure and pain, as well as that of selfish behaviour, are basic in Hobbes' moral philosophy. The combination of these two constitutes the essence of egoistic hedonism" (Drakopoulos 1991, 23).

John Locke's (1632–1704) political philosophy elevated the role of property in the lives of society and its members to almost mythical proportions. Like Hobbes, Locke also saw society in part as a series of exchanges between property owners—"The theory which ... was to become in the eighteenth century almost a religion, was that expressed by Locke, when he described property as a right anterior to the existence of the state ... only the freeholders constituted the body politic, and they could use their property as they pleased" (Tawney 1936, 258; see also Locke 1946, 1960).

Locke also developed further the notion that: "Moral values arose from sensations of pleasure and pain, the man calling 'good' what experience showed to be productive of pleasure ... Just as Newton had seemed to substitute a rational law of nature for unpredictable and often malevolent forces, Locke appeared to have disclosed the scientific laws of the human mind, which would allow men to reconstruct society on happier and more rational lines" (Hampson 1968, 38–39; see also Locke 1946, 1960).

Locke and Hobbes were to have a very significant impact on Enlightenment thought, and the impact of their work continues to be felt. They are in a very real sense the shapers of much later political theory, as we shall see. Macpherson has described this type of philosophy as "The Political Theory of Possessive Individualism", highlighting the break with an ethical code moulded by the Church Fathers and the Schoolmen, and noting its momentous significance in the history of European development (Macpherson 1962, 263–264).

5.3.4 A Century of Revolution

The seventeenth century was indeed a century of revolution. The revolutions of the Civil War and of 1688 were accompanied by scientific and philosophical changes of huge magnitude. Early Puritanism had promulgated a belief system which promoted thrift, industry, a duty to labour, religious individualism modest living and charity. By the end of the seventeenth century this had become transmuted in England, at any rate, into an ethic which endorsed competitive trade and interest charging, condemned charity as inappropriate, was economically and theologically individualistic, and had been separated from the heart of economic theory by rationalism and Newtonian mechanistic world-views. The scene had also been set for removing theology from theories of society, ethics, and sociology.

5.4 Industry and Enlightenment: Eighteenth Century England

If the seventeenth century was the century of revolution, than the eighteenth can fairly be said to have been a 100 years of industry and enlightenment. As in the preceding century, the fabric of society and its understanding of itself changed dramatically. Urbanisation, the growth of factories, and the French revolution are of particular note amongst the many catalysts for changes which we will now review. Although the proper object of our study in this century is the development of ideas in England, nonetheless European and Scottish thought are of great importance, and no rigorous artificial divide between the intellectual and industrial progress of England and her neighbours will be attempted.

5.4.1 Socio-Economic Trends

At the end of the 1730s food prices began to fall back, whilst the price of industrial products rose. Real wages increased gradually, as did disposable income. Workers could choose to work less, and employers began to complain of shortage of workers, and to invest in rudimentary mechanisation. These complaints of idleness, and drunkenness among workers contributed to the increasingly prevalent industrial ideology that maintained that the poor would only be saved from their own sin if kept poor (Hampson 1968, 44, Coleman 1977, 92–94). Nonetheless, in the early eighteenth century, most people still lived in the countryside, and carried out traditional communal farming. Some changes in crops grown, and improvements in feedstock, seed-drills and ploughs were beginning to take place, as well as consolidation of land-ownership in the hands of the rich (Coleman 1977, 117; Lane 1978, 32). Moves to individualistic farming did not become significant until the later half of the eighteenth century, and by 1740, only three enclosure acts were passed on average each year (Coleman 1977, 124). "Industry was almost equally traditional in its methods, organisation and outlook. Guild regulations-perpetuated customary processes, restrained production and protected established interests. Between 1725 and 1740, industrial output grew at only about 1 %" (Hampson 1968, 45–46). In the area of international trade England was growing beyond simple exporting of a few staple products, and a surge of imports such as tobacco, silk, tea, coffee, spices, cotton, sugar from America and Asia took place, much of which was re-exported. Trade, in contrast to industry, doubled between 1715 and 1740 (Hampson 1968, 45–46). England was also involved in the slave trade, dominated shipping, finance, insurance and European fashion. In terms of infra-structure, the ports of Glasgow and Liverpool, grew very rapidly over this period, due to transatlantic trade, and improvements were made to many rivers, especially within the North and Midlands. New roads were built, and newspapers began to be produced in the provinces. The seeds of the Industrial Revolution had been sown, and bore fruit in the second half of the eighteenth century.

The period from 1750 to 1850—the Industrial Revolution—saw a remarkable adjustment of the economic, industrial and social foundation of England. This in turn had a huge impact upon the dominating ethical and religious mindset, and contributed not inconsiderably to the creation of an enterprise ethic. The industrial revolution is also the heroic era of enterprise, and acts as an iconographic symbol for much of the late Twentieth Century Enterprise Ideology. The growth and development of industry across England was facilitated by great improvements in transportation, with new roads being built and existing roads improved. A system of canals was constructed which by the turn of the century extended for some 600 miles (Lane 1978, 166, 171–174): "Exports doubled between 1720 and 1760, and then under the impact of the American War and its immediate aftermath fell away until 1780. Then between 1780 and 1800 exports more than trebled in value ... The great surge in the value (and volume) of exports provided the major stimulus to British manufacturers and inventors" (Lane 1978, 107).

These manufacturers and inventors were to change English life forever. Carding machines, shuttles, Hargreaves's spinning jenny, and Arkwright's spinning frame all began the process of automated production. It was, however, too big to be housed in a cottage, which necessitated the building of special workshops, near sources of power, often rivers, and gave birth to the factory system. The need to be near engineers prompted entrepreneurs to build their mills near towns, and the increasing need for labour swelled the populations of towns substantially. These mills were usually small, employing around 150–300 people, often women and children, and in labour shortages Poor Relief recipients from other cities could be transported around the country. As mills were established in towns, so the population drifted in from the surrounding countryside, so that by 1851: "... for the first time over half the population of England and Wales lived in urban areas with populations of over 50,000 people" (Lane 1978, 98).

This massive move to the towns and the growth of the industrial cities throughout the industrial Revolution was exacerbated by the enclosure of common land in the countryside: "in 1700 about half the arable land of the country was cultivated under the open-field system. By 1830 almost all agricultural land was enclosed" (Lane 1978, 41). Within 130 years, then, the enclosure of land which had provided grazing for the stock of the rural poor was taken into private ownership, and they had little choice but to become labourers on the new farms of the rich, or to move to the cities in search of work. The urbanisation caused by the growth of factories had a profound social, as well as economic effect on the working classes. The first trade unions and friendly societies began to be formed, partly because large numbers of workers lived very close together for the first time. The removal from the village, with its established customs and behaviour, centred largely around the church, disrupted the social life of the poor, who often found no Anglican church in the vicinity of their new homes. This left them open to the approaches of the Nonconformist churches, and the importance of dissenting sects grew significantly towards the close of the eighteenth century.

Throughout the eighteenth century, whilst Anglicanism remained the faith of the ancien regime, (the landowners, gentry and aristocracy), Coleman confirms that Dissent was appealing to small merchants, traders, artisans, manufacturers, and emergent capitalists" (Coleman 1977, 108). He is sceptical, however, that the so-called Protestant Ethic had anything more than a "permissive" effect on the development of industrialisation, developing instead what might be termed the weak Weberian line: "To 'keep your accounts punctual', to believe in sobriety and frugality, to worship a God who is supposed to help those who help themselves: such creeds were unlikely to have done very much for the more spectacular acts of risk-taking and profitmaking, but they may have given a helping hand to the vital substructure of capitalism which consolidated and extended the market economy" (Coleman 1977, 108).

Responsible to a significant degree for the implementation and exploitation of the Industrial Revolution, eighteenth and nineteenth century entrepreneurs have acquired mythical status in contemporary analysis, polemic and comment. Of special interest for us, however, is the fact that whether such people were aristocrats, industrialists or commercial novices, many of them shared membership of the Nonconformist sects: "There was a disproportionately larger number of Quakers, Congregationalists, Baptists, Presbyterians and Unitarians among the entrepreneurial class. Non-conformists made up only about 3 % of the population of England and Wales in the 1770s, yet about 50 % of the early inventors and main entrepreneurs of the Industrial Revolution were Nonconformists" (Lane 1978, 143).

5.4.2 Philosophy

In the early eighteenth century, the relative peace and economic growth enjoyed by continental Europe was mirrored by an optimistic belief in the benevolence of providence. As the scientific discoveries of the past century were assimilated and extended, thinkers began to see order and systems in all manner of things. And behind this observable, rationally-ordered framework, was seen the hand of God. Belief in a systematically designed cosmos, which was understood increasingly to be created for man's benefit, naturally engendered belief in a benevolent divine architect. Hampson examines this trend of the early to mid-seventeen hundreds, and notes a number of astonishing examples which were used to illustrate this beneficent Providence, from dark fleas being visible on pale skin (Bernadin de St Pierre), tides helping ships come into port (I'abb6 Pluche), and the most useful metals being close to the surface of the earth (Clement de Boissy; see Hampson 1968, 79–84, Pluche 1735–1736).

These examples demonstrate that the divine will as expressed in creation was aimed at the provision of a world ordered in all respects for the good of man. The discoveries of order in Physics in particular lent credence to these beliefs in a Beneficent Provident. Leibniz in particular has come to be associated with this Optimism, and his particular philosophy maintained that our cosmos was de facto the best of the compossibles which God could have chosen at the moment of Creation. That is, simply by being the Universe which God had created for mankind and himself, it must perforce be the best that there could be. Evil and imperfections were, in this type of religious philosophy, seen as necessary obstacles for man to overcome on his journey towards godliness (see Leibniz 1898, 1934).

Leibnizian Optimism has (at least) two significant implications for this argument. Firstly, as the deity becomes ever more the object of reasoned quasi-scientific argument, He is less and less the traditional Christian God of revelation: "To treat the term God as little more than a scientific working hypothesis must, however, be clearly distinguished from the traditional belief in a particular revelation" (Vereker 1967, 20). Secondly, and related to this, is the continued emphasis on religious individualism. The Reformation and the translation of the Bible into demotic language reduced the importance of the clergy as mediators and translators between man and God, and this theological independence came to be reflected in notions of economic independence and especially in the possessive individualism of Hobbes, Locke et al. As thinkers began to apply their reason to the understanding of God, as well as increasingly identifying God with the ordered natural world ("Nature"), the importance of Scripture was downplayed. The reduction of the importance of the shared Scripture in favour of the application of personal reason and reaction to nature as mechanisms for understanding God increased religious individualism (Vereker 1967, 30).

Although Leibniz only acknowledged that good *could* overcome evil, Pope followed the doctrine of Optimism to its logical conclusion and decided that, as with the Universe, whatever existed must be for the best. This jump in philosophical thought was to have enormous subsequent consequences, which may explain why the following section from Pope's Essay on Man (1869, first published 1732) is among the most frequently cited pieces of English verse, particularly in critiques of the Enlightenment:

All nature is but art, unknown to thee;
All chance, direction which thou canst not see:
All discord, harmony not understood;
All partial evil, universal good:
And, spite of pride, in erring reason's spite,
One truth is clear, Whatever is, is right.
(Pope, Essay on Man 1869, Epistle 1, 11 285–294.)

From such Optimism it is possible to draw out a conclusion which contains the germ of much subsequent thought. Since "whatever is, is right", a sensible explanation needs to be found for evil, and in particular for the greed and individualism of contemporary enterprise, the explosion of which must have seemed especially shocking in England after the restraint and asceticism of Puritan businessmen. The response is that even self-love is good, because it leads towards the greater common good. These assumptions are implicit in the two couplets below, extracted from Books Two and Three of Pope's Essay on Man:

Thus God and Nature linked the general frame
And bade self-love and social be the same
(Pope, Essay on Man 1869, Epistle 111, 317–318).

To comprehend the enormous jump that this represents in ethical thought, Pope's verse should perhaps be compared with de Mandeville's Fable of the Bees, which scathingly noted the importance of vice in the economic progress of England, and which ironically proposed that increased wealth and progress could be achieved by allowing play to unfettered selfishness, hedonism, envy and greed (de Mandeville 1725). Published in 1704, the poem was banned by the state (see Fussfeld 1990, 16). Yet just forty years later Pope's Essay on Man could be lauded as expressing the optimistic and positive spirit of the age, for voicing these same sentiments. Furthermore, the contemporary perception of the Universe as designed, as functioning mechanistically towards a given end, combined with optimistic spirit of the age, promoted the notion that this end was mankind's happiness (Vereker 1967, 36).

For earlier thinkers, it was legitimate for wealth to be acquired as a by-product of an ascetic, hardworking life. It was acceptable from the Church Fathers onwards for wealth to be created as a resource for the provision of charity. The mid-eighteenth century represents the very first appearance of an explicit and firm acceptance of selfish wealth-creation, as a means of promoting overall economic growth. Taken in conjunction with the rejection of charity and provision for the poor, with the religious individualism noted above, and with the thrift and hard work promoted by the Puritans in the previous century, most of the facets of the generic ideal type of enterprise values can now be seen to be in circulation.

Providentialism also undermined literal belief in the power of the Fall, and Original Sin - if this is the best of all possible worlds, and God has created man so as to improve it still further as man strives to be godlike, then it is hard to also see the world as a fallen, inherently corrupt arena. Mankind as a whole and individual men could achieve some significant degree of rightness with God, and progress in the temporal sphere towards a more perfect world was possible. The traditional endless cycle of sin and depravity, only to be overcome for the elect by the grace of God, has no part in the Enlightenment philosophy. Salvation and redemption are to be found in secular striving towards social and economic improvement, and education (Vereker 1967, 21–22).

Whether man was free or not was also a matter of some debate. Increased trust in mankind's abilities as reasoners and experimenters—perhaps best witnessed to by the amazing scope of the French Encylopedie (1986 edition)—led to questions as to whether this ability was circumscribed by predeterminism. Since nature, or God, was seen to have created a cosmos which followed laws, however, did this not suggest strongly that some form of determinism prevailed? Equally, if man was ruled by reason, then acting in a reasonable, consistent manner to the unchanging rule of nature could also be seen to imply determinism. The thinking on this subject in the eighteenth century ranges from the evasive (Pope, in Hampson 1968, 113–114) to the confusingly casuistic. Leibniz, for example, felt that man, like God, was essentially motivated by goodness, and that his decisions were determined but contingent upon the fact that in this Universe behaviour was dictated by the pursuit of the good. Perhaps the most helpful comment on these abstruse concepts is made by Vereker, who notes that "The hallmark of freedom was less choice than attainment, the achievement of the best possible ends" (Vereker 1967, 26).

Curiously, given the prevalence of Optimism and Providentialism in the first half of the eighteenth century, they were to suffer a significant reversal in the second half, with even adherents (like Voltaire) abandoning their confidence. Following the wars of 1740–1748 and 1756–1763, and further developments in science, a move away from early eighteenth century beliefs in the bienfaisance and underpinning, if indirect, significance of God is evident. It is customary, although not unchallenged, to date the change in attitudes from the catastrophic earthquake in Lisbon, in November 1755. Voltaire's reaction to this disaster, which effectively undermined his belief in a benevolent nature, was articulated in Candide, which mocked the Optimism he himself had held in earlier years (Voltaire 1967). In the light of the recurrent wars in Europe, and the horror of Lisbon, educated Europeans found it ever more difficult to believe in the ordered progress of a kindly nature, watched over by a personal and benevolent God.

Yet, if the optimistic spirit of the early enlightenment died with the forty thousand victims of the Lisbon earthquake, many of its tenets outlived the philosophy itself. The mechanistic understanding of nature and economic activity was not challenged, but rather became eLabourated and developed. Only the concept of a benevolent Nature / God was largely dropped from this Newtonian paradigm. Geology—in particular the beginnings of an understanding of evolution—and mistaken experiments purporting to show life being generated, all led to a new attitude which: "... emphasised the complexity of matter and its apparent capacity to generate life, the existence of anomalies in nature and the revolutionary transformation of nature itself over an immense period of time. Science ... seemed to have dispensed with the need for God as a necessary factor in its explanation of the universe" (Hampson 1968, 91). Indeed, the new findings of science went rather further than this, since it was becoming increasingly difficult for educated men to reconcile what they learned from nature with belief in the literal truth of the Bible, and especially the Flood and Genesis. Having dispensed with the Bible in terms of religious philosophy, leaving it behind scientifically may seem but a small step.

We have seen how Hobbes and Pope sow the seeds of modern economic theory, and these were reaped most notably by Adam Smith. His major contributions to economics are summarised succinctly by Fussfeld: "According to Smith, self-interest in a free society would lead to the most rapid progress and growth a nation was capable of achieving. People would save in order to improve their own positions and in so doing would add more capital to the nation's resources. They would use that capital in the most profitable way and in so doing produce the things that others wanted most. In the system of natural liberty there were only three legitimate functions of government: the establishment and maintenance of justice, national defence, and 'erecting and maintaining certain public works'" (Fussfeld 1990, 26). Vereker notes that in Smith's work: "Providence itself was all in all. Human co-operation ...had been pre-arranged by God, acting through nature, to ensure the results he had in mind" (Vereker 1967, 43). This first articulation of modern economic theory, then, is couched in language and ideas that are fundamentally religious in nature, and conceive of a Providentialist God who has so shaped economic laws that the pursuit of individual happiness and wealth lead naturally to the betterment of society.

Immediately after Smith published the Wealth of the Nation, the French Revolution and American War of Independence led to strong retrenchment in England by the political elite. Conservatism was to delineate the remainder of the century, and the national intellectual conscience was largely occupied with preventing any spark of liberalism turning into the conflagration of revolution. The Napoleonic Wars then took centre stage, and only after the Congress of Vienna in 1815 did Dissent once again give voice to the battle for freedom in religion, trade and economics.

5.4.3 A Century of Re-structuring

The eighteenth century, then, saw the massive changes in economic and social structure which we noted above; industrialisation, urbanisation, development of the national infrastructure and the heroism of enterprise. The optimistic Providentialism and Natural Theology of the earlier part of the century emphasised the bienfaisance of an ordered, regulated cosmos, within which even the selfish pursuit of wealth led to positive outcomes. Although the mid-century chaos led to abandonment of the cheerfully positive enthusiasm of Pope and Leibniz, their inheritance of a mechanistic and divinely maintained environment persisted, finding expression, *inter alia*, in Smith's economic theories. Other characteristics of this school of thought have been noted as a move away from doctrines of Original Sin and the Fall, towards a faith in man's abilities to help in the perfection of the temporal sphere, and a uneasy debate over determinism and freedom, with freedom being seen as less to do with choice and more to do with achievement.

5.5 Freedom and Enterprise: Nineteenth Century England

5.5.1 Industry and Society

Bendix (1963) has written extensively on "ideologies of management in the course of industrialisation", and notes that nonconformist entrepreneurs remained broadly at odds with the Anglican establishment and nonconformist evangelism among the working classes was extensive. This preaching taught that idleness and poverty were sinful, and that nothing positive could be done by employers to improve the lot of the poor: "The masses of the people were said to be immoral, their distress the result of indolence or sin. No educational or institutional device would improve their evil habits; only hunger could accomplish that. . . All the means for their relief, namely moral conduct and the postponement of marriage, were within their power and within their power alone" (Bendix 1963).

This position is in line with English thought from the late seventeenth century onwards, but we should nonetheless remind ourselves that it contrasts significantly with the paternalistic theologies of the ancient regime, where charity and care for the subordinate poor was the duty of the elite within the inherently feudal system. An increasing trend of radical Protestantism from Calvin on through Cromwell and the Enlightenment was the importance of the individual and his direct relationship with God. The relegation of structural sin to the theological storeroom in the eighteenth century also opened the way for a focus on those individual vices which undermined social progress. Thus, it is almost inevitable that idleness and frivolity became the most perilous sins a man could be tempted by. This is especially so given the contemporary moral rectitude of the self-interested pursuit of wealth, which essentially crossed greed, envy, selfishness and obsession with money off the list of vices.

5.5.2 Free Trade and Dissent

Nineteenth century dissenters developed an ideology that demanded religious and commercial liberty as the concomitant of individual hegemony. This allowed them to develop their businesses unfettered by state control, but also to pass responsibility for the lives of their workers into the hands of the labourers themselves (Bendix 1963). The belief in dependence was rejected by Dissent, although it remained a shibboleth of the Tory Anglican philosophy, which tried to implement reforms aimed to educating and feeding the poor on a national level, and protecting them in the workplace. These social reforms were rejected by the entrepreneurial dissenters as an attack on individual liberty and responsibility, as well as a threat to the economic well-being of English industry. Alongside the wholesale transference to individuals of theological and social responsibility, there arose a literature which promulgated the belief that, for those who practised the thrift and hard work preached by the non-conformists, there was a real hope of social and economic advancement. The most famous of the writers of these tracts was Samuel Smiles, whose writings told of successful young men working and studying to better their lot: "The doctrine of self-help proclaimed that employers and workers were alike in self-dependence, and that regardless of class each man's success was a proof of himself and a contribution to the common wealth. There was evangelical zeal in this appeal of employers to the drive and ambition of the people" (Bendix 1963; see also Smiles 1866).

Honeyman (1982) has demonstrated that in fact, very few of the entrepreneurs of the industrial revolution came from humble origins, but rather that the middle and upper classes dominated economic activity during and after industrialisation just as they had before it. She notes that Smiles' work instead of reporting the reality of opportunities available to all through hard work and determination, told a tale that people wanted to believe, a tale of hope: "Smiles was reiterating in popular form what the contemporary public wanted to hear. Industrialisation had produced so many unpleasant consequences for the working man that the notion of a beneficial concomitant was likely to be well received. Smile's views were extensively believed at the time, and the idea that new opportunities for social mobility emerged late in the eighteenth century has been largely accepted ever since" (Honeyman 1982, 1, 60).

The identification of Nonconformist Dissent with enterprise shaped much of the liberalism which was the trademark of England in the nineteenth century. Still barred from holding political posts, whether locally or nationally, the Dissenters turned to business and commerce to find their area of self-expression and public activity: "They consciously advocated free trade to benefit commerce and bestowed their blessings upon expanding industrial enterprises. The morals proclaimed from their pulpits - thrift, honesty, and diligence—belonged to the market place (Cowherd 1959, 15). The crusade for religious freedom became interwoven with the movement demanding free trade, as evidenced by the work of the Anti-Corn Law League, and for the fight for political reform, as demonstrated by the Chartists. The fight against slavery was equally led by the Dissenters. However, the history of the victories won by Dissent in these areas was not a smooth and steady accumulation of rights. Rather, the barometer of public and political support for their demands altered dramatically throughout the first half of the nineteenth century, and was affected by the abundance of food and work, the tone of the protest, and so on.

It was in the new northern industrial towns of Manchester, Leeds and Birmingham, that Dissent found its greatest following. There were few Anglican churches in these cities, and they had neither their own bishops, nor members of Parliament. The men who had led the growth of industry were barred from participation in the town corporations because of their religious beliefs. The great reformers of the nineteenth century rose from this background—Cobden, Bright, and Attwood—and fought long and hard for freedom in religion, politics and trade. Yet their belief in the paramount importance of freedom was such as to oppose the New Poor Laws, preferring charitable care for those in poverty, and also to attack plans for state, rather than church, education, and even legislation to protect children working in factories. John Bright expressed the spirit of Dissent, (echoing Adam Smith on these issues) in a speech on education in the Commons: "If there is one principle more certain than another I suppose it is this, what a people is able to do for itself, their government should not attempt to do for it" (Parliamentary Debates, see also Bright 1868, for more along these lines).

The forces of Dissent then, rallied to the banner of freedom, and won the repeal of the Test and Corporation Act (1828), the Reform of Parliament (1832), participation in Municipal Corporations (1833) and Freedom of Marriage, (1836). All these changes promoted the liberty of individuals to live lives free from government control, for the middle classes to take responsibility for their own destiny. Yet in those areas where other legislation was called for, mostly by paternalistic Tory High Churchman, to protect and ameliorate the lot of the poor, these were not supported by the Dissenters, who saw the threat of state power being re-imposed on part of life they believed properly belonged in the hands of the people. Some of these arguments have a familiar ring to readers cognizant with late twentieth century Enterprise Ethics, as a description of the position of the Dissenters vis-a-vis industrial reform shows: "Shorter industrial hours would destroy competitiveness in overseas markets, slash profits and wages and promote idleness and debauchery (Ward 1970, 25).

Clark (1985) argues strongly for the doctrinal roots in these disputes between the ancien regime and the bourgeois entrepreneurs. The ancien regime, from the late seventeenth century, was marked out by its belief in the divine authority of the head of the state, and the head of the family, as analogous to the hierarchy of power in the divine sphere (Clark 1985, 79). This theology was challenged by the discoveries in Physics, which suggested that as God had withdrawn from active participation in his creation, allowing it to follow the newly discovered laws of nature, so: "... man, if living in a self-sufficient world, would be free to treat the state as a machine and to use or remodel it at will for his purely secular purposes" (Clark 1985, 217). The discussion of the previous two centuries would give support to Clark's position. Still greater challenge was posed by the Arians and Socinians, who believed that Jesus was not truly God, not a full partner in the Trinity. From this belief led the conclusions that there could be no atonement, no original sin (and therefore that man was fundamentally good and could be left to run his own life free from state or church intervention), no apostolic succession of the clergy, and hence no hierarchy within the church, or, by analogy, outside it (Clark 1985). The position of the radical dissenting campaigner Price is a good example of the Arian theology translated into the socio-political sphere, and his position bears some of the hallmarks of the (secularised) enterprise ideology of the 1980s in Britain: "Original sin was rejected as inconsistent with free will. Restraint on the individual conscience was the definition of arbitrary power. Free will was identified as good by the individual's obligation to pursue his religion as his private judgement led him: a concept of natural rights thus filled the vacuum created by the disappearance of Christian obligation. Civil liberty in general seemed to flow from Price's preoccupation with religious liberty" (Clark 1985, 330). Although Dissent returned to the Trinitarian told by the early nineteenth century, and the national leaders of dissent, especially Wesley, preached the old doctrine of subordination to church and state, and supremacy of the monarchy, church and parliament, Clarke maintains that at the grass-roots level "Dissent ultimately implied a gesture of defiance against the idea of a hierarchical, deferential Anglican society" (Clark 1985, 378). This religious revolt, and the huge rise in the numbers of nonconformist Christians, gave birth to the challenges to the ancient regime described above. There is little wonder that among the demands of the nineteenth century radicals was the disestablishment of the Church, or that a number of key votes on reform in the Lords were overturned by the votes of the bishops.

5.5.3 A Century of Enterprise

The nineteenth century was certainly a hundred years of enterprise, in industrial, political and religious terms. Freedom became a rallying cry of the dissenters, who built on enlightenment economic theories to demand the market place be liberated, and economic agents within it freed to sink or swim. What is also apparent is that the poor, who were also brought into the dissenting fold in large numbers, were fed an ideology of enterprise which effectively suppressed state care for them as a corollary of the extension of market place mechanisms. Original sin was laid firmly to rest, as inconsistent with the all important doctrine of freedom. Freedom of choice, of economic activity, of religious expression dominated the century and was understood in a highly individualistic sense. Freedom as liberation or justice for any outside the industrialist class is not at issue. Here, indeed, many of the key aspects of (Thatcherite) Enterprise Ethics come together in an important manner.

Conclusion

Whilst the period was one of enormous complexity, the three centuries dealt with in this chapter are the cradle, in many ways, of the Enterprise Ethic of the late twentieth century. Most of the ideas of importance to the Thatcherite Enterprise Ethic reach their fruition in this period, although they may not held together at any one moment in time. Firstly, a radical alteration in perceptions about self-love and self-interest is clear, with these now being acceptable because they promote the common good, and recognise the significance of the individual's relationship with his God. From Pope's Essay On Man, and Adam Smith to the dissenting entrepreneurs, self-interest is given positive ethical value. Freedom in religion, politics and—especially—trade has also become a clarion call, also reflecting an individualistic ontology. Myths are promoted which encourage the working man to take control of his own destiny through frugality and hard work, so that he too can enjoy the fruits of success. The ancien regime is challenged for being elitist, paternalistic and archaic, but struggles to protect the poor from the excesses of industrialisation. The radicals who opposed the Corn Laws in the interests of free trade—and the need to feed the poor—will not subscribe to factory legislation because it interferes with freedom and threatens profits. All of these themes are to reappear within the Thatcherite ideology of enterprise. Yet the themes that dominate Thatcherism in the twentieth century were, in the late eighteenth and early nineteenth, generated within a religious context and strongly based on doctrinal positions.

English Puritan Protestantism, during these three centuries, then, moved from Calvin's opposition to wealth creation untrammelled by a strong traditional ethical code, to one which endorsed all manner of practices anathema to Scholastics and Reformers alike. By the late seventeenth century, English divines had moved towards a position which endorsed competitive trade and interest charging, condemned charity as inappropriate, was economically and theologically individualistic, and had been separated from the heart of economic theory by rationalism and Newtonian mechanistic world views.

The Providentialism of the eighteenth century reinforced religious individualism, and began the process of rejecting such traditional doctrines as Original Sin, the Fall, Determinism, Mystery and Scriptural revelation. The Non-conformists of the industrial revolution carried these views further still, and emphasised the self-help morality which would enable any willing and hard working man to make his way in the world to the greater glory of God. Deeply individualistic, this theology saw charity as an evil which created dependence and lethargy, instead of stimulating the poor to better themselves. The Victorian ethos of self-help and enterprise reached its zenith in the writings of Samuel Smiles, whose work exhorted all men to take control of their own destiny and fulfil their duty to God and family by wealth creation.

(continued)

Only in the England of the Industrial Revolution and Victoria, does a fully articulated enterprise theology occur, unfettered by the constraints of charity and agape. Only here do we find that the individual has pride of place as against his neighbour, only here do we discover an alliance between free trade and entrepreneurial Protestantism, only here is charity roundly condemned, and the free practice of wealth creation not only cautiously sanctioned but exhorted.

Such a full and open enterprise theology marks a point of radical discontinuation from the tradition which preceded it. Until this point, the aim of most religious writers had been to curtail and contain enterprise within acceptable bounds of Christian teaching-controlled money lending, extensive donations to charity, God and neighbour as of more importance than self, labour as a humble duty not the sole route to salvation, and the Christian Community as the locus of salvation via charity, and modest service. This is the tradition which survived from Clement of Alexandria through the Scholastics to Calvin, Luther and the early English Puritans like Baxter. The dramatic shift in English theology that took place during the Industrial Revolution broke with this tradition, and laid the ground for the beliefs of 1980s Enterprise Theologians.

References

Anderson AR, Drakopoulou-Dodd SL, Scott MG (2000) Religion as an environmental influence on enterprise culture—the case of Britain in the 1980s. Int J Entrep Behav Res 6:5–20

Bacon F (1975) In: Armstrong WA (ed) The advancement of learning. Athlone Press, London

Bendix R (1963) Work and authority in industry. Harper and Row, New York

Bright J (1868) In: JET (ed) Speeches on questions of public policy Rogers. Macmillan, London, 2 Vols

Bunyan J (1969) In: Adrian DB (ed) The Pilgrim's progress. Airmont, New York

Clark JCD (1985) English society 1688-1832. Cambridge University Press, Cambridge

Coleman DC (1977) The economy of england 1450-1750. Oxford University Press, Oxford

Cowherd RG (1959) The politics of English dissent. The religious aspects of liberal and humanitarian reform movements from 1815 to 1848. The Epworth Press, London

de Mandeville B (1725) The fable of the bees private vices. Publick Benefits, London

Descartes R (1968) In: Sutcliffe FE (intro) Discourse on method and the meditations. Penguin Books, Harmondsworth

Descartes R (1984) In: Cottingham J, Stoofhoff R, Murdoch D (trans) The philosophical writings of Descartes, 2 vols. Cambridge University Press, Cambridge, p 439

Drakopoulos S (1991) Values and economic theory—the case of hedonism. Aldershot, Avebury

Drakopoulou Dodd S, Gotsis G (2007) An examination of the inter-relationships between entrepreneurship and religion. Int J Entrep Innov 8:93–104

Drakopoulou Dodd S, Gotsis G (2009) 'Enterprise values' in the new testament and antecedent works. Inte J Entrep Innov 10:101–110

Fussfeld D (1990) The age of the economist Scott, 6th edn. Foresman and Company, Glenview, IL

Gassendi P (1972) In: Brush CB (trans and ed) The selected works of Pierre Gassendi. Johnston Reprint Corporation, New York

Hampson N (1968) The enlightenment. Penguin, Harmondsworth
Hill C (1966) The century of revolution 1603-1714. Norton Library, New York
Hobbes T (1946) Leviathan. Oxford University Press, Oxford
Honeyman K (1982) Origins of enterprise. Business leadership in the industrial revolution. Manchester University Press, Manchester
Hudson W (1959) Protestantism and the Spirit of Capitalism. In: Green RW (ed) The Weber thesis and its critics. Heath, Lexington, Washington, DC
Lane P (1978) The industrial revolution, the birth of the modern age. Weidenfield and Nicholas, London
Leibniz GW (1898) The monadology and other philosophical writings. Oxford University Press, London
Leibniz GW (1934) The philosophical writings of Leibnitz. Morris, M (compiler), London
Locke J (1946) In: Gough JW (ed) The second treatise of civil government and a letter concerning toleration. Oxford, Basil Blackwell
Locke J (1960) In: Laslett P (ed) Two treatises of government. Cambridge University Press, Cambridge
Macpherson CB (1962) The political theory of possessive individualism. Oxford University Press, Oxford
Newton I (1952) In Motte A (trans) Cajori F (revisor) Mathematical principals of natural philosophy. Encyclopaedia Britannica, Chicago
Nussbaum FL (1953) The triumph of science and reason. Harper Row, New York
Pluche MA (1735–1736) Le Spectacle de la Nature. Utrecht
Pope A (1869) In: Pattison M (ed) Essay on man. Clarendon, Oxford
Robertson H (1959) A criticism of Max Weber and his school. In: Green RW (ed) The Weber thesis and its critics. Heath, Lexington, Washington, DC
Shaw H (1968) The levellers. Longman, London
Smile S (1866) Self-help with illustrations of character, conduct, and perseverance. Murray, London
Smith P (1962) Origins and modern culture 1543–1687. Collier Books, New York
Sombart W (1959) The role of religion in the formation of the capitalist spirit. In: Green RW (ed) The Weber thesis and its critics. Heath, Lexington, Washington, DC
Tawney RH (1936) Religion and the rise of capitalism. Murray, London
Thomson A (1976) Church history: new movements. Reform, rationalism, revolution 1500-1800. SPCK, London
Vereker C (1967) Eighteenth century optimism. Liverpool University Press, Liverpool
Voltaire de (Arouet, Franqois-Marie) (1967) In: Brumfit JH (ed) *Candide* (in French). Oxford University Press, Oxford
Ward JT (ed) (1970) Popular movements @1830-1850. Macmillan, London
Weber M (1990) The protestant ethic and the spirit of capitalism, parsons (trans, 1930). Allen Unwin, London

Chapter 6
The Stationary State: Deadlocks and New Perspectives

Cosimo Perrotta

6.1 The Idea of the Stationary State

The concept of the stationary state refers to a non-growing economy, where people confine themselves to re-produce in the same quantities the goods they consume yearly. This idea was successful in the nineteenth century and in the first decades of the twentieth. It was used as a "methodological fiction" by Marx (in his model of simple reproduction) and by others up to Pigou, above all in comparison with the concept of growth.[1]

The stationary state can also be seen as the conclusion of the capitalist accumulation process. Schumpeter distinguishes a pessimistic vision of such a perspective and an optimistic one. The first view was expressed by Malthus, Ricardo and others. For them the stationary state inevitably derives from the limits that nature imposes to growth. The other view is represented above all by J.S. Mill, K. Marx and J.M. Keynes. The latter authors see the stationary state as the outcome of abundance, once this has been reached.[2]

The model of Malthus and Ricardo nearly disappears in the middle of the nineteenth century. But in the last decades it has revived, thanks to the problems of environment pollution, which is produced by industrial development.

I explained, orally and roughly, the ideas of this paper at the conference of the "Associazione di Storia dell'Economia politica" (Storep), held in Gaeta (Italy) in June 2013. I thank the participants in that debate and in the debate held in Volos.

[1] Cp. Schumpeter [1949], IV.7.3.a, 964–966.

[2] See for ex. Mill (1848), III.5.6, 570–574.

C. Perrotta (✉)
Faculty of Humanities, University of Salento (formerly called University of Lecce), Via Cosenza, 3, 73100 Lecce, Italy
e-mail: cosimoperrotta@gmail.com

G.C. Bitros, N.C. Kyriazis (eds.), *Essays in Contemporary Economics*,
DOI 10.1007/978-3-319-10043-2_6

6.1.1 *John Stuart Mill*

The recent crisis of mature economies stimulates some reflections on the Mill–Marx–Keynes's approach. Mill maintains that,

"the richest and most prosperous countries would very soon attain the stationary state, if no further improvements were made in the productive arts, and if there were a suspension of the overflow of capital from those countries into the uncultivated or ill-cultivated regions of the earth."[3]

Mill writes that previous economists (for ex. Smith and McCulloch) saw this as a gloomy, although inevitable prospect. They preferred "the progressive state", i.e. development without end (ibidem).

On the contrary, he adds,

> I am inclined to believe that it would be, on the whole, a very considerable improvement on our present condition. I confess I am not charmed with the ideal of life held out by those who think that the normal state of human beings is that of struggling to get on; that the trampling, crushing, elbowing, and treading on each other's heels, which form the existing type of social life, are the most desirable lot of human kind, or anything but the disagreeable symptoms of one of the phases of industrial progress. (ivi, 3).

Thus the stationary state appears to Mill as a superior level of civilization. It can be reached once the population growth is checked and excessive inequalities are eliminated:

"we may suppose this better distribution of property attained, by the joint effect of the prudence and frugality of individuals, and of a system of legislation (...)."

This way, society can have

> a well-paid and affluent body of labourers; no enormous fortunes, except what were earned and accumulated during a single lifetime; but a much larger body of persons than at present, not only exempt from the coarser toils, but with sufficient leisure, both physical and mental, from mechanical details, to cultivate freely the graces of life. (p. 4).

In 1848, the year of utopian ideas, Mill concludes:

> It is scarcely necessary to remark that a stationary condition of capital and population implies no stationary state of human improvement. There would be as much scope as ever for all kinds of mental culture, and moral and social progress; as much room for improving the Art of Living, and much more likelihood of its being improved, when minds ceased to be engrossed by the art of getting on. Even the industrial arts might be as earnestly and as successfully cultivated, with this sole difference, that instead of serving no purpose but the increase of wealth, industrial improvements would produce their legitimate effect, that of abridging labour. (p. 6).

---

[3] Mill (1848, 2).

6.1.2 Marx

The last sentences quoted from Mill recall the vague references that Marx did on the communist society. The latter can be considered as the Marxian version of the stationary state. Social wealth, Marx maintains, depends on labour productivity and on production conditions.

> "The realm of liberty only begins when labour imposed by necessity ends". Beyond the latter "the development of human potentialities starts. It is an end in itself, it is the true realm of liberty, which however can flourish only on the basis of the realm of necessity."[4]

Note that the realm of necessity, as Marx affirms many times, is led to an end by capitalism itself, which allows so huge an accumulation of wealth that necessity can be overcome. This is what he calls the "historical mission" of capitalism.[5]

Marx also explains that the advent of the stationary state (that is: communism) does not eliminate the increase in social productivity; on the contrary it even fosters it. But the new situation allows so big an increase in leisure time that the latter becomes "the measure of wealth" and supplants the old measure of labour time.[6]

6.1.3 Keynes

Keynes's optimistic approach is very evocative. In 1930 he describes the crisis of his time as a transition towards a higher civilization. His expressions fit well also for today's situation:

> We are suffering, not from the rheumatics of old age, but from the growing-pains of over-rapid changes, from the painfulness of readjustment between one economic period and another. The increase of technical efficiency has been taking place faster than we can deal with the problem of labour absorption.[7]

And, a little further:

> We are being afflicted with a new disease of which some readers may not yet have heard the name, but of which they will hear a great deal in the years to come—namely, *technological unemployment*. This means unemployment due to our discovery of means of economising the use of labour outrunning the pace at which we can find new uses for labour. But this is only a temporary phase of maladjustment. All this means in the long run *that mankind is solving its economic problem*. I would predict that the standard of life in progressive countries one hundred years hence will be between four and eight times as high as it is to-day.[8] (p. 3)

---

[4] Marx (1864–1965), ch. 48, 3, 933.

[5] See for ex. ibidem, ch. 51, 996–997.

[6] Marx (1857–1858), notebook VII.2, Competition, vol. 2, 405.

[7] Keynes (1930, 1).

[8] According to Zilibotti (2008, 38) the increase in welfare has been even higher than Keynes's prevision.

Then "the *economic problem* may be solved, or be at least within sight of solution, within a 100 years. This means that the economic problem is not—if we look into the *future—the permanent problem of the human race*" (p. 4).

The very problem then will be to adapt oneself to a cultural context which is completely new. Mankind has always struggled against scarcity. His nature was forged through this struggle. The end of scarcity will force human nature to undertake a difficult change. In the new context,

> The love of money as a possession—as distinguished from the love of money as a means to the enjoyments and realities of life—will be recognised for what it is, a somewhat disgusting morbidity, one of those semi-criminal, semi-pathological pro-pensities which one hands over with a shudder to the specialists in mental disease. All kinds of social customs and economic practices, affecting the distribution of wealth and of economic rewards and penalties, which we now maintain at all costs, however distasteful and unjust they may be in themselves, because they are tremendously useful in promoting the accumulation of capital, we shall then be free, at last, to discard.(pp. 5–6)

6.2 Saturation

6.2.1 The Utopian Element

These last sentences confirm what already appeared in Mill and Marx: the idea of stationary state contains a strong utopian component (in the sense that it cannot be accomplished). The reasoning of these authors goes as if, once the satisfaction of basic needs is achieved, the search for profit disappears. However experience shows that satisfaction of needs does not make "the love of money" disappear.[9] The latter seems to be a natural attitude in many individuals; and today there are many extreme manifestations of it.

On the other hand, investments are not always undertaken for the sake of a "semi-pathological" or an "elbowing" thirst for money nor is labour always performed out of necessity. Most of the time there is also the wish of creating something, a professional or entrepreneurial pride. This is a positive component of human nature, and it too is not eliminable.[10]

Beside the utopian feature, the idea of stationary state also has a "conservative" element: the distrust towards future economic development (utopian attitude and conservative view are not incompatible, as we can often see in the history of social thought). In fact the main shortcoming of this idea is that it conceives the essential needs as fixed once and for all. It neglects the teaching of Enlightenment authors.

Enlightenment, after more than 2,000 years, finally got rid of the Aristotelian distinction between natural (i.e. essential) needs and "artificial" needs; the latter

[9] Cp. Leijonhufvud (2008).

[10] Similar statements can be often found in the comments to Keynes's article in Pecchi and Piga (2008), like those by Solow, Phelps, Freeman, etc.

being not really wants, rather they are created by human fancy. As Millar, Genovesi and many others explained, all human needs are both natural and artificial. They belong to human nature and to its permanent evolution, but at the same time even the most elementary needs are moulded by culture.[11]

The Enlightenment approach provides a view of development based on the permanent creation of new needs. New goods are in the beginning luxury goods, but gradually they become essential needs for all. Then the full satisfaction of a society will never arrive. Marx expressed this concept by saying that it is production—not consumers—that creates the new needs, in order to keep accumulation going. Although this is often true, such a view should imply that, after the breakdown of capitalism, essential needs will not increase any more.

6.2.2 The Realistic Element

However the creation of new needs, and consequently of new goods, does not eliminate the prospect of saturation and of a stationary state. Increase in per capita consumption is only one factor of capitalist accumulation. The second factor is the extension of traditional goods to others. On turn, this extension can be external (export) or domestic (access of lower classes to some non-basic consumption).

Export was the driving force of accumulation during the middle ages and up to the end of the seventeenth century. Nowadays it is fundamental for China, Germany, Japan, etc. On the other hand, the enlargement of domestic markets has become more and more important. From it the steady increase of middle classes derives, which has stabilized development.

All the structural crises in the past are due to the lack of one or both these factors. About the 1930s crisis, export did not help because five centuries of colonialism had impeded the growth of a market in the backward countries. On the other hand the domestic market of mature economies was blocked by low wages and the consequent scarcity of demand.

Only the post-world war boom ended definitely the 1930s crisis. It increased demand thanks to Keynesian deficit spending and to welfare policies. These factors extended the structural increase in consumption even to the lowest classes. This huge increase in consumption generated a 25-years boom. Housing, health care, social security, education, public transports; the diffusion of cars and household appliances; the general growth in food, clothes, entertainment consumption; all this, beside extending enormously employment, increased human capital productivity. The new mass employment of women pushed up both production and consumption. The non-western market remained too poor, suffocated as it was by neo-colonialism. But the domestic market widened until its very limit.

[11] Millar (1771), 180–188. Genovesi (1765) X.10, 231n; X.13, 234–235; and (1767) I.174. For other authors, see Perrotta (2004), ch. 11.6.

6.2.3 The Crisis

In the end the limit was reached. In the 1970s the roaring increase of both productivity and consumption led to a general saturation that the authors of the stationary state had foreseen. After the lowest classes had joined the rest of society in a relative welfare, the internal market could not enlarge any longer at the previous speed and accumulation could not go on. The creation of new goods and new needs went on, but it was not enough to support the general development, because of the nature of new technologies (see below).

Saturation, instead of leading to a rich and peaceful economy, led to bitter social conflicts, to unproductive investments, finally to the present crisis. Competition among producers became more and more ruthless.

Only a few years before there was an opposite situation. The boom was driving accumulation towards the post-Keynesian main goal: full employment.[12] This tendency had strengthened workers in the industrial relations. Wages grew beyond the increase in productivity, to the detriment of profits. This stimulated a strong opposition by the entrepreneurs, who defended what Marx had called the industrial reserve army.[13] At the academic level Keynesianism was accused of cheating workers through inflationary wages (Milton Friedman). The welfare state was accused of unbalancing the state budget to the detriment of investments. But saturation, the very cause of the crisis, was never mentioned.

When accumulation started slowing down, human capital was applied to less and less productive uses (production of repetitive goods). Social expenditures, instead of being an investment, ended up by being a weight on profits and on the public budget. In the middle of the 1970s, James O'Connor spoke about the fiscal crisis of the state.[14]

In the end social spending and state intervention were discredited; and so was solidarity to the poor and to backward countries. In western countries deregulation and the idea of an unlimited free competition took the upper hand. A simplistic slogan gained momentum: "less state, more market" (in fact it meant less public controls and less protection of the workers).

Saturation led capitals in excess towards four main types of employment. All of them are profit-producing. But only two of them are also wealth-producing: the creation of new goods and the investments in emerging countries (globalization). The other two are not productive of social wealth. They are: the production of repetitive goods; financial and real estate speculation.

As we will see, in mature economies *all* these destinations dramatically lowered the demand for labour and increased unemployment. Abundance and high

---

[12] On full employment, see Pollin (2012).

[13] Marx maintains that the unemployed, being ready to accept lower wages, push the wages of employed workers down. To this end, capital always keeps this reserve army: Marx (1867) ch. 23.3, 688–701.

[14] O'Connor (1973).

productivity, instead of reducing labour time, have increased it, have lowered wages and worsened labour conditions. Unemployment is the very core of the present crisis. *While in the previous crises unemployment was caused by the lack of investments, today—in mature economies—it is caused by investments themselves.*

6.3 Consequences of Saturation: New Technologies and Investments Abroad

6.3.1 New Technologies Produce Unemployment

It is now 30 years that investments in high-tech products lead growth (although a lower and lower one) in mature economies. This shows that, contrary to the forecast of the stationary state, there is always room for innovation and for production based on profit.

However high-tech products are not sufficient to avoid stagnation. In the nineteenth century the increase in productivity relied on investments in machinery (growth of fixed capital), which kept demand high. But gradually productivity growth was based increasingly on another tendency: the growth of workers' skill.

In the 1930s the latter tendency gained momentum. Since then technical progress was increasingly based on the relative diminution of fixed capital in terms of costs that is on a tendency opposite to that of the nineteenth century. Innovations became more and more capital saving. This means that investments in human capital relatively increased. Keynes himself, as we have seen, sensed that technological unemployment was bound to trouble accumulation.

When industrial production started to decline, the role of human capital increased even more. Post-industrial technologies, in any sector, use materials which are so cheap that investment costs are very low. Then they do not activate demand and employment sufficiently to stir up a general growth. It is not any longer the time when, for example, automatic weaving, steam boiler, railways, or cars dragged development by themselves. Today the increase in productivity, based on human capital, is able to save, not only on the costs of fixed capital and on the number of workers, but even on skilled labour, which is the central factor of present development. Especially the new information technologies are dismantling larger and larger production sectors.

Apparently there is nothing new, because technical progress always consists in substituting human labour with mechanical labour. In the past this process was compensated—at least in the long run—by the increase in productive investments, which was allowed by the increase in profits (in its turn due to the increase in productivity) as Ricardo explained to the Luddites.[15] But in our period this process

[15] Ricardo (1821) ch. 31.

has proceeded so fast that the increase in productivity, per unit of added investment, makes both capital and labour exceeding in great quantities.[16]

In the present market, dominated by the logic of profit, the very high productivity of new technologies, instead of abridging labour time and giving welfare, generates unemployment, poverty and the worsening of labour conditions.

6.3.2 Globalization Destroys Manufactures in the Mature Economies

Saturation in the mature markets is pushing industrial investments towards the emerging economies, where they find both lower labour costs and a growing demand. Of course this tendency is positive, in so far it helps global accumulation and takes enormous masses of people out of poverty. But at the same time it is destroying a very big part of western industry.

Such a tendency has been fostered by globalization, i.e. the liberalization of international exchanges, which was promoted by western countries themselves. In order to overcome market saturation, western countries implemented in the 1970s the free exchange of finance capital, and imposed it on developing countries. In the 1980s they also implemented the liberalization in the trade of goods, mainly through commercial treatises.

But globalization had an unintended effect: emerging economies developed far beyond expectations, and became strongly competitive with western economies. Now they export to western markets cheaper products, which tend to substitute local production; and attract western capital for investment. Meanwhile their internal demand is growing fast. These tendencies are producing the so called delocalization of western industry, and causing huge unemployment in western countries.[17]

Of course competition on labour cost by the poor countries is not new. As early as 1728 Daniel Defoe wrote about China's and India's exports, produced with very low wages. Defoe gave the problem the same answer that at present has been advanced: England, he said, having the highest wages in the world cannot compete on prices for her exports, but she competes on the high quality of the products.[18]

Defoe's thesis still holds, but only partially. Emerging countries are gaining momentum also in product quality. For example, in education and human capital's skill, many Asian countries today are more advanced than western countries.

[16] On information technologies, see Gualerzi (2010).

[17] See for ex. Reinert (2004) and Chang (2008).

[18] Defoe (1728), 36–68.

6.4 Saturation Consequences: Repetitive Goods and Speculation

Investments in the emerging countries by western excess capital, instead of overcoming saturation and re-launching western economy, have devastating effects on it. But the unproductive employment of this excess capital produces even worse effects. It is leading to a real degeneration of the accumulation process, by increasing parasitism and tending to destroy the basic rules of economic community.

6.4.1 *Repetitive Goods*

In a relevant portion, excess capital is still employed in the saturated sectors. It tries to force the market by producing what we can call *repetitive goods*. These are new items of goods already present in the market. In general repetitive goods are advertised as being better than the previous items, but quite often the supposed advantage does not exist or is negligible.

There are many ways to support the sale of repetitive goods: massive advertising (the subliminal one included); fashion; use of less durable materials, costs being equal; technical structure of the goods, which impedes to change only one part of them; protected markets and control of distribution; etc.

Repetitive goods have a decreasing utility. Quite often consumers would prefer to pay for other more useful goods (for example, public green, non-polluted air, efficient public transports, household services) instead of buying a second or third TV device, car or coat, etc. In fact the present structure of the market is based on the consumption of private, mainly material goods. It rarely allows a real alternative choice, because the demand for the first type of goods is not able to become effective.

Production of repetitive goods gives profit to the enterprises but does not increase real wealth in the society. Workers too who produce repetitive goods are in excess. They form the disguised unemployment of mature economies.[19] Thus production of repetitive goods is socially unproductive.

There can be several reasons for insisting in the production of repetitive goods. First of all, many small/medium enterprises are hardly able to innovate, on the technological or financial or cultural level. On the other hand big enterprises tend to reinforce their oligopoly positions. So they can keep or even increase their profits, thanks to the expulsion of marginal enterprises from the market. Besides, many enterprises and their workers got used to public assistance. Even institutions find it

[19] The concept of disguised unemployment first appeared in development economics, in order to measure backwardness. For ex., if in agriculture 100 labourers without caterpillar produce the same quantity than 10 labourers who use a caterpillar, in the first case there is a disguised unemployment of 90 workers (less the cost of the caterpillar, measured in wages).

easier, and more popular, to provide assistance than to innovate or change useless production.

Paradoxically unproductive production is encouraged by the radical idea that market failures can be solved only through competition. In fact in the market of repetitive goods competition is increasingly harsh, but this does not add any real advantage to the consumers in terms of satisfaction of needs. On the contrary it hinders the production of new goods for new needs.

The subject of repetitive goods is important for two reasons. First, it gives an answer to the problem of consumerism. Second, it calls in question the Keynesian deficit spending as a solution of the present crisis.

Criticisms to consumerism began as early as the 1960s. In the last decade, to the traditional argument of moral corruption (used, for example, by Bauman), the argument against pollution have been added (Latouche uses both arguments).[20] Stiglitz, too, uses the concept of consumerism in order to explain why in the US the Keynesian forecast of a stationary state was not fulfilled.[21]

Stiglitz in some aspects reminds the argument on repetitive goods, but he relies on individual preferences, and confuses consequences and causes of the crisis due to saturation. Even the old, effective analysis of Fred Hirsch does not explain much. It sees consumerism as promoted by capitalism as such. The latter creates illusions and proposes impossible goals in order to push people to earn and spend more and more.[22]

However, Smith reminds us that, whilst the consumption of necessaries is limited, that of "luxuries" is not.[23] The shortcoming of the anti-consumerist view is this: it does not make a difference between new goods (and needs) and repetitive goods. Such a distinction should be kept in mind also about the Keynesian policies to increase demand (of any good). For instance Krugman believes that these policies are sufficient to get out of the crisis.[24] This can be true in the short run, but if the production of repetitive goods is encouraged also in the long run, this will worsen the negative consequences of saturation. The latter can be overcome only through big investments in goods which now are scarce.

6.4.2 Speculation

Finally an increasing part of the excess capital moved to financial or real estate speculation, or to illegal hoarding in the fiscal havens. Here we will hint only to

[20] Baumann (2009) and Latouche (1995).

[21] Stiglitz (2008).

[22] Hirsch (1976).

[23] Smith (1776), I, XI, part II, 165. Cp. Ricardo (1821), ch. 21, 195.

[24] Krugman (2012).

financial degeneration, although similar arguments hold for the other types of speculation.

The huge literature on financial speculation of the last decades stresses that such a sector has gone through a spectacular and pathological growth.[25] Such a growth does not help any longer the production of goods and services as it should, rather it substitutes such a production. Financial investments usually give better and speedier yields (when they are successful). But their appeal is strongly reinforced by the saturation of traditional production in mature economies.

The abnormal increase in financial investments generates such a distortion in the market that it has often spoiled the economic agents' behaviour. Often it destroys professional ethics, loyalty in transactions, sense of cooperation, respect of one's own customers. All these things—economists have always warned—are necessary to the good functioning of economy.

Before the last two decades it would have been unthinkable that managers earned 500 or 1,000 times more than their employees, or that banks cheated their own customers, or that enterprises counterfeited their budgets in order to increase the managers' benefits or bet on derivatives and hedge funds to the detriment of the enterprise, etc.

This professional and moral degeneration is now partly extended to the level of real production, and inevitably leads to deprive employees of their basic rights.

6.5 New Needs and Production of Wealth Without Profit

Thus, when the conditions were realized for a stationary state, of supposed abundance and abridged labour, the same conditions led to an endless crisis, which in turn drove to economy's degeneration. This crisis also generated enormous inequalities at all levels (incomes, properties, education, culture, real rights, wages, and working conditions),[26] disruptive unemployment, poverty, great sovereign debts.

However the rationale of the stationary state—radically different from the logic of profit—can help us to get over the present crisis and its biggest evil: the widespreading unemployment. We should think of an economy where—beside (not instead of) the production for profit, promoted by private initiative—other sectors can grow which finally produce the new goods demanded. Precisely the goods which fulfil needs that the present market cannot express as effective demand.

Before examining the new sectors, let's stress two points. First, even in the production for profit many things can be done in order to defend employment. For

[25] Just two examples: Soros (2008) and Gallino (2011).

[26] See, among the many data, those of the Economic Policy Institute (USA) cited by Fullbrook (2013): in the period 1979–2011 the average income of 90 % of US population (the less rich) rose from 27,000 to about 31,000 (+15 %); that of the richest 5 % (minus the top 1 %) rose from ca. 105,500 to 165,500 (+134 %); the average income of the richest 0.1 % of population rose from 570,000 to 2,000. 160 ca. (+279 %).

example transforming, partly, the assistance to the unemployed into a support to solidarity contracts, or into incentives to abridge labour time. Second, the growth of the new sectors needs state's intervention. No wonder about this. In the past many periods of strong development have been promoted and led by the state. For example, the take-off of capitalism in sixteenth to seventeenth c. England, under the Tudor governments; the development in the nineteenth c. of Germany, then of Japan; the great boom in western European states in 1950–1975.

6.5.1 Basic Investments Implemented by the State

The state should implement the basic investments for development, while stimulating private participation. Many basic investments are too big for private capital, or their yields arrive only in the long run. Sometimes they give only a social yield, not a specific profit.

Today the basic investments consist of big infrastructures, networks for transports or for information and communication technologies; universal health care; universal and high quality education; diffusion of green energy; a non-polluted environment; hydro-geologic protection; town-planning; archaeological restoration. Some of these big projects can be financed with bonds or taxes bound to specific outcomes. The most important investment for development is to increase the productivity of public bureaucracy.

6.5.2 Non-profit Production (Public and Private)

We should free ourselves from the traditional idea that wealth is formed only through profits. In the capitalist economy a relevant part of wealth production has always been without profit. It is the case of public administration, of professionals, of independent producers (peasants, artisans, retail traders).[27]

In the long run, independent producers did not disappear; while public administration, besides supporting profit production, gradually provided autonomous goods (infrastructures, education, research, health care, information, social security).

However, it was the world of professionals that guided the revolution in the production of wealth. These autonomous highly skilled producers are today the main source of wealth. Their importance grew along with the complexity of economy; but their take-off came in the 1980s, when post-industrial economy prevailed.

---

[27] About the latter, see Smith (1776), b. I, ch. 6 and b. III, ch. 3. Marx (1867), ch. 24.7, 823–826; (1861–1863), vol. I, *Appendice*, 12.f, 606–609.

Post-industrial economy broke the polarization of the industrial production (mainly divided into dependent labour and capital owners). Because of the decrease in capital costs and the high skill of human capital, new productive processes were born, more creative, differentiated and ductile. Many of these processes are external to the logic of profit, sometimes even external to the logic of immediate utility (sale). The profit market is now too narrow to measure the quantity of wealth produced.[28]

Thus a myriad of new professions and professionals was born. A similar change happened also for consumption. Once material needs of the individual or the household are fulfilled, new and more complex needs appear, which require new services.

A part of the new jobs fulfils the new needs in research, culture, art, education, health care, skilled handicraft. Another part refers to the applications and functioning of the new technologies. Still another provide personal and household services of various kind, especially for the aged, ill, handicapped persons, or children and mothers (note that personal services have a better quality when they are provided by non-profit labour). Finally many new jobs provide collective services, new or improved, like transports, urban planning, and the infinite services aimed at a non-polluted environment.

Not always these new services or goods are public. Most of the times they are not. Often they are collective, but can be run by private, although non-profit, associations, cooperatives or even individuals.

6.5.3 *Fighting Poverty*

Fighting against poverty is another sector which produces wealth without profit, and could increase employment. It applies to both the mature economies and the poor countries. Poverty in mature economies is increasing again, making also human capital poorer. It is a process opposite to that of the boom of 1945–1975, which was sustained by the growing skill and productivity of human capital. It is urgent to change the present negative tendency, because today's economy is mainly non-material, and human capital skill is the pillar of development. The expenses against internal poverty is for developed economies an investment in the long run.

Also the expenses against poverty in the poor countries are an investment. In the past, poverty relief has been often the main way for development. We remind the assistance to the poor in Elisabeth I's England; the welfare policy implemented by Bismarck; the Marshall Plan after World War II; finally the welfare policies in Europe in the 1950–1960s.

---

[28] Marx realized such an evolution and put limits to the classical theory of labour value: M. (1957–1958), notebook VII.2, 403–406.

In all these cases, in the short run, the Keynesian mechanism held: assistance increased demand with multiplied positive effects. But in the long run the positive effects were even higher, because—along with demand—productivity increased. Besides, in the case of the Marshall plan, aid raised productivity of the receiving country. This allowed to increase the interchange between the donor and the receiver, fostering development for both. Today developed economies could put to work millions of their unemployed thanks to assistance.

Of course similar interventions hold at one condition: that they generate an autonomous development, not charity (and corruption). Development projects should be based on two pillars: implementation of infrastructures and native human capital formation at all levels.

Conclusions

Our conclusions are somehow paradoxical. We started looking what, of the idea of stationary state, that is an economy without development, can actually be applied. But we end up thinking the opposite: how to make development re-start. However there is not a real contradiction. Both ideas, stationary state and new way of developing, suggest a kind of society less unequal, where the logic of profit, while keeping its role, does not hinder the main goal: welfare for all.

Economists often forget that a part of our society does not like permanent risk, the frenzy of competition and a steady quest for enriching, i.e. the features of profit economy. Then, beside profit economy, we should allow other types of economy to grow: those based on autonomous labour, cooperation, non-profit production, solidarity.[29]

But, in order to achieve this, we should abandon the idyllic vision of J.S. Mill, Marx and Keynes. It is not true that the new economy grows up spontaneously. It needs long-lasting efforts and also hard struggles against those who defend their own privileges. Above all, inequalities in income and in social opportunities have to be reduced. Excessive inequality narrows both supply and demand of new goods, and feeds rents and parasitism.[30]

The confusion between productive and unproductive investments, and between production of wealth and production of profit, has caused in developed economies the abnormal increase of parasitic rents and a standstill in production, despite so many unsatisfied new needs.

[29] Of course an economy with a vast non-profit sector does not mean a centralized or socialist economy, as some authors believe (see for ex. Trainer 2011, 80).

[30] Cp. Solow (2008), 92–93.

References

Baumann Z (2009) Capitalismo parassitario. Laterza, Roma-Bari, 2011

Chang HJ (2008) Bad Samaritans. The myth of free trade and the secret history of capitalism. Bloomsbury, New York

Defoe, D (1728) Plan of the English Commerce, being a complete prospect of the Trade of this Nation, as well Home as Foreign, reprint. Kelley, New York, 1967

Fullbrook E (2013) Score card: 16% vs. 288%. Real World Economics Review Blog, January 29

Gallino L (2011) Finanzcapitalismo. Einaudi, Torino

Genovesi A (1765) Lezioni di commercio ossia di Economia Civile, parte I. In: Custodi P (ed) Scrittori classici italiani di economia politica. Destefanis, Milano, pp 1803–1816, parte Moderna, 7 & 8

Genovesi A (1767) Lezioni di commercio ossia di Economia Civile, parte II. In: Custodi P (ed) Scrittori classici italiani di economia politica. Destefanis, Milano, pp 1803–1816, parte Moderna, 8 & 9

Gualerzi D (2010) The coming of age of information technologies and the path of transformational growth. Routledge, London

Hirsch F (1976) I limiti sociali allo sviluppo (social limits to growth). Bompiani, Milano, 1981

Keynes JM (1930) Economic possibilities for our grandchildren, on-line, scanned from Keynes, Essays in Persuasion. Norton, New York, pp 358–373, 1963

Krugman P (2012) End this depression now! Norton, New York

Latouche S (1995) La megamacchina (La Megamachine). Bollati Boringhieri, Torino, 2008

Leijonhufvud A (2008) Spalmando il pane sottile sul burro. In: Pecchi L, Piga G (eds) Il ventunesimo secolo di Keynes. LUISS U.P., Roma, 2011, pp 115–121

Marx K (1857–1858) Lineamenti fondamentali della critica dell'economia politica (Grundrisse). La Nuova Italia, Firenze, 1968, reprint 1978, 2 vols

Marx K (1861–1863) Teorie sul plusvalore. Editori Riuniti, Roma, 1961, reprint 1972, 2 vols

Marx K (1864–1865) Il Capitale, III. Editori Riuniti, Roma, 1968

Marx K (1867) Il Capitale, I. Editori Riuniti, Roma, 1964

Mill JS (1848) Principles of political economy, b. 4, ch. 6 ("Of the stationary state"), on line ed. 2000 Liberty Fund, http://www.econlib.org

Millar J (1771) The distinction of ranks in society. Murray, London, in-4

O'Connor J (1973) La crisi fiscale dello stato (The fiscal crisis of the state). Einaudi, Torino, 1977

Pecchi L, Piga G (eds) (2008) Il ventunesimo secolo di Keynes (Revisiting Keynes). LUISS U.P., Roma, 2011

Perrotta C (2004) Consumption as an investment, The fear of goods from Hesiod to Adam Smith. Routledge, New York

Pollin R (2012) Back to full employment. MIT Press, Cambridge, MA

Reinert E (ed) (2004) Globalization, economic development and inequality. Elgar, Northampton, MA

Ricardo D (1821) Principles of political economy and taxation. Dent, London, 1973

Schumpeter JA (1949) History of economic analysis, 1954, reprint. Routledge, London, 1997

Smith A (1776) Ricchezza delle nazioni (Wealth of nations). ISEDI, Milano, 1973

Solow R (2008) I nipoti di chi? In: Pecchi L, Piga G (eds) Il ventunesimo secolo di Keynes. LUISS U.P., Roma, 2011, pp 89–94

Soros G (2008) Cattiva finanza (The new paradigm for financial markets). Fazi, Roma

Stiglitz J (2008) Verso una teoria generale del consumismo. In: Pecchi L, Piga G (eds) Il ventunesimo secolo di Keynes. LUISS U.P., Roma, 2011, pp 49–88

Trainer T (2011) The radical implications of a zero growth economy. Real World Econ Rev 57:71–82

Zilibotti F (2008) 'Possibilita' economiche per i nostri nipoti': una prospettiva globale 75 anni dopo. In: Pecchi L, Piga G (eds) Il ventunesimo secolo di Keynes. LUISS U.P., Roma, 2011, pp 37–48

Chapter 7
Leon Walras on Social Justice

Panagiotis G. Korliras

7.1 Pure and Social Economics

Léon Walras is best known among economists as one of the protagonists of the so-called "marginal revolution" and as the founder of general equilibrium theory. Yet, Léon Walras was much more than a proponent of the use of mathematics in economic analysis; the corpus of his writings indicates that Walras was a genuine French intellectual, with a view of the "economy" that developed parallel to, and embedded in, his view of the "society". For Walras the theoretical economist, we have the standing verdict of Joseph Schumpeter, who said that "as far as pure theory is concerned, Walras is in my opinion the greatest of all economists" (Schumpeter 1954, 827). For Walras the social thinker, much less is known or discussed by economists, except for the work of the "Walras group" in Lyon (Dockès 1996). In fact, "pure theory" was only one of the three branches of economics that Walras was teaching from 1870 to 1892 at the University of Lausanne. His celebrated *Éléments d' Économie Politique Pure—Théorie de la Richesse Sociale*, aptly translated as *Elements of Pure Economics* (Walras 1954), was to be complemented by two other volumes: the *Études d' Économie Sociale—Théorie de la Répartition de la Richesse Sociale* or "Social Economics" (Walras 1896), and the *Études d' Économie Politique Appliquée—Théorie de la Production de la Richesse Sociale*, or "Applied Economics".[1] In that grand scheme, the 'pure" economic theory was

[1] Throughout the text, for the Éléments we use the English translation by William Jaffé as "Elements of Pure Economics", (1926). For the Études d' Économie Sociale we use the new edition as volume IX of the "Auguste et Léon Walras: Oevres Économiques Complètes" (1990). Walras' Études d' Économie Politique Appliquée was published in the same series as Volume X.

P.G. Korliras (✉)
Department of Economics, Athens University of Economics and Business, 76 Patision Street, Athens 10434, Greece
e-mail: ckorlira@otenet.gr

G.C. Bitros, N.C. Kyriazis (eds.), *Essays in Contemporary Economics*,
DOI 10.1007/978-3-319-10043-2_7

only meant to be a basic and abstract framework about the fundamental properties of what came to be known as the "general competitive equilibrium", although Walras himself made clear that his "pure" economics must be read in connection to his "social" and "applied" economics. According to William Jaffé, the *Elements* were designed not as a study of men as they live and move, and think in the "ordinary business of life" (as Alfred Marshall had said), but as a theoretical representation of a "just economy" from the standpoint of "justice in exchange"; "distributive justice" called for separate treatment in the *Études d' Économie Sociale* (Walker 1983, 348).

To better understand the economic thought of Walras, it must be pointed out that he agreed with John Stuart Mill that "the Distribution of wealth is a matter of human institutions only", in contrast to Production, the laws of which "partake the character of physical truths" (Mill 1871, 199–200). In that respect, Walras, like Mill, recognizes an implicit divide between "ontology" and "deontology" in economics. Laying-out his own fundamental concepts in the *Elements*, Walras says that political economy is "simultaneously a natural science and a moral science. . .on the one hand, we have a moral science the aim of which is to determine how wealth *ought to be* distributed as equitably as possible; and on the other hand, we have a natural science the aim of which is to determine how wealth *is* produced as naturally as possible". Thus, "we shall divide political economy into a natural science, a moral science, and an art" (Walras 1926, 56–57). Clearly, the "is" corresponds to "ontology" and the "ought to be" to "deontology"; furthermore, the "ought to be" must be examined from two points of view: (a) expediency or material well-being, which leads us to applied science (and applied economics) or *art*, and (b) equity or justice, leading to a moral science (and social economics) or *ethics* (Walras 1926, 60). For Walras, the distinction between science and art, and the distinction between art and ethics, must be understood "methodically after taking into account the freedom and cognitive nature of the human will" (Walras 1926, 62). He concludes as follows: "such, then, are the distinguishing characteristics of science, art and ethics. Their respective *criteria* are the *true*; the *useful*, meaning material wellbeing; and the *good*, meaning justice" (ibid, 67). The *Elements of Pure Economics* is an idealized presentation of the "true"; the *Études d' Économie Politique Appliquée* are concerned with the "useful"; and the *Études d' Économie Politique Sociale* are concerned with the "good", at the centerpiece of which we have Walras' theory of economic justice. But these are three intrinsically connected aspects of Walras' vision of political economy as both a natural and a moral science.

In the fourth "Lesson" of his *Elements*, before he begins expounding his mathematical theory of general equilibrium, Walras gives to the reader his thoughts, rather his guidelines, which are necessary in order to connect his "pure theory" with his "social economics". According to him, "industrial production must not only be abundant, but also properly proportioned. . .the distribution of social wealth among the members of a community must be equitable. Social disorder is as much to be eschewed as economic disorder. . .it is claimed that the system of laisser-faire, laisser-passer, harmonizes apportionment with abundance. . .in production, man's will is guided by considerations of material well-being, in distribution his will is guided by considerations of justice" (Walras 1926, 75). Moreover, "the appropriation of scarce things or social wealth is a phenomenon of human contrivance and not a natural phenomenon. . .the appropriation of things by persons or the distribution of social wealth among men in society is a moral and not an industrial phenomenon (ibid, 76, 77). Finally, since "property is a phenomenon involving the concept of justice: it is a right" (ibid, 78), Walras concludes thus: "Appropriation being in essence a moral phenomenon, the theory of property must in essence be a moral science. *Ius est suum cuique tribuere*—justice consists in rendering to each that which is properly his. . . If, therefore, any science espouses justice as its guiding principle, surely it must be the science of the distribution of social wealth, or, as we shall designate it, *social economics*" (ibid, 79). For Walras, Distribution is a socio-ethical problem, and "not one for which a solution can be ground out simply by turning the crank of an analytical engine" (Walker 1983, 210–212). It is in fact interesting that not a single title of the eight major parts of the *Elements* or of the 42 "Lessons", contains the word "distribution" or its equivalent in any relevant sense. Even "marginal productivity", which plays a role in the "pure theory", is a mere extension of the theory of production, almost as a mathematical by-product, not a "theory of Distribution". As Walras himself says in his *Elements*: "Though our description of free competition emphasizes the problem of utility, it leaves the question of justice entirely to one side, since our sole object has been to show how a certain distribution of services gives rise to a certain distribution of products. The question of the (original) distribution of services remains open, however" (Walras 1896, 257). The issue of Distribution belongs to "social economics", to be examined from a different perspective in the *Études d' Économie Sociale*.

7.2 Justice and Order

Walras' social economics, where the issue of "justice" arises, can only be understood as an "economy" imbedded in "society", in the context of a quasi-holistic philosophical stance. The "society" consists of "persons", but Walras affirms that "moral persons (and personal ethics) exist only within the society and through the society", and that "if every moral person is an essential element of society, society is an essential element of all personal ethics" (Walras 1990, 132, 133). Then Walras goes from "society" to the "state", affirming that "the state is not a pure and single collection of individuals", that "the state has an existence of its own and which exceeds the sum of existences of all the individuals", thus "society is a natural and necessary fact, and not al all conventional and free" (ibid, 136, 137). By explicitly rejecting the notion of a "social contract", Walras not only adopts a holistic approach, but he also deprives himself from the option to deduce the "principles of ethics", and thus the "principles of justice", from any supposed free and rational choices of the members of the society (as Rawls did in the twentieth century). In fact, Walras takes a further stance, by asserting that "social ethics is a geometric science. Justice is not induced nor is it confirmed a posteriori from and by experience. It is deduced a priori through abstract definitions of the experience" (Walras 1896, 427). Thus, having explicitly rejected the contractarian foundation of ethics, Walras now rejects the consequentialist foundation of ethics, which means that he implicitly rejects the basic tenets of utilitarianism; the "good" is not simply the "useful", and thus justice is not expediency. In essence, Walras, who as a "pure theorist" employs the concept of utility as the principal founding stone of his theory, condemns the consequentialist utilitarian view of ethics with his holistic and natural-law point of view (Dockès 1996, 75–85).

From the views of Léon Walras presented so far, let us retain two points critical in assessing his theory of justice: First, that "social ethics is a geometric science", and second, that ethics and justice are "deduced a priori". The first point implies that for Walras, the problem of "justice" must be examined in conjunction with another important social issue, which for him is the "problem of order". The second point implies that Walras must propose a definition of justice which is suitable for his "social geometry". The two problems of "order" and "justice" are, then, to be examined by means of a pair of "criteria" which conform to Walras' ultimate goal: to expound a theory about the "democratic ideal". These criteria are "liberty" and "equality", drawn from "*la devise révolutionnaire*: *Liberté*, *Egalité*" (with *Fraternité* missing). The abundance of production, or else the material efficiency of the economy, is not an issue of "social economics", and in a sense it is taken for granted whatever it is: Walras, the pure theorist, has in the *Elements* demonstrated the conditions under which an economic system can be very efficient, even though he himself admits that these conditions are not universally applicable, as the principles of pure competition cannot be applied to, e.g. the cases of natural monopolies. But if Walras were a utilitarian, he would accept the conclusion that an economic system which produces the maximum material well-being, is "good", i.e. "just". Such would be the consequentialist point of view. To that economic efficiency, Léon Walras superimposes an additional (and a priori) definition of justice, which he then combines with the "problem of order" under the criteria of liberty and equality. Thus, Walras' theory of justice is one element of his grand scheme of "social geometry", and that theory of justice is presented at the sixth lesson of his long essay titled "Théorie Générale de la Société" contained in his *Études d' Économie Sociale*.[2]

Léon Walras distinguishes two types of "justice', the "commutative justice" and the "distributive justice". "Commutative justice presides over exchanges, and we can represent it as a sort of 'balance': in a running competition, we want all runners to start from the same line; distributive justice implies that the runners will be compensated according to their capabilities, i.e. according to the time that each runner touches the finish line. It is to violate justice if some of the contestants are

[2] Walras' "general theory of society" is generally ignored by historians of economic thought, because his theory is beyond the scope of what is acceptable as "economic theory". This is due to the fact that the "old" division between pure and applied and social economies has been abandoned. With one notable exception: the influential (and translated in many languages, including English) Histoire des Doctrines Économiques by Charles Gide and Charles Rist (1913, 671–674).

given considerable prior advantages; we equally violate justice if we pretend that they all finish at the same time. The problem of social justice is to discern the respective spheres of equality and inequality" (Walras 1896, 139). Walras' athletic example would lead us to think of "justice as fairness", (à la Rawls), but such "fairness" has to be seen in the context of the broader scheme of "equality and inequality". For Walras, the principle of social justice is summarized by the dictum "*égalité des conditions, inégalité des positions*" (ibid, 129). The "equality of conditions" refers to the general social conditions in a democratic society, and it can be interpreted as equality of opportunity or a society of equal opportunities for all, irrespective of the final outcomes.[3] The "inequality of positions" refers to the particular situations of the individuals in the framework of a free-market system; individuals, seen as economic agents, are entitled to pursue their interests and to enjoy the fruits of their capabilities and efforts, so that the "inequality of positions" is a legitimate outcome of the fair-play in a competitive economic system. Thus, the Walrasian notion of social justice comprises both equality and inequality.

To complete his "social geometry", Walras proposes a solution to the "problem of order", by discerning the respective spheres of "liberty" and "authority": "*liberté de l' individu, autorité de l' État*" (Walras 1896, 129). Liberty or freedom for the individual has to be combined with the authority of the State, since individuals, as moral persons, live naturally only in and through society. The State is presented as a guardian of the rules of civilized social co-existence, and individuals are free to pursue their interests and well-being only in the context of the rules of an orderly democratic society. This is how Walras completes his "general theory of society": liberty combined with authority solves the problem of order, and equality and inequality solve the problem of justice. "Liberty of the individual; authority of the State. Equality of conditions; inequality of positions. This is then, in the final analysis, the supreme law of the organization of a society on the basis of order and justice" (ibid, 140).

It remains to be seen to what extent Walras' "distributive justice" can also be considered as "re-distributive". As mentioned in the first section of this paper, Walras was well aware of the question of the "original distribution of services", or, in modern terminology, we should call them "endowments". Despite the fact that Pareto, Walras' successor at the University of Lausanne, defined an "optimal" situation, when no one can improve his position without worsening the position of someone else, and despite the fact that later general equilibrium theorists "proved" that any general competitive equilibrium is a "Pareto optimum", it is well known that any redistribution of initial endowments will lead to a different

[3] The expression "égalité des conditions" was first coined by Alexis de Tocqueville in his Democracy in America (English translation, edition of 2004). Its meaning has been narrowly rendered as "equality of status" (Brogan 2006, 275, also 351–352), or, more accurately, as "égalité devant des chances de la vie" (Leroy 1962, vol. 2, 528), i.e. equality of opportunity. Tocqueville thought that the "equality of conditions" was the principal characteristic of a democracy, and in this sense we adopt Leroy's version in order to assume a common, to both Tocqueville and Walras, concern for the democratic ideal. See also Boson (1963).

final allocation which is equally Pareto optimal. How can, then, the unrestricted economic forces, be prevented from creating more inequality than what is consistent with the Walrasian notion of "justice"? In the same vein, coming to the other pillar of Walras' social geometry, what is it that can prevent either the encroachment of individual liberties by the strengthening of the powers of the State, or, inversely, how can the State react, in the name of "society", to an overgrown liberty of individuals? On the question of order, Walras who presented himself as a "liberal socialist", or even a defender of the democratic ideals of the French Revolution, said that "the requirements of order would rather demand a restoration of liberty against the invasion of authorities", while on the question of justice he said that "the requirements of justice demand a restoration of equality against the invasion of inequality" (Walras 1896, 143). These statements, made in the context of the political and intellectual milieu of France at the end of the nineteenth century, may sound too specific to that milieu, but we can easily reflect on them in different places and times: the Walrasian social geometry is simple but malleable, indeed the basis of a political economy of a democratic society. In that sense, Walras' "distributive justice" can also be considered as "re-distributive", provided that a delicate balance is preserved in the respective spheres of the twin criteria of liberty and equality for the twin problems of order and (social) justice.

7.3 Walras in Perspective

To place the notion of justice of Léon Walras in perspective, we have, first, to clarify the exact meaning of his terminology, and second, to relate his notion with the principal currents of thought on this issue. In his "Théorie Générale de la Société", Walras uses four terms: "*justice*", "*justice commutative*", "*justice distributive*", and "*justice sociale*". The term "justice" is used to describe a very broad state of affairs, is unavoidably vague and never defined, and the only specific use made by Walras is when he writes about "the problem of justice" in the context of his "social economics". The term "commutative justice" is used with two meanings: it relates to justice in exchange, and then it relates to his "equality of conditions". In modern terminology, commutative justice means something different: it means full commutation of deserts into rewards or punishments, and corresponds to the notion of suum cuique, i.e. render unto each his own. The egalitarian (as far as conditions are concerned) meaning of the Walrasian commutative justice is absent from the modern terminology, which, in fact, implies that "inequality" is not inconsistent with commutative justice. The term "distributive justice" is used by Walras to denote the commutation of deserts based on abilities, and thus is related to the 'inequality of positions". In modern terminology, distributive justice is usually meant to imply that reward and punishments are distributed as they ought to be; in fact, distributive justice is in the normative domain, and has a presumption of equality and it can even be re-phrased as "redistributive justice".[4] It seems, therefore, that using the Walrasian terminology of commutative and distributive justice, one must distance himself from the modern usage of this terms, or else, to reverse their meaning as far as the issues of equality and inequality are concerned. At any rate, however, both terms are related to equality-inequality as operational rules in the context of an economy-in-society.

The term "social justice" is used by Walras to describe the combined effects of commutative justice with equality of conditions, and distributive justice with inequality of positions, as the solution of "the problem of justice" in the context of his social geometry. It is, therefore, a notion with a wider meaning, expressing not only a state of affairs, but also the set of institutional arrangements and policies in the normative (or ought-to-be) domain. Social justice is, for Walras, a desired state of affairs, which would exist if certain rules and practices are or are made to be in operation. In that sense, "social justice" must not only be related to the issue of equality vs inequality, but must be examined and assessed in combination with the other problem, the "problem of order", which relates to the issue of liberty vs authority. Social justice, in Walras' scheme, has meaning only in the context of the joint solution of the puzzle: justice with equality-inequality and order with liberty-authority. Thus, social justice is intimately related to the issues of liberty and equality (liberté-égalité).

As social justice belongs to the sphere of normative economics and politics, it has been the object of much controversy among philosophers and economists in the twentieth century, and the cause of a vast literature.[5] At this point, we can limit our references to two prominent figures in this controversy, F. A. Hayek and John Rawls. In his *The Mirage of Social Justice*, Hayek attacks the concept of social justice (or economic justice, as he says), because it is "regarded as an attribute which the 'actions' of society, or the 'treatment' of individuals and groups by society, ought to possess", so that social justice came to be "essentially the same as that in which the expression 'distributive justice' had long been employed" with the result that "this conception of 'social justice' leads straight to full-fledged socialism" (Hayek 1976, vol. 2, 62–64). Although Léon Walras claimed to be a socialist, Hayek's version of social justice is not the same as Walras'. Whereas Hayek sees in the notion of social justice an ideological bias towards re-distribution in an egalitarian sense, Walras includes the "inequality of positions" as an integral part of his scheme, and re-distribution is only called forth when, and if, there is too

[4] On these issues, see the survey articles by Anthony de Jasay 1998: "Justice" and by Helmut Kleimt: "Distributive Justice", both in the New Palgrave Dictionary of Economics and Law (1998). Although "justice" is also, and for some primarily a legal notion, economists and philosophers, from John Stuart Mill to Léon Walras to John Rawls, adopt a broader meaning of that notion, serving as a fertilizer to the field of "law and economics".

[5] Merely as indicative of that literature, we mention the volume of reading by Edmund S Phelps (editor): *Economic Justice* (1973), the book by Serge-Christophe Kolm: *Modern Theories of Justice* (1996), and the survey article of James Konow: "Which is the Fairest One of All? A Positive Analysis of Justice Theories", in the *Journal of Economic Literature* (2003).

much inequality. Thus, contrary to Hayek's notion of social justice, Walras' notion is not fundamentally redistributive.[6]

As a set of rules and institutions which corresponds to desired state of affairs in an economy-in-society, Walras' notion of social justice is closer to the same notion in the work of John Rawls. In his *Theory of Justice*, Rawls says that "the principles of social justice provide a way of assigning rights and duties in the basic institutions of society and they define the appropriate distribution of the benefits and burdens of social cooperation" (Rawls 1971, 4). These principles "regulate the choice of a political constitution and the main elements of the economic and social system" (ibid, 7). Thus, "a conception of social justice is to be regarded as providing in the first instance a standard whereby the distributive aspects of the basic structure of society are to be assessed" (ibid, 9). Then, in his *Political Liberalism*, Rawls poses a "fundamental question", namely "what is the most appropriate conception of justice for specifying the fair terms of social cooperation between citizens regarded as free and equal, and as fully cooperating members of society" (Rawls 1993, 3), so that such a conception becomes "a shared basis for settling such a fundamental question as that of the most appropriate family of institutions to secure liberty and equality" (ibid, 8). With its emphasis on social cooperation and institutional arrangements, as well as on the issues of liberty and equality, the Rawlsian notion of social justice is quite similar to the Walrasian notion, despite the fact that Rawls was apparently not aware of Walras' "social economics".

This proximity of the theories of Léon Walras and John Rawls is, however, evident only at the very general sphere of socio-economic and institutional arrangements, which correspond to a modern social-democratic ideal (Dockès 1996, 127–135). There is, indeed, a major difference between the two theories. Walras "imposes" a notion of social justice conceived a priori, in a holistic approach which pre-supposes that "justice" together with "order" are indispensable characteristics of a well-ordered socio-economic system. Rawls, on the other hand, "derives" a notion of social justice from rational decisions of the members of a society, in the context of a "social contract". As Rawls says: "the guiding idea is that the principles of justice for the basic structure of society are the object of the original agreement. They are the principles that free and rational persons concerned to further their own interests would accept in an initial position of equality as defining the fundamental terms of their association" (Rawls 1971, 11). The theory of Rawls is "contractarian", a philosophical stance explicitly criticized and rejected by Léon Walras (Walras 1896, 132), because for him persons are "moral entities" only "within and through society", and thus not conceived as "deciding" about the

[6] The view of F. A. Hayek is reviewed, and supported, in the survey article by Julia Stapleton: "Social Justice", in the *New Palgrave Dictionary of Economics and the Law* (1998). It must be noticed, however, that the tendency to dismiss the notion of "social justice" as a mere theoretical device to promote re-distributive or socialistic doctrines, and the ensuing debate, was since the 1970s sparked by the work of John Rawls, and principally his influential book *Theory of Justice* (1971). If Walras' version of "social justice" were known, at least in the English speaking world, the arguments in that debate would probably have been different.

terms of social co-operation "before society" (Walras 1896, 132; Dockès 1996, 100–102).

One final note on the Walras–Rawls relationship: Walras never added to the "*Liberté*, *Égalité*" the remaining "*Solidarité*" in order to complete "la devise révolutionnaire". Rawls, however, does refer to "fraternity" in conjunction with "liberty" and "equality", by linking his "difference principle" (thus, his maximin rule) with the notion of fraternity: "the difference principle does seem to correspond to a natural meaning of fraternity: namely, to the idea of not wanting to have greater advantages unless this is to the benefit of others who are less well off" (Rawls 1971, 105). In the work of Rawls, such an idea of "fraternity" can emerge in the context of his contractarian philosophy. For Walras the same notion might have been considered as superfluous in the context of his view that society, and social co-operation, is a datum. Exposing his theory as an economist and social thinker, Walras was addressing the problem of resolving potential causes of instability in an economic system based on the working of competitive markets, and a society which, in his view, needs both "order" and "justice". In the end, what Walras and Rawls seem to have common, is a political economy of a democratic society.

References

Boson M (1963) La Pensée Sociale et Coopérative de Léon Walras. Institut des Études Coopératives, Paris

Brogan H (2006) Alexis de Tocqueville: a life. Yale University Press, New Haven, CT

de Jasay A (1998) Justice. In: The new Palgrave dictionary of economics and the law, vol. 2. Macmillan, London, pp 400–409

de Tocqueville A (1850) Democracy in America (trans: Goldhammer A). The Library of America, New York (1998)

Dockés P (1996) La Société n'est pas un Pique-Nique- Léon Walras et l' Économie Sociale. Economica, Paris

Gide C, Rist C (1913) Histoire des Doctrines Économiques. Sirey, Paris

Hayek FA (1976) The mirage of social justice. In: Hayek FA (ed) Law, legislation and liberty, vol 2. Routledge, London (1978)

Kliemt H (1998) Distributive justice. In: The new Palgrave dictionary of economics and the law, vol. 1. Macmillan, London, pp 630–635

Kolm SC (1996) Modern theories of justice. MIT Press, Cambridge, MA

Konow J (2003) Which is the fairest one of all? A positive analysis of justice theories. J Econ Lit XLI:1188–1239

Leroy M (1962) Histoire des Idées Sociales en France, vol 2. Gallimard, Paris

Mill JS (1871) Principles of political economy, the 1909 Ashley edition. Augustus Kelley, Fairfield, NJ

Phelps ES (ed) (1973) Economic justice-selected readings. Penguin, Baltimore, MD

Rawls J (1971) A theory of justice. Harvard University Press, Cambridge, MA

Rawls J (1993) Political liberalism. Columbia University Press, New York

Schumpeter J (1954) History of economic analysis. Oxford University Press, Oxford

Stapleton J (1998) Social justice. In: The new Palgrave Dictionary of economics and the law, vol. 3. Macmillan, London, pp 468–475

Walker D (ed) (1983) William Jaffe's essays on Walras. Cambridge University Press, Cambridge

Walras L (1896) Études d' Économie Sociale (prepared by Pierre Dockés). Economica, Paris (1990)
Walras L (1926) Elements of pure economics (trans: Jaffé W). Richard Irwin, Homewood, IL (1954)

Part III
Institutions and the Free Market System

Chapter 8
Surprising Institutions

Carl Hampus Lyttkens

8.1 Introduction

The following is a report of an episode of conflicts over property rights, an episode that highlights some interesting (and possibly entertaining) features of individual decision making in a world of imperfect information. Perhaps I should point out that the possibility of recording this experience for the benefit of posterity did not occur to me until the final surprise was delivered by the court of appeal.

This is an unusual approach in economics, but if you read scientific medical journals, you will from time to time encounter articles which essentially are reports of "one case of X". The X in question could be any sort of unusual medical experience. Some such reports stand out more than others. For instance, there is Pinheiro et al. (2003) who reported in the *American Journal of Forensic Medicine and Pathology* the death of an otherwise healthy fisherman who put a fish between his jaws in order to free his hands for work. The fish unfortunately squirmed its way into the larynx and so the fisherman choked to death despite the efforts of the fisherman's friends with pliers. The presumption in the literature is that there is something to be learned from such singular cases. One effect can be that other similar reports emerge (death by fish has been discussed more than once). Let us now turn from fish to institutions.

Institutions fulfil several important roles in society. Institutions constitute the rules of the game and reduce the uncertainty in human interaction. Unfortunately, as Douglass North (1981) has made us aware, when we look around us and back in history we can see that efficient institutions are an exception rather than the normal state of affairs. Eggertsson (2005), who focus particularly on the possibilities of reform (or lack thereof), points out that individuals frequently rely on incomplete social models (mental constructs to cope with uncertainty and complexity in the

C.H. Lyttkens (✉)
Department of Economics, Lund University, P. O. Box 7082, 220 07 Lund, Sweden
e-mail: carl_hampus.lyttkens@nek.lu.se

G.C. Bitros, N.C. Kyriazis (eds.), *Essays in Contemporary Economics*,
DOI 10.1007/978-3-319-10043-2_8

environment). We are often ignorant about the likely responses of other actors in the economy, and the feedback we receive on our actions do not necessarily improve our mental images of how the world functions (North 2005).

The relative efficiency of an institution depends on how it affects behaviour in the economy, which in turn depends on the extent to which it is understood by the different actors. This paper focuses on the extent to which an actor knows about and understands an institution.

It is usually *not* a good idea to assume that everybody has perfect information about everything. On the contrary, our information is frequently not only limited but also erroneous and we often carry incorrect beliefs about the world surrounding us.[1] One aspect of this is that we are often mistaken about the nature of the institutional structure in our society. Institutions need not be well-known, the institutional structure is not necessarily transparent and the characteristics of a particular institution may come as a surprise to us. This is true even with respect to property rights in Western Europe, where such rights are usually assumed in the literature to have been secure and stable for centuries.

The two dimensions—efficiency and transparency—are obviously related. For example, an institution that would be efficient if it was well understood may be rather less than efficient if individual actors do not know enough about it. In the latter case, resources can be wasted, for example, in terms of transaction costs, when people act on an erroneous belief about the nature of the rules of the game.

The following story illustrates several kinds of institutional surprises. It is based on my personal experience of a series of institutional discoveries; the discoveries were made when I ventured to protect my property rights with respect to a piece of land owned by my sister and me (around 210 hectares) and located in southern Sweden. The opposing team counted among the players not only a multi-national corporation but also (this being one of the surprises) a Swedish government agency with a long history. It is not at all obvious that the experience has made my beliefs about the institutions in this area more correct than before.

8.2 Background: A Swedish Institution with a Long History

Anno domini 1600, Karl IX—the Swedish King-to-be—engineered the beheading of five leading aristocrats. This event later became known as The Carnage in Linköping and represented an important step on Karl's way to the Swedish throne.[2]

[1] As noted in behavioural economics, our beliefs tend to be wrong on average, for example, because we are overconfident, we conclude from too small samples, and we expect our future preferences to be close to the present ones, cf. DellaVigna (2009).

[2] Even today, Karl IX seems to have a less good reputation in this part of Sweden compared to the rest of the country where Karl's efforts to present himself as the bulwark against *papism* (suspect

After the death of Karl's brother Johan, Johan's son (Karl's nephew) Sigismund became King of both Poland and Sweden. However, by playing on anti-Catholic feelings and the fact that Sigismund largely was under obligation to stay in Poland, Karl IX gradually seized control over Sweden, until in 1607 he formally was crowned King of Sweden.

The main source of opposition to Karl's take-over lay within some groups of the Swedish aristocracy, and they suffered for this. During the period when he manoeuvred to take power, Karl had more than 20 aristocrats summarily executed (Petersson 2009). Since he did not trust the aristocracy, Karl followed the example of his father Gustavus Vasa and relied to a large extent on commoners as secretaries and administrators. He however also instituted several of the magistracies (held by members of the aristocracy) which would serve as the basis of Swedish administration in the following century.

When Karl was not busy knocking off aristocrats, he took a deep interest in his personal income and later also in government revenue. He banned trade in the countryside, favouring trade in the towns where he could tax it.[3] He tried to regulate the export of iron products (Petersson 2009).

The legacy from Karl IX was taken over by his son King Gustavus Adolphus, who put Sweden on the political map of Europe during the 30 years' war. After the death of Gustavus at the Battle of Lützen in 1632, Sweden was ruled by the regency of Queen Kristina. Head of the administration was Count Axel Oxenstierna (powerful already during the reign of Karl IX). Oxenstierna further developed Swedish government bureaucracy, which was to undergo a metamorphosis during his time in power[4] and served as a basis for Swedish administration in the centuries to come.

It was under the leadership of Oxenstierna that the government agency "Bergskollegium" was formed in 1637, an agency ordained to direct mining affairs which it continued to do until 1857. In 1649 Bergskollegium was seen as important enough to be put on an equal footing with the five main branches of government (finance, foreign policy, jurisdiction, war and fleet).[5]

In 1857 Bergskollegium was abolished and its duties taken over by Kammarkollegium. The organization of government agencies dealing with the mining issues was divided into districts; these districts were subsequently gradually amalgamated during the twentieth century, until in 1998 the whole of Sweden became one district. The mining inspectorate received a new name—"Bergsstaten"—and was put under the leadership of one "Bergmästare", a title

friendliness towards Catholicism) seems to have worked better (Petersson 2009). Linköping is situated in the County of Östergötland, which incidentally is where our property was situated.

[3] This is of course no surprise to those who believe in the predatory model of the state, cf. Levi (1988), Lyttkens (1994), North (1981).

[4] Sweden was relatively early with many public institutions. For example, the Bank of Sweden (Sveriges Riksbank) was founded in 1665, and in 1749 demographic statistics were collected for the first time making Sweden and Finland the countries with the longest continuous records of that kind.

[5] Heckscher (1936, 688).

that goes back to the medieval period and continued in use over the centuries. The head office is now in the city of Luleå (in the north of Sweden) with a subsidiary office in the city of Falun in the County of Dalarna.

This is the background to the government agency Bergsstaten, which is an important actor in what follows.

8.3 Tasty Left-Overs from the New Institutional Economic Smargasbord: Surprising Institutions

New Institutional Economics (NIE) has brought several features of the institutional structure in contemporary society to the attention of other economists. It has influenced mainstream economics which now regularly incorporates, for example, considerations of transaction costs and social norms. Much of NIE is now conducted within this (extended) neo-classical paradigm.

However some of the most intriguing notions of NIE remains to be explored. One of these is the importance of the belief systems of the actors in the economy and in particular the fact that these may entail erroneous beliefs about the world. Furthermore it is by no means certain that the feedback individuals receive on their actions make their beliefs about society more correct than they were before (North 1990).

Institutions—defined here as the rules of the game—play an important part in this. One example of incorrect beliefs is when the existence of an institution is poorly known in general or in detail. If that is the case, a citizen will likely be surprised when he finds out about the rules of the game in that particular sphere of society.[6] What surprises an actor of course varies across nations and with the experiences of how actors behave. For a contemporary Greek, it is, for example, probably surprising to come to Sweden and find that you can phone a government official (or nowadays email her) and receive a quick, straightforward, and usually correct answer to a question. A citizen of Athens in the classical period would on the other hand have been anything but surprised if he learnt that a government official had embezzled the money entrusted to him.[7]

To the extent that the institutional structure is unknown to us, the feedback we get on our decisions may include information about these previously unknown

[6] Institutions are sometimes defined as shared beliefs, e.g., Aoki (2001). This obviously makes it pointless to talk about surprising institutions. However, the phenomena I deal with in this essay would still have to be considered.

[7] The overarching principle behind the extensive rules and regulations in classical Athens was "that absolutely nobody is to be trusted" (Davies 1994, 204). Similarly, Hansen (1999, 310), concludes that "the Athenians had the characteristic of being honest with themselves about themselves. [. . .] they went on the basis that, given the chance, every one of them would have his hand in the till and make a profit out of political activity, and they took every possible means to limit the chances."

institutions. When this is the case the institutions might be consonant with what we believe about society so that they come as no big surprise. It can also happen however that the institutional set-up turns out to be substantially different from what we expected, in which case information about them may well increase rather than reduce the uncertainty we experience.

In this essay we will encounter some different ways in which the institutional set-up can turn out to be surprising, even to a supposedly well-informed citizen.

8.4 Learning About Your Property Rights: A Surprising Story

8.4.1 A Letter: Not Nice, But No Surprise

In early spring 2006, I receive a letter. It is addressed to my sister and me, and informs us that Lundin Mining Exploration AB (henceforth Lundin Mining) has requested permission to search for minerals on our piece of land. So we are dealing with a big multi-national company with organisations in several European countries.

The property in question is all covered with forest, and it has been in the family since the 1930s, when my grandmother bought it. My sister and I took over the property in 1994 when we bought the 50 % that were owned by our cousins. It is always a great pleasure to visit the forest and learn more about planting, clearance, thinning, etc. The property is situated some 450 km from where we live, in the county of Östergötland, where Linköping is the most important city (residence of the King's governor etc.).

We very much enjoy the visits to "our forest." We use to meet there with a forester—an employee of the government authority that regulates forestry in Sweden ("Skogsstyrelsen"). He knows everything about forestry and we always learn a lot and have a great time generally. Furthermore, the visits make a nice change to my normal professional activities and it provides my sister and me with a useful income. Furthermore, I view (my part of) the property as a substitute for an old-age pension scheme, since I plan to sell my half to my sister's side of the family when I approach retirement.

But now a mining company has decided to search for minerals in my forest! And it is a big multinational one too, with activities in many European countries so it seems unlikely that they will be unable to afford it. This is worrying because I believe that Swedish law gives them the right to start mining if they find something worth mining. They will own the mining business of course. And even though the letter mentions that we will receive 1.5 ‰ of the value of the ore (an improvement compared to previous legislation when the landowner received nothing), this is no real comfort. It seems highly likely that the beautiful views will be destroyed.

I strongly suspect that it will ruin the forest in its capacity as income insurance for old age.

What to do? I decide to phone the government agency that administers such cases. I can see from the letter that it is called Bergsstaten, and the letter is signed by an official entitled "Bergmästare". I ask him if there is any chance of success if I try to protest against the plans of Lundin Mining. The answer I receive is a simple and straightforward "no"—there is nothing I can do to stop them from getting the concession to prospect on my land for 3 years. I sigh and hope that they will not find anything worth mining. Lundin Mining receives the permission on March 21.

8.4.2 Another Letter: Let's Trust Coase

Time passes, and in this case no news is good news (it must mean that they have not found anything worth mining). Then in the end of March 2009, I receive a new letter from Bergsstaten. It informs us that Lundin Mining has asked for a 1-year extension of their concession, until March 21 in 2010. Bergmästaren has granted them this extension. This time however I was in a more obstinate mood. "Let's see if at least I cannot create some transactions costs. Perhaps if I am difficult enough the company will give up?" It is a vague hope, but at least a hope. If I am sufficiently annoying, perhaps Lundin Mining will give up and shift their interest to property with owners less inclined to write complaining letters to the authorities?

Coase (1960) showed that transaction costs make the distribution of rights matter for resource allocation, and I do have some rights on my side. However I do not have great hopes because, being an economist, I can see that it is likely to be an economically efficient rule that individual land owners cannot stop a mining project. Following Coase's line of argumentation, it could easily be prohibitively costly to contract with all the landowners who have property that would be needed to start a mining project, even if the income from the mining project in principle would suffice to make every one better off. This is because each landowner could engage in opportunistic behaviours (a major source of transaction costs, as we know from Oliver Williamson (1985)), and try to appropriate the whole surplus of the mining operation.

So on March 25th I write a letter to appeal the decision to the County court of Dalarna—the court of appeal for the decision by Bergsstaten to grant Lundin Mining an extension (cf. Table 8.1 for a time table of the whole process).[8] I note with some interest that the letter with my appeal should be sent to Bergsstaten and not to the court of appeal, (cf. below on capture theory).

In the letter, I emphasize that our property includes areas of great natural beauty, which most likely would be destroyed if Lundin Mining is allowed to start mining

[8] The county court of Dalarna has been assigned this function as a court of administrative law (Förvaltningsrätt).

Table 8.1 Time table of LYTTKENS vs. Bergsstaten and Lundin Mining

Date	Event	Surprise?
2006-03-21	Lundin Mining receives a 3 years concession to search for minerals on the property of LYTTKENS. It is valid until 2009-03-21.	No, not really
2009-03-11	Bergsstaten receives an application from Lundin Mining for a 1-year extension of their concession (Dnr BS 201-390-09).	
2009-03-18	Bergsstaten decides in favour of the application from Lundin Mining.	Pretty quick handling, or don't you think?
Around March 20th	LYTTKENS are informed about the application from Lundin Mining and the decision by Bergsstaten.	
2009-03-25	LYTTKENS lodge a protest to the County court in Falun against the decision by Bergsstaten.	
2009-04-14	Bergsstaten/Bergmästaren argues that the decision should stand.	
2009-05-06	LYTTKENS argues that the extension should be denied, because Lundin Mining has not shown that they have carried out purposeful investigations.	
2009-06-02	Bergmästaren notes that LYTTKENS is right: the extension ought not to have been granted on the grounds stated in the original application; however, Lundin Mining ought to be allowed to add other grounds for granting them an extension.	Yes indeed. Twice
2009-06-17	LYTTKENS complain that Bergsstaten is not impartial and adds some further arguments against the extension.	
2009-07-09	Lundin Mining complements their application, adding the other grounds indicated by Bergsstaten 2009-06-02.	No way.
2009-07-01	Bergsstaten states that the reasons that Lundin Mining now gives when applying for an extension are such that it should be granted.	Hardly.
2009-07-12	LYTTKENS argue that even if the area forms part of a larger area under investigation, Lundin Mining has still failed to show that the investigations will in fact be carried out within the time of extension.	
2009-07-29	LYTTKENS note that a final comment from Lundin mining does not add anything principally new.	
September 1st 2009 (approx.)	The case is ready for a decision by the court.	
2010-03-22	The extension expires.	Somewhat.
2010-12-01	The court decides in favour of LYTTKENS in the case of LYTTKENS vs. Bergsstaten and Lundin Mining, but since the extension has expired, no further action is taken.	Yes.

there (and I point out that Lundin Mining already has had 3 years at their disposal). As I said, my hopes are not great, because if I remember correctly from my earlier phone call, such considerations would be taken into account later in the process. If Lundin Mining find minerals, the value of the nature will probably be taken into consideration when it comes to the decision whether to allow them to start mining or not (fat chance that we would be able to stop them then, if we had not done so before, but what the h—k, I do not expect to be successful, I expect to be a nuisance).

The next letter I receive is a statement dated April 14th from Bergmästaren to the County court regarding our appeal. He states that there is no reason not to grant Lundin Mining their extension. The value of the nature will be considered if and when it ever comes to a potential mining project. Furthermore, Bergmästaren notes that according to Swedish law, a party should be granted extension if the said party has conducted "meaningful investigations"[9] and Bergmästaren notes that we have not made any objections as regards the meaningfulness of the investigations carried out by Lundin Mining.

8.4.3 The First Institutional Surprise: The Rules of the Game Are Not Totally Against Us

This made me curious. I had not noted this concept of "meaningful investigations" in the first letter about the extension. And I had been given the opportunity by the County court to comment on the new statement from Bergmästaren. So in order to explore every avenue of success, and Sweden being the kind of country that it is (cf. Sect. 8.3), I contacted the County court (or was it Bergsstaten? I simply do not remember) and asked for a copy of the original letter where Lundin Mining asked for an extension. I also spent some time reading up on the legislation (the web is a wonderful thing).

When shortly afterwards I receive the copy, I find that Lundin Mining describe their activities until today in two parts. In the whole area covered by their concession, which includes many more properties than just our forests, they have carried out geophysical measurements and have been drilling. But in the particular are where our property is situated, all they say is that they have carried out "geological visits in the field" ("...*har geologiska fältbesök gjorts*").

Now this looks like a possible opening—what a nice surprise. The facts may be more in my favour than I had expected. In my new letter (May 6th), I point out that what Lundin Mining—according to their own application—to date has done what could be translated into plain non-bureaucratic Swedish as "been there and taken a look." This, I now argue, could hardly be the kind of "meaningful investigations"

[9] In Swedish: "ändamålsenliga undersökningar". Minerallagen, 2 kap, § 6.

that was mentioned in the law, when it states that extension is almost automatic if such investigations have taken place.[10]

I was reasonably satisfied with my crafting of the reply, but I still did not really think that I could succeed in stopping Lundin Mining. A telephone call to a friend who happens to be a judge did not give me great hopes of success. He took a look at the legislation and concluded that it was heavily biased in favour of the mining company. For example, he told me that nobody actually had to inform me when someone obtained the right to look for minerals on my land.

So I was pleasurably surprised when I received a copy of the comment that Bergsstaten had delivered as a response to my new letter (dated June 2nd). Bergmästaren states that after careful consideration of the facts, he has found that Lundin Mining *had not* in fact showed that they had carried out "meaningful investigations", and that they ought not to have been granted an extension on this account.

I have won! Or then again perhaps not.

8.4.4 The Second Institutional Surprise: It Looks as Though Bergsstaten Is a Player on the Other Team

Keeping on reading the statement of Bergsstaten, I find to my surprise that *Bergmästaren* also notes the following: even if there have not been any meaningful investigations, a party shall (according to the law) have the right to an extension if the party has "acceptable reasons" for not having carried out such investigations. An example of such acceptable reasons would be that the area under consideration forms part of a large area where investigations are carried out. Bergmästaren argues that it is likely that Lundin Mining would have been granted an extension if they had stated this as a reason in their application and consequently—Bergmästaren argues—Lundin Mining ought to be given an opportunity to complement their original application.

This was indeed an institutional surprise (and an unpleasant one at that) Not only is the law very favourable to those who wish to look for mining opportunities, but in addition to this it now seems to be the case that the government authority that supervises these activities is in fact a player on the team of those who want to start mining. In fact, when the County court eventually makes a decision in our case (more on this anon), Bergsstaten is listed as my adversary together with Lundin Mining. I had not counted on this, I must admit.

My way of summarizing the statement from Bergsstaten in a new letter to the County court (dated June 17th) is that Bergmästaren now says that Lundin Mining should have been denied an extension on the basis of their application, but that they

[10] Mineralförordningen SFS 1992:285, § 7.

ought to have been granted an extension if they had written a different application, and that therefore they should have the right to write a new application.

I suggest to the County court that Bergsstaten does not behave like an impartial agency, and I question if this is in accordance with Swedish law. In addition, I try to be imaginative and dig up a few more aspects from my reading of the relevant legislation: A extension of the permission based on the grounds cited by Bergsstaten would require: (1) that the project as whole stretches over more than 3 years, which Bergsstaten has not in fact shown, and (2) that it is probable that the investigations on our land would in fact be carried out within the time specified in the extension (i.e., 1 year), which again had not been shown. Both these aspects seem to be necessary conditions for an extension.

I add that a company like Lundin Mining ought to be aware of what they should specify in order to have their extension granted, and should therefore not be allowed to bring more arguments to the case (admittedly not a watertight argument, but as I said—trying to be a nuisance).

8.4.5 No Surprise at All

It comes as no reprise when we receive a copy of a statement from Lundin Mining (dated June 22nd), where they apply for an extension of their right to search for minerals on the grounds that our property is part of a larger area where investigations are carried out, i.e. precisely those arguments that Bergmästaren pointed out would have been acceptable as a reason for not having performed sufficient investigations. One supposes that Lundin Mining has employees who can read.

Similarly, it is hardly surprising that Bergsstaten in a new comment (July 1st) states that the reasons that Lundin Mining now gives for applying for an extension are such that it should be granted according to the law. The new arguments brought forward by Lundin Mining constitute a sufficient excuse for not having performed any thorough investigations, according to Bergsstaten (anything else from them would indeed have been a surprise, since this is what they wrote already on June 2nd). Bergmästaren adds that as an impartial official he ought to have pointed out to Lundin Mining that they should have given other reasons for an extension in their original application.[11]

In a new comment (July 12th), we argue that even if our property is part of a larger area under investigation, Lundin Mining has still failed to show that the investigations will in fact be carried out within the time of the extension. In fact, Lundin Mining has not even commented upon this aspect of the case.

[11] I hate to admit it, but this sound reasonable. It still feels unfair though, when you as an individual is confronting a major company.

In a letter to the Court of July 29th, we note that a final comment from Lundin Mining (in mid-July) does not add anything principally new. This is where the exchange of letters ends.

8.4.6 What Will Happen Now? More Surprises?

Not having heard anything for a while, I phone the County court in late August or early September 2009 to ask what is going on. I receive the answer that as far as the County court is concerned, the case is ready for a decision (*avgörandeklart*). It stands in line.

This sounds sort of OK but I can now start thinking about the fact that the County court is situated in the same small Swedish city as the subsidiary office of Bergmästaren (Falun).

A main idea in the capture theory of regulations is that a regulating agency over time will tend to become captured by those it is set to regulate. There are several reasons for this. For example, employees of the government agency are likely to see a future career as employees of the regulated firms. For the firms it is of course very useful to hire people who know a lot about how the regulator thinks and plans. Furthermore the employees of the government agency and the firms will often meet regularly in committees etc. Hence to me as an economist it looked as decidedly bad news that the court selected to handle cases concerning mineral rights was in fact geographically located in the same city as the government agency that was siding up with Lundin Mining against me.[12]

8.4.7 The Third Institutional Surprise Should Perhaps Not Have Been Much of a Surprise?

After a while, I forget about the case. So it is with a certain amount of surprise I open a letter about 9 months later. Dated 2010-05-21, it informs me that Lundin Mining's permission to search for minerals on our land had expired on March 22, 2010. In other words, is seems that their right to extension was upheld while the case was going on. I had in fact read something of this nature when I browsed the legislation in the area. So perhaps I ought not to have been surprised. Given what my friend the judge had told me about the general tendency in the legislation in the area, I ought to have expected this even though it seemed unfair.

[12] The fact that Lundin Mining wrote such a sloppy application could be seen as an indication that they firmly believe that Bergsstaten will be on their side and will grant them an extension anyway.

8.4.8 The Fourth and Fifth Institutional Surprises: A Letter Can Be Nice But Also Useless

I am definitely surprised when I receive a new letter in December 2010. It reports the verdict delivered by the County court on December 1st with respect to our case.[13] The court begins by noting that the time for the 1 year extension has expired (in fact it expired 7 months earlier). The court however also argues that we as plaintiffs have a reasonable interest in having the case tried by the Court.

With respect to the actual case, the court finds that: (1) Lundin Mining has not conducted meaningful investigation and (2) Lundin Mining has provided acceptable reasons for not having had time to conduct such investigations, but (3) Lundin Mining has not shown that it is likely that the investigations on our land would be carried out within the 1-year extension. Therefore, *there has not been sufficient reason to grant them an extension*! We won!

The court however also notes that since the extension has expired, the court will not take any further action in the case. So we also lost? Surprise, surprise?

8.5 Discussion

So we have won, but lost, the game vs. Lundin Mining and Bergsstaten. Does this mean that there has been no capture? After all, the court has decided in our favour. We may note that the county court was amalgamated with anther County court in February 2010, which would make capture potentially less likely. On the other hand, the case was ready for a court decision in September 2009, with half a year left of the extension, but a court decision did not appear until 8 months after the extension had expired. This delay could be an easy strategy to give Lundin Mining what they wanted, but could of course also be due to other bureaucratic reasons.

The case has featured a number of surprises. The potentially biggest one is that it is possible for an "ordinary citizen" to win a case against a multinational corporation, and against a government agency with more than 350 years on its neck. At the same time, this comes with another surprise, namely that even if you win, you lose.

So ex post it seems that we may have created a lot of transaction costs in vain. On the other hand, perhaps precisely these transaction costs will make at least Lundin Mining less eager to search for minerals on our land in the future? Perhaps they will turn to another European country.

Institutions can be surprising in many ways. You can be ignorant of the existence of some of the rules of the game (a feeling fervently experienced by non-Americans trying to watch a game of American Football or (worse) baseball), you can be mistaken about the meaning of a rule that you are aware of, the interpretation of a

[13] Förvaltningsrätten i Dalarna, Dom 2010-12-01, Meddelad I Falun, Mål nr 394-10, Enhet 2.

rule can depend on the presence of other rules or conditions (for example, that the bureaucratic delay means that you lose even if you win a case of extension).

This uncertainty is inevitable, so the big question in a way is whether the feedback we received made us better informed than before. Has uncertainty been reduced and have our expectations about consequences of an action become more correct? The answer to at least the first question seems to me to be "no"—we feel as unsure about the possibility of success in a case like ours as before we began the whole process. On the other hand, it definitely shows that it is possible to create some transaction costs, which is always nice to know.

8.6 Epilogue

We have now sold our property to a descendant of Birger Jarl, ruler of Sweden in the thirteenth century (founder of Stockholm) and probably at least as ruthless as Karl IX.[14] We wish the new owner the best of luck against Bergsstaten and big business in the future.

References

Aoki M (2001) Toward a comparative institutional analysis. The MIT Press, Cambridge, MA
Coase RH (1960) The problem of social cost. J Law Econ 3:1–44
Davies JK (1994) Accounts and accountability in classical Athens. In: Osborne R, Hornblower S (eds) Ritual, finance, politics. Clarendon, Oxford, pp 201–212
Della VS (2009) Psychology and economics: evidence from the field. J Econ Lit 47:315–372
Eggertsson T (2005) Imperfect institutions. University of Michigan Press, Ann Arbor, MI
Hansen MH (1999) The Athenian democracy in the age of Demosthenes: structure, principles, and ideology. University of Oklahoma Press, London
Heckscher E (1936) Sveriges ekonomiska historia från Gustav Vasa. Första delen, före frihetstiden, andra boken. Albert Bonniers Förlag, Stockholm
Levi M (1988) Of rule and revenue. University of California Press, London
Lyttkens CH (1994) A predatory democracy? An essay on taxation in Classical Athens. Explor Econ Hist 31:62–90
North DC (1981) Structure and change in economic history. W. W. Norton, New York, NY
North DC (1990) Institutions, institutional change and economic performance. Cambridge University Press, New York
North DC (2005) Understanding the process of economic change. Princeton University Press, Princeton, NJ
Petersson E (2009) Den skoningslöse – en biografi över Karl IX. Kultur, Natur
Pinheiro J, Cordeiro C, Vieira DN (2003) Choking death on a live fish (Dicologoglossa cuneata). Am J Forensic Med Pathol 24:177–178
Williamson OE (1985) The economic institutions of capitalism. The Free Press, New York, NY

[14] For the record, however, the buyer himself is one of the more friendly persons we have ever met.

Chapter 9
The Middle Class and the Market

Elias Katsoulis

9.1 Review of the recent literature

In their book *Winner Take-All Politics*, J.S. Hacker and P. Pierson observe that "in an era in which those at the top reaped the massive gains, the economy stopped working for middle—and working—class Americans. We know that the rich grew fabulously richer over the period. We know that relative to rich, the rest Americans lost ground...When we look at the DNA evidence on US incomes, we find that most Americans experienced extreme modest gains over the era in which the rewards at the top multiplied". (Hacker and Pierson 2010:19).

Hacker and Pierson's graph (T. Piketty, E. Saez, data updated through 2007) http://elsa.berkley.edu/saez/tabfig2007.xls portrays the development of the richest 1 % Share of National Income (including capital gains 1960–2007). According to this, the upper 1 % of the population increased its share in the national income from 10 % in 1960 to 24 % in 2007. The spectacular rise of the wealth of the few seems to have occurred at the expense of middle and working class income. The relevant literature is consistent to this conclusion although there have been various explanations pertaining to its causes.

Without challenging the above theories, in his last book *The Next Convergence*, M. Spence shifts his attention to the emerging middle classes in developing economies. A more careful study of Spence's analyses indicates the deeper causes of middle class dwindling in the developed countries, especially in the USA. Risking to be oversimplifying, he defines middle class strictly according to income and concludes that "middle-income transition refers to that part of growth processes that occur when a country's per capita income falls into the range of $5000 to

---

This paper derives from Katsoulis (2012).

E. Katsoulis (✉)
Ypsilantou 47, 15451 Neo Psychiko, Greece
e-mail: ikatsoulis@hol.gr

G.C. Bitros, N.C. Kyriazis (eds.), *Essays in Contemporary Economics*,
DOI 10.1007/978-3-319-10043-2_9

$10000". Above this level, the industries that drove the growth in the early period start to become globally uncompetitive due to rising wages. These labour-intensive sectors move to lower-wage countries and are replaced by a new set of industries that are more capital knowledge-intensive in the way they create value". What happens with the development of middle incomes, Spence argues, "is a combination of positive and negative forces. As income rises, labour-intensive processing industries with relatively low value added become internationally uncompetitive relative to other countries in a less advanced state. They are replaced by higher-value-added industries and functions within industries, both upstream in the value-added chain in product development and more capital-intensive parts of manufacturing, and downstream part with marketing, global reach, and brand building...The new emerging economy is more capital-, human capital- and knowledge intensive. The pattern of importing knowledge and technology starts to shift from importing technology to developing and exporting it, part of the journey to advanced-economy status". (Spence 2011:100–103).

In his Cowen (2013) book *Average is Over, Powering America beyond the Age of Great Stagnation,* T. Cowen continues the research he started with the e-book "The Great Stagnation" (2011). He ascertains that the median salaries of American employees have stagnated during the last 40 years while those of others have skyrocketed. Cowen records the causes of such a development concluding that technological advances are responsible for the phenomenon: "the increasing productivity of intelligent machines, economic globalization, and the split of modern economies into both stagnant sectors and some very dynamic sectors...workers more and more will come to be classified into two categories. The key question will be: Are you good at working with intelligent machines or not? Are your skills a complement to the skills of the computer or is the computer doing better without you? Worst of all, are you competing against the computer? If you and your skills are a complement to the computer, your wage and labour market prospects are likely to be cherry. If your skills do not complement the computer, you may want to address that mismatch. Ever more people are starting to fall on one side of the divide or the other. That's why average is over."

These three studies of middle class shrinkage—or otherwise social strata shrinkage—in developed societies present the problems that arise from the development in labour markets and the ensuing progress in the fields of science, technology, economy etc. Hacker and Pierson maintain that only a low 1 % "take-all" winning group will profit from the general growth globally.

Spence encourages the transfer of intensive labour sectors of production to low-wage countries. At the same time he points out the gradual climb of these countries in the value added ladder suggesting that even capital intensive and high paying labour positions are transferred to developing countries or that, in the event they remain in developed countries, they suffer substantial wage cuts. In other words, there is growing pressure for lower wages on those fragments of the middle classes that are unable to meet the new demands of international labour division. (This issue is also addressed by Elsby et al. (2013)). This argument is further supported by Cowen's observations. If you cannot cater to the needs of computerization, it is better to retire or, at least, keep away from the domain of new technologies. To conclude, many low specialization job positions as well as jobs of low capital composition are lost or off shored. This trend is expected to deepen as long as emerging economies continue to climb in the quality ladder.

Nevertheless, there are exceptions to this trend of low specialization jobs which are lost over to other countries resulting in high rates of unemployment among the middle class. Such is the case of Germany and the Scandinavian countries. On the other hand, an increasing number of developing countries have opened up to the international markets importing goods, technologies and expertise. This has led to the creation of a middle class whose membership has increased remarkably in the last 20 years. References on the development of middle class in the emerging economies of China and India—to cite but a few—appear in up-to-date bibliography. According to some estimations (Karras 2010), US and European middle classes comprised 54 % of the world's middle classes in 2009 but are expected to fall to 32 % in 2020 and to 21 % in 2030. In contrast, they are expected to rise from 28 % to 54 % and 68 % respectively in Asia. This phenomenon is attributed to a generalized trend marked by the shift of the world's economy from its traditional North Atlantic markets to new Pacific markets.

As the prospect of a dwindling middle class continues to loom in the horizon, so does scepticism among analysts of trends in the developing world. Middle class is usually defined by income criteria. Thus, according to the World Bank, citizens and families with income ranging from 0.75 % to 1.25 % of median wage-rate belong to the middle class. Other researchers disregard this income criterion and apply qualitative criteria to the definition of middle class. Today there is rich bibliography in regards to the development of middle class showing that what create its huge dynamics are international trade and the gradual integration of developing countries into the markets. According to calculations by Freeman (2005), during the last 20 years the global workforce increased from 1, 5 to 3 billion. The transfer of capital, technology, expertise, research etc. (outsourcing) was followed by the transfer of vacancies, especially toward the sector of services (offshoring). In developing countries agricultural economy was abandoned and those working in the fields were streamed to new jobs in the cities (urbanization) gradually becoming initiated to manufacturing and new technologies. Now, as we are already marching in the second decade of the twenty-first century, emerging economies pass into a second phase of development. They invest their own capitals to create infrastructure in the sector of production and train their workforce in highly skilled and highly specialized jobs thus fueling the growth of peak technologies. For example, China has evolved into the greatest power of our age in the field of photovoltaic energy, while Chinese, Indian, Russian and Brazilian enterprises go international, enter the world market dynamically and end up being competitors of multinationals in developed countries.

Global Trends 2030, in *Alternative Worlds* of the American National Intelligence Service journal, states that during the next 15–20 years global economy and politics will experience a kind of "tectonic shifts" the most important of which will be the growth of "middle class". According to the article, it will be the first time that "the majority of the world population will not become poorer and middle classes will rule the most important social and economic sectors in the majority of countries all over the world". A research carried out by Goldman Sachs on middle class worldwide points out that, even without taking into account the emerging middle classes of China and India, the inflows into the middle classes will be the greatest the world has seen in many years. All too often now relevant literature refers to the rapid creation of the educationally and economically strong layers which presumably will trigger the creation of an internal market that will boost consumption. In turn, it will lead to the gradual appearance of a strong middle class which will substitute the diminishing middle classes in developed countries. On the whole, there is a spectrum of theories regarding the explanation of middle class shrinkage in developing countries.[1] Of all theories, I can single out the one that concerns an implicit explanation deriving from the analyses of economic developments in relevant literature. It is the research carried out in the context of new economic geography.[2] Pivotal in this research are two key factors; firstly, production *proximity* i.e. workers, consumers and enterprises and secondly, *location*, an essential attraction in the competition for capital and foreign direct investment which is closely linked to the issue of offers on the best terms. Essential as location may be, factors like rapid development of communications, technologies and reduction of transport cost among others have undoubtedly diminished the importance of some of its advantages while they have increased that of others.

In any case, the qualitative characteristics of location, such as institutions, political stability, infrastructure, human capital, training, consensual procedures etc., not only remain effective but also increase in importance as time and space are squeezed due to globalization. Considering the above, I find it necessary to bring out the "new paradigm" that is currently being formulated in the ranks of the new economic geography. This evolutionary practice, known as *offshoring*, concerns the transfer of specific vacancies from developed economies to developing ones. It refers to vacancies in the sector of production of goods but mainly to services since it is new technology that makes this transfer possible and profitable.

The transfer of vacancies concerns first of all low capital intensity jobs e.g. those of unskilled workers. According to Grossman and Rossi-Hansberg (2006), offshoring procedures are becoming crucial for the economy of all countries involved, both importing and exporting and also for global economy. Offshoring produces three kinds of effects: labour-supply effects, relative-price effects and productivity effects. In short, we face an evolution in which: (1) Labour supply from the developing world to the international markets increases, (2) Prices of goods and services in international markets decrease due to wage reduction in low skilled jobs and (3) Production return rates increase due to increases in productivity.

Consequently, the repercussions of offshoring are significant for the welfare of both developing and developed countries. The afore-mentioned authors maintain

---

[1] For example, Gigliamaro and Mosler (2009:15) argue that the reaction of middle classes can be explained on the basis of a diminution of their internal cohesion. Middle classes are weakened because "every time its members become different to each other and less able to cooperate. The middle class decline has been here conceived in terms of reduction and inner cohesion".

[2] In the following, I make use of part of the analysis of my book "The Return of Politics" (Athens, 2012, 208–305).

that contrary to what politicians and citizens in developed countries may believe, this development has an overall positive effect for all parties concerned even if scholars may have their reservations. J. Stiglitz, for example, detects positive and negative aspects in this new trend. A good one is that workers' wages will be boosted in developing countries. A negative one is that unskilled workers' wages are expected to drop dramatically in developed countries.

Grossman and Rossi-Hansberg—among many others—strongly oppose the above conclusions. They argue that the transfer of vacancies to the developing countries opens up new prospects for reforms consistent with the demands of the market economy since they promote technological change, improve infrastructure and enhance education. They estimate that production and transport cost reductions of goods and services will drive the wages of low skilled workers upwards in the countries of origin, i.e. the developed countries. This seemingly paradoxical conclusion is based on the assumption that wage reduction in offshored low skill employment influences indirectly the wages of low skilled employees that remain in their country e.g. in the developed countries, so that productivity increases along the whole length of the production or service chain. Conclusively, "reduced but clear productivity in the developed country, with legally set minimum wages, is transferred out of the country, so that, part of the production chain that migrates to low wage countries, reduces total and proportionate prices of the good or service produced on the market and this again raises the value of all related tasks involved in the production chain". In addition to its positive effect on Labour compensation, offshoring also raises the competitiveness of the produced goods or services due to the simple fact that effected decrease on production costs allows for the proportionate decrease of their market price.

This price drop in the markets modifies the terms of trade in the countries of origin and elevates their position not only in terms of the international division of Labour but also in terms of competition. All this triggers chain reactions in the total amount of productivity and profitability of enterprises in these countries. Therefore, the two positive effects of offshoring, productivity increase and subsequent price drop, produce the next effect related to the increase in labour supply. This in turn means that the transfer of low skilled jobs to low wage Labour states frees the work force in the countries of origin i.e. the developed ones resulting in the increase of a bulk of labour supply which according to the law of supply and demand should lead to a decrease of the price of labour. Surprisingly enough, this is not the case, though.

On the contrary, offshoring brings about an increase of labour offer (labour-augmenting supply tasks) while technological progress affects production positively (factor-augmenting technological process). Thus, the widening of the labour market and the effect of technological progress on Labour allow or rather mandate that the workers—who were laid off to due to offshoring—be absorbed by a market whose composition has changed. The phenomenon of low skilled work migration, which is expected to deepen and widen in the years to come, reduces the supply of low skilled workers in domestic markets. On the other hand, it diversifies and promotes the supply of workers who are trained in new skills and new services in the same markets. As a result, demand for highly specialized and highly trained Labour will increase.

Demand for highly specialized workers generates but also imposes the improvement and diversification of education of the work force, a fact that contributes to the creation and accumulation of human capital, which then is multiplied in the form of social capital, joins the ranks of production and improves the total amount of productivity (total factor productivity), the epitome of every economy, be it developed, emerging or developing. In this way society functions better, the position of the country of origin is elevated in the international division of lab or and in the markets and the terms of international trade improve. At the same time the markets of the developing countries become integrated paving the way for development in the Third World. That is no less than a total win-win situation.

All these developments and many others yet to appear cannot in any way be intercepted. On the contrary, a new unprecedented situation is spawned throughout the international market, so countries unable to face the new challenges will be bypassed by the dynamic and adaptable economies of developing countries. As eloquently stated in the Economist, January 18, 2014:7

> Shunning progress would be as futile now as the Luddite's protest against mechanized looms were in the 1810s, because any country that tried to stop would be left behind by competitors eager to embrace new technology

It is logical to deduce from all this complex reorganization of the job market in the developed and developing world that instead of offshoring causing a decrease in unskilled labour wages in the country of origin, as argued by Stiglitz, it causes their increase. Low skilled workers' wages have not fallen until now and this is due to the combined forces of evolution, terms of trade and amendment of total factor productivity. Needless to say, the explanation of this positive development is that profits from productivity increase along the whole chain of production combined with the trend to offshore tasks from enterprises in developing countries is generally conducive to wage increase. This defeats the fears of the enemies of globalization and offshoring among statesmen, publicity and also part of the academic community.

Full of optimistic messages about short term advances, Spence (2011) enhances his last book with perceptions that I believe complete the image of forthcoming progress as presented by Grossman and Rossi-Hansberg. Spence presents three ideas that underscore our points of interest. First, he speaks about the "quality ladder". This qualitative ladder concerns the improvement of production methods of goods and services generated by offshoring in all countries involved. Then, he mentions the technological ladder and last, climbing the value-added chain in which are involved developed but mostly developing countries. As far as the latter are concerned, this climbing i.e., modernization as a condition for the creation of the higher levels of value-added chain, is a matter of a further development or stagnation. It is the kind of development that another researcher, Blinder (2007) called "climbing the comparative advantage ladder". Finally, this stream of observations and new ideas accompanying current trends is accentuated by the witty concept of leapfrogging put forward by Freeman (2006), who compares the evolutionary process of offshoring with leaps over many obstacles. Should all these positive developments be considered in the influx of innovations in all sectors of production and in all aspects of human endeavour, optimism about prospective changes is a foregone conclusion.

The New Growth Theory considers that new discoveries, innovations, new products and the like overwhelm us daily in rates beyond our understanding. They set into motion the deepest evolution ever witnessed and are expected to affect the next generations in such a way that the existent system of shortage of goods that has governed the course of humanity until now will gradually be replaced by a system of affluence. Both P. Romer and M. Spence have referred to this new system in their studies while Diamandis and Kotler (2012), Prahalad (2010) have devoted their research to discussing the anticipated future trends. Prahalad sees in new technologies the means that will help Third World countries exit the dead end situation in which they have been trapped for centuries.

9.2 What Are the Implications of All This for the Developed World?

Literature examining factors that are crucial for offshoring procedures argues that the transfer of capital, employment, scientific knowledge, research etc. from developed to developing countries will help the creation of a consumer oriented middle class in these countries which will overshadow the shrinkage of consumption capacity of the middle classes in the developed countries of the West (The Economist, January 25th 2014 "China loses its allure"). Nonetheless, evolution in the emerging and developing countries, which has already been sketched in this study, especially that concerning climbing the value-added chain and the quality ladder, increases the power of the cost of working force in the emerging and developing countries to such a degree that the comparative advantage of cheap Labour starts to retreat. Already since the end of the first decade of the twenty-first century there have been signs of a meek return to employment in manufacturing positions. "The rapidly rising wages, which have been outpacing productivity gains, have steadily increased the unit Labour costs of production". (Dolega 2012:10). Widespread evolutionary trends inhibit the offshoring process, also known as *reshoring* or *onshoring* in economics terminology. Such are the risk of transporting goods to remote areas (including the risk of piracy), high transportation costs due to the constant rise of oil prices, delays in completing agreed upon projects, political instability and even armed conflicts, to mention but a few. All this increases costs and reduces the comparative advantages of offshoring in manufacturing.

According to up-to-date data, it seems that it is manufacturing the sector that benefits the most from the increased costs of offshored employment. Similar experience is now being recorded in other activities also, as for example service jobs and telecommunications. Beyond this, available information regarding the intentions of the new Chinese government allows for the assumption that radical changes are being modelled for the country's economic growth. More specifically, China is expected to experience a shift from extroversive policies i.e. from being export oriented, to introversive ones i.e. internally led growth e.g. improvement of the standard of living and increase of purchasing power. To achieve this it will need to stream its production toward meeting the needs of its urban and rural population. Implicit in the Chinese government's intention to gradually float its currency, the remninbi, in international markets by 2020 is the message that major changes are going to occur in the international economic system and in offshoring/outsourcing procedures towards reshoring.

If this is the case, then we can predict that the appearance of a large and powerful consumptive middle class in the emerging and developing world will counterbalance the consumptive gap created by the decrease of the purchasing power of the middle class in the developed world.[3]

Equally important is the realization that if we could generalize our experience from the evolutionary trends in the developed countries of the West, then we can expect that the appearance of middle classes in the context of the internalized economic growth of emerging and developing countries will create conditions necessary for the reinforcement of democratic procedures. Even if these conditions do not completely comply with the historic model of western countries, they will lay the foundations for those human, political and social rights that are indispensable to and the basis of democratic regimes. Besides all its political, social, economic and cultural differences, the democratic world will be a better world.

Using a wealth of studies concerning contemporary developments in offshoring/outsourcing and resourcing/onsourcing, the Economist (Special Report, Outsourcing and Offshoring, 19 January 2013, p. 6 ff.) mentions a study by Boston Consulting Group (April 2012) on American manufacturing companies with yearly sales rates greater than $1 billion. Of these, 37 % declared that they plan to transfer their production facilities from China back to the USA, while 48 % of enterprises with sales rates above $10 million stated that they have already repatriated (came out as recourses). The Economist (op cit.) refers to yet one more study (of many that see the light of publicity) conclusive to similar results. It argues that the outflow of manufacturing jobs from high cost to low cost countries is expected to deteriorate during the next 2 years while resourcing will double compared to the 2 previous years.

As the head of the project observes, "the offshoring of manufacturing is now rapidly moving towards equilibrium". It goes without saying that new countries in Asia, Africa, Latin America and the former communist countries appear on the international market now possessing the comparative advantages of cheap labour

[3] See The Economist, Burgeoning Bourgeoisie, A Special Report on the New Middle Classes in Emerging Markets, Feb. 14, 2009. Already half of the world's population is estimated to belong to the emerging middle classes including those parts of the population whose purchasing power (PPP) ranges between $2 and $13 per capita daily.

and great demand for investment and consumption. This development—already in progress—foresees that the offshoring/outsourcing process will continue, this time with the involvement of emerging economies that will "expatriate low intensity capital and productivity".

Should this be the case, as the literature attests, middle classes in developed countries will continue suffering the pressures. One way to cope with all these pressures has already dawned on us; it is middle class veering round to the kind of employment that fills the gap created by outsourcing/offshoring processes on the one hand and by resourcing/onsourcing processes on the other. If anything, this will entail veering round to value-added ladders which will have to be climbed unremittingly.

References

Blinder A (2007) Offshoring: big deal, or business as usual? CEPS Working Paper, no 149, June

Cowen T (2013) The average is over. Powering America beyond the age of the great stagnation. Penguin Group, New York

Cowen T (2011) The great stagnation. How America ate the low-hanging fruit of modern history, got sick and will (eventually) feel better, Dutton, Penguin Group, New York, NY

Diamandis P, Kotler S (2012) Abundance. The future is better than you think. Free Press, New York, NY

Dolega M (2012) Offshoring, onshoring, and the rebirth of American manufacturing. Special Report, TD Economics, 15 October

Elsby M, Hobijn B, Sahin A (2013) The decline of the US labour share. Economic Studies at Brookings, September

Freeman R (2005) What really Ails Europe (and America): the Doubling of the Global Workforce. The Globalist (www.theglobalist.com), June

Freeman R (2006) The great doubling: the challenge in the new global labour market. Berkley University, August

Giglienaro Ch, Mosler K (2009) Measuring middle-class decline in one and many attitudes. Quaderno di Ricerca, no 333, November

Grossman M, Rossi-Hansberg E (2006) The rise of offshoring: it's not wine for cloth anymore. Federal Reserve Bank of Kansas City, August

Hacker JS, Pierson P (2010) Winner-take-all politics. How Washington made the rich richer-and turned its back on the middle class. Simon & Schuster, New York, NY

Katsoulis E (2012) Η Επιστροφή της Πολιτικής. Χρηματοπιστωτικός Καπιταλισμός και «Νέα» Παγκοσμιοποίηση, Αθήνα, Ποταμός (The Return of Politics. Finance Capitalism and "new" Globalization, Athens, Potamos)

Karras H (2010) The emerging middle class in developing countries. OECD Development Center, Working Paper, No 285, January

Prahalad CK (2010) Fortune at the bottom of the pyramid: the eradicating poverty through profits. Pearson Education, Wharton School Publishing

Spence M (2011) The next convergence: the future of economic growth in a multispeed world. Farrar, Straus and Giroux, New York, NY

Chapter 10
A Moneylender in Venice: Costantino Bogdano 'da Patrasso', c. 1800–1844

Ioanna-Sapfo Pepelasis and Angeliki Tzavara

10.1 Introduction

The moneylender has been a permanent figure in many societies throughout history, yet the most famous of all times is a 'fictional' persona, Shylock in Shakespeare's *The Merchant of Venice*. Moneylending is an activity that is largely hidden from the public eye and has left behind few records. The facts concerning real-life moneylenders are veiled in mystery compared to those of other financial actors. There are a few exceptions to this, most of which concern England in the early modern period, two examples being the sixteenth-century Thomas Sutton and the seventeenth-century spinster Joyce Jeffries (Shipley 1976, 456–76; Tittler 1994, 249–63).

Far removed in time and space from these is Costantino Bogdano 'da Patrasso' (i.e. from Patras), a moneylender who arrived in Venice shortly after the fall of the Republic in 1797 and lived there until his death on 2 July 1844.[1] Having no heirs, he bequeathed his Venetian estate to the Scuola di San Nicolò dei Greci, the Greek Community.[2] Thanks to this generous gesture, there exists at the Istituto Ellenico in

We thank Professor Chryssa Maltezou, Director of the Istituto Ellenico di Studi Bizantini e Postbizantini di Venezia, for her support, and Professor Franco Amatori for his comments and suggestions. We also thank George Derpanopoulos, Apostolis Rigas and Cristina Sofianou for their research assistance. Alexandra Pel kindly offered editorial advice. We are grateful to the Department of Economics of the Athens University of Economics and Business for providing research funds.

[1] When we refer to Greek names we use the Italian versions, to underline that this is a story taking place in an Italian context and locality.

[2] For the history of the institution of the 'Scuola' or 'Community di San Nicolò dei Greci', see Maltezou (1999).

I.-S. Pepelasis (✉) • A. Tzavara
Department of Economics, Athens University of Economics and Business, 76 Patision Street, Athens 10434, Greece
e-mail: ioannasapfopepelasis@gmail.com

G.C. Bitros, N.C. Kyriazis (eds.), *Essays in Contemporary Economics*,
DOI 10.1007/978-3-319-10043-2_10

Venice the recently catalogued Bogdano Archive, which contains valuable information regarding his wealth at the time of his death and his credit transactions.[3] Bogdano died exceptionally rich for someone in his station. At over 5,500,000 Austrian lire (hereafter abbreviated as AL) his wealth was roughly equal to one-third of the assets of each of two of the most important local banking houses at the time, both of which belonged to noble families, the Papadopoli and the Jewish Treves de' Bonfili (Zorzi 2003, 247–8; Bernardello 2002a, 586–7, refs. 42–4).

This was an amazing achievement for an outsider. Our starting point for unfolding the story of our intriguing money lender is a brief background sketch of Venice.

10.2 Venice at the Time

Bogdano's long sojourn in Venice occurred in an era that has attracted relatively little scholarly attention and during which the city has been described as having '. . .lost its place in the history of Europe. . .' (Greenfield 1939, 320; Ginsborg 1979). No longer a global merchant empire but under foreign imperial rule (briefly Napoleonic, but mostly Austrian), Venice was impoverished in comparison to its glorious past and to contemporaneous prominent economic centres of industrialisation. The size of its population was dwindling, unemployment was widespread, poverty was endemic, and ready cash was in short supply. Within this general picture of decline, which became especially pronounced between 1815 and 1830, there were some signs of regeneration. In 1830 Venice became a free port, which initiated a significant rise in trade within the Mediterranean and further afield. Commercial revival was accompanied by important public works schemes. Among the most emblematic achievements were the construction of the new railway bridge connecting Venice with the mainland and the gas illumination of the city. Moreover, new products appeared, steam power driven factories were built, and new banks were founded. Large joint-stock companies were introduced as a new form of business organisation. The two leaders in this area were the 'Imperial Regia Privilegiata Strada Ferrata Ferdinandea' (est. 1837), known as La Ferrovia Milano–Venezia and one of the most important railway projects in pre-unification Italy, and the 'Società Veneta Commerciale' (est. 1839). The latter had its own ships and 'was likened by the local press to the East India Company.'[4] Lastly, but

[3] For the Bogdano Archive, in the classification of which Angeliki Tzavara participated, see Maltezou (2008), especially 241–243. The Bogdano Archive corresponds to number 129 of the Archival Series, hereafter abbreviated to A.E.I.B., E1, N. 129.

[4] Pezzolo (2007); A'Hearn (2003, 351–381). For economic decline see also Cipolla (1970, 202–214); Kindleberger (1996, 56–59, 63–67). For the poor see Greenfield (1939, 325, ref. 43). For interesting information on signs of economic expansion, see Bernardello (2002b, 5–66); Bernardello (1996); Cafagna (1973, 278–87); Greenfield (1939, 313–333); Zorzi (2003, 72, 247–248).

not least, unemployment became less acute, and by the early 1840s the recorded number of objects left at pawnshops dropped continuously, which may hint at the existence of higher liquidity among the abundant number of poor. A new sense of civic pride was emerging.

Despite these developments and although the Austrians are considered to have taken initiatives in driving modernisation, there was mounting social tension against the regime and dissatisfaction among the populace and the rising business elite. The members of the new elite, among which bankers held a prominent position, 'prided themselves on their code of business ethics, on their conservativism, sturdy credit and speculation'—and Bogdano, as we will uncover below though 'simply' a moneylender, epitomised these traits (Greenfield 1939, 329, 333; Ginsborg 1979, Chap. 1). It is fascinating to observe the strategy of this successful informal financier: he operated, on the one hand, within the time frame of what is internationally considered 'the classic era of merchant banking' (Cameron and Bovykin 1991, 5, ref. 15); on the other, he lived and worked during an epoch of transition (and mixed ambience) in Venice, which *ex post* becomes all the more absorbing as it approached the tail end of a still-divided Italian nation (Gilmour 2011, 113–47).

10.3 Biographical Background of Bogdano

Our moneylender was born in 1765 in the Theou Odigitrias parish of central Patras, the major port-city of the Peloponnese, which was at the time under Ottoman rule. His father, Paolo, a merchant, moved with the family to the island of Corfu at some point during the Orlov Rebellion in the Peloponnese (1768–1774).[5] Costantino remained on Corfu and reportedly moved to Venice as an already wealthy adult after the fall of the Republic in 1797. He had purportedly arrived there by 1800, but it was only in 1803 that his name first appeared in the official registry of the Greek Community, a group declining in fortune and with a dwindling population of just over a hundred people, mostly merchants (Xanthopoulou-Kyriakou 1977, 12–14; Triantafyllou 1967, 192–5; Triantafyllou 1980, 1330–2).[6]

Migration to Venice did not entail a break with his past. Throughout his life he retained property, deposits and perhaps other business interests on Corfu.[7] In addition, having lived there for so long, he was already familiar with Venetian practices, as the island had been under Venetian rule between 1386 and 1797.

[5] For the Orlov Rebellion, see Gritsopoulos (1967).

[6] Triantafyllou did not examine the archive in its final form, as he looked at some loose papers, and in his works he often does not give a clear and precise citation of the documents he studied. In this piece we refer to him for what he considers to be correct and when no other source exists for what we wish to comment on.

[7] A.E.I.B., E1, N. 129, b. 21, doc. 1 (from now on Will). See also Triantafyllou (1967).

Moreover, between 1796 and 1866, one-fourth of Greeks residing in the 'City of Water' declared Corfu as their place of origin.

The personal life of our moneylender is clouded in some mystery as no diaries or letters have survived. Some biographical events are mentioned in bibliographical sources. However, a 'direct' and rather detailed impression of his way of life and character traits as an elderly man can be gleaned from studying his will, which was drawn up on 13 April 1844, and the judicial transcription of his wealth at death (*Inventario*), completed on 19 July 1844 under the supervision of the Venetian authorities and in the presence of the testamentary executor and representatives of the Greek Community.[8]

Bogdano clearly lived in comfort. He had two homes in the city of Venice and seven servants. His main residence at the time of his death, a home in San Geremia, was well-furnished, replete with expensive mirrors, carpets and chandeliers. For executing his professional duties he owned three scales, which had accompanying weights (*pel denaro*) for diverse types of coins, quite a few table clocks and portable writing desks. As would be expected from a man of some culture, Bogdano possessed some books and had a chessboard. His home in San Geremia also contained two oil paintings (one of which was a depiction of a bacchanal), 6 watercolours and 47 etchings/engravings.

As was the European custom of the rich of the day, Bogdano drank coffee and chocolate. He took care of his appearance and had a large wardrobe, which contained among other things a chest of 47 white shirts in perfect condition and a black fur coat. Though westernised, he was nevertheless a devout Greek Orthodox and owned icons and other Orthodox devotional objects. He had an iron pit for roasting lambs, as has been the perennial culinary tradition of all Greeks, especially at Easter. Although he had land in the countryside, he did not maintain a country house. Bogdano may have gone hunting from time to time (as he owned binoculars for hunting and two rifles), but it seems unlikely that he was very active at least at the end of his life as he was rather sickly and died the owner of 505 handkerchiefs and some 20 *sputerole* (spitting bowls).

A rather private and idiosyncratic person, Bogdano remained a bachelor throughout his life. Though it was customary for wealthy individuals to have many godchildren, to our knowledge he had only one, Paolo Drossopoulo, who originated from Corfu. According to Bogdano's will, his closest two friends at the end of his life were the elderly landowner Pietro Maino, to whom in a sentimental gesture he left his French gold cigarette case, and Dr Giuseppe Calucci, his personal lawyer and executor of his will. The latter served as the Governatore of the Greek Community in 1845. An eminent legal scholar, he was also a friend of Daniele Manin, the leader of the 1848 revolt in Venice, and was a deputy of the Assembly of

[8] A.E.I.B., E1, N. 129, b. 25, doc. 1 (from now on *Inventario*), ff. 16v-17r.

the city. In his business transactions, as discussed below, Bogdano was also close to Angelo Papadopoli, a member of the noble banking family (Triantafyllou 1967, 205, 208; Zorzi 2003, 94, 104, 188, 246).

Bogdano's sole blood relative in Venice was his elder brother Nicolo, who arrived there from Corfu in 1824/1825, i.e. roughly 24 years after he did. He was in commerce and hence a rather typical Greek émigré. There is no surviving evidence of Nicolo having been in business with Costantino, although he lived with him up to his death at the age of 72 in 1835. Nicolo's widow, Marietta, together with his beloved servant Demetrio Vlassopoulo, became the recipients of the usufruct of the Venetian estate of Costantino upon his death. It was peculiar for a servant to receive such a generous gift, so we may assume that he was very dedicated and in some way exceptional to our moneylender. It is improbable that he had been of assistance with Bogdano's financial transactions, for he did not even know how to write: he put a cross instead of a signature when he was asked to sign the *Inventario* of his employer's estate in July 1844.

Bogdano may have been something of a loner, but nevertheless he sought out a presence in the public sphere. He served on the board of the Greek Community as Governatore in 1816 and Contraditore in 1821 and stood without success (1826, 1830, 1831 and 1838) for the office of Guardian Grande (president). In the end, he offered more to his compatriots after death than during his life, as his endowment was vital to the survival of the Greek Community, which had been experiencing financial difficulties since 1797. Our moneylender overshadowed by far the other benefactors of the 1800s: Conte Giorgio Mocenigo, who died in 1839; Giorgio Edoardo Pickering, who passed away in 1843; and the merchant banker Conte Giovanni Papadopoli, who died in 1862. The combined amount of those three bequests amounted to some 150,000 AL—a minuscule amount compared to the Bogdano endowment of over 5,000,000 AL. Indeed, the latter enjoyed wider notoriety. The rumours surrounding the size of the estate were such that the leaders of the 1848 revolt declared in October 1848 the obligatory participation of the Bogdano estate in the internal loans it was planning to raise. While the post-mortem fame of Bogdano outside the Greek Community was rather transient, within it his eminence as a major patron has lived on. In 1951 his remains were reburied in the Greek Community Church of San Giorgio dei Greci at the side of those of the other famous great benefactor, Tommaso Flangini (1579–1649) (Triantafyllou 1967, 187–8, 191; Xanthopoulou-Kyriakou 1977, 58–65; Papaioannou 1986, 114, ref. 128; Zorzi 2003, 247–8; Mertzios 1939). Significant as Bogdano's legacy as a philanthropist may be, we propose that his unwitting 'gift' of the surviving evidence he left to posterity on moneylending in the unique setting of nineteenth-century Venice is of wider significance, and so we now turn to an analysis of this.

But first a few words about the wider context of the Greek diaspora: there is a large literature on the activities of Greek merchant-entrepreneurs living outside of Greece who were involved in the transnational trade in such bulk commodities as grain and cotton (as for example, Katsiardi-Hering 2004). Fewer are the case studies on Greek Diaspora financiers and in this context the story of a moneylender involved in the local economy and its citizens, is a rarity.[9]

10.4 Wealth at Death

Let us begin by taking a glimpse at Bogdano's early days in Venice. In 1803, when he first registered with the Greek Community, he entered the word 'Landowner' next to his name. This may not have been an entirely accurate description of his position, but neither was it false as he already owned land on Corfu.[10] Whether during his first years in Venice Bogdano lived solely as a rentier is not recorded. There is evidence that by 1811 at the latest he was involved in moneylending and that by 1814/1815 he had an income from local real estate and the co-ownership of a *livello* (an emphyteutic lease). This information is provided from the *Inventario* and the '*Quaderno della sostanza lasciata dal fu signor Costantino Bogdano*'. This was a supplementary list, composed by the administrators of his estate, providing additional information on properties owned and rented and of outstanding loans. These two documents offer a detailed picture of Bogdano's wealth at death (see Table 10.1). His objects and personal items (discussed in some detail above) included a few ornaments in precious metals and jewellery, such as a gem-encrusted piece with 47 *brillianti* diamonds[11]: though Bogdano was not a pawnbroker, he relied in some part on the mechanism of taking valuable objects as security for the short-term credits he granted.[12] At a little over twice the value of his gold and silver ornaments and his jewellery, the cash he held at death consisted of the following monies: Austrian lire and talleri (dollars), croccioni cut in Milan, Genoese doppie, fiorini, Venetian zecchini, French coins—the so-called franchi and Luigi d'oro—and a small amount of ongari (Hungarian) gold coins. That our moneylender held the above mixture of cash is not surprising given the time and place. During the 1800s these types of currencies circulated widely among the cities of Northern Italy, necessitating some degree of money-changing (Kindleberger 1993, 137–8). Bogdano at death held—in twice the value of what he had in cash—shares in the two leading sociétés anonymes: the 'Società Veneta Commerciale',[13] among whose founders were the bankers Giacomo Treves de' Bonfili and Spiridione Papadopoli; and the 'Strada Ferrata Ferdinandea', of which Spiridione Papadopoli was also a director (Zorzi 2003,72, 247–8). By owning

[9] Up to now, the most well known case of a Greek diaspora financier is that of Andreas Syngros. See Pepelasis Minoglou (2002); Also Angelou and Chatziioannou (1997).

[10] Will and Xanthopoulou-Kyriakou (1977).

[11] For the fact that he would collaborate with the pawnbroker Angelo Chielin, see the *Inventario*.

[12] As was certainly the practice of Venetian bankers in the fifteenth and sixteenth centuries: Lane (1937), pp 187–206.

[13] Alias 'Veneta Società Mercantile' in the *Inventario*.

Table 10.1 Wealth at death of Bogdano in Venice

Composition	Austrian lire
1. *Personal items*	
Books	96.60
Furniture and other personal items	4,716.70
Total	4,813.30
2. *Gold, silver, jewels and other valuables*	
Gold and silver pieces/ornaments	7,507.69
Jewellery	3,961.00
Total	11,468.69
3. *Money assets*	
Cash	23,638.81
Shares	45,600.00
Total	69,238.81
4. *Outstanding debt*	
Dry bills of exchange and other	520,852.78
Mortgage loans	278,192.29
Total	799,045.07
5. *Real estate—Livello*	
Urban and rural property	4,734,521.31
Livello (half)	35,609.20
Total	4,770,130.51
6. *Other*	
Ownership share in brigantine	3,578.00
Grand total[a]	5,658,274.38

Source: Compiled from: A.E.I.B., E1, N. 129, b. 25, doc. 1 (*Inventario*). *Quaderno della sostanza lasciata dal fu signor Costantino Bogdano fu Paolo*, 1844–8, ff. 43v-57r. See also Triantafyllou (1967)

[a]The Grand Total is a gross estimate of his wealth. For the net amount of his estate bequeathed to the Greek Community we must deduct the 4,164.58 AL spent on expenses mostly for his illness and funeral; and some 32,000 AL left to his close friends and some servants. He also made a bequest to Giuseppe Calucci, which he described 'as a 4 % on his *sostanza*'. We cannot calculate what sum this represented as Bogdano did not state in his will whether the latter was to include also his real estate property. A.E.I.B., E1, N. 129, b. 25, doc. 1 (*Inventario*), ff. 16v-17r

shares in (only) these two companies Bogdano in a way became part of the story of the rising modern business sphere in Venice. The ownership of shares had more of an emblematic significance, as the outstanding debt of his clients was by far his largest intangible asset.[14] As we will see below, substantial sums were involved in his moneylending operations. He carried out this business in private, as a one-man show, and there is no evidence that he had formal partners or owned a financial 'firm' of some sort. However, he did participate in a brigantine named *L'Ammirabile*, which was under the flag of Austria and which according to other

[14] For full details see Section III below.

sources was 234 tons.[15] He also had half-ownership of a *livello* in the Noventa area of Padua.[16] Bogdano's largest asset at death was real estate. Of his properties, 36 were dispersed in Venice and two were large landed estates in the Dolo district. The administrators of his estate made valuations for only 25 of his 38 properties. These alone had a total value which was over four times the outstanding debt owed to him at his time of death. Among his properties was a deserted monastery of the Order of the Carmelitani (Scalzi) in the Cannaregio neighbourhood of Venice. Its building was eventually bought back by the friars after Bogdano's death and the adjacent land was confiscated in the 1850s for the construction of the Venice railway station.[17] The acquisition of so much real estate made good business sense. It enhanced Bogdano's 'respectability and power' in his adopted city and was a gateway to the legitimisation of wealth deriving from the hidden economy.[18] Furthermore, it was a means for diversification and, we may argue, speculation (speculative profits), for Bogdano appears to have purchased a large part of his property prior to 1830 when prices were rock-bottom.

How typical was the composition of Bogdano's wealth for a moneylender? Although it is almost impossible to answer this question, some useful comparisons can be made. One much earlier example, the also childless sixteenth-century (Tudor-Stuart) moneylender Thomas Sutton, left a large endowment to charity and his records largely survived as a result. 'Richie Sutton', as was the case with Bogdano, also had other business activities. Moreover, the greater part of his wealth was invested in landed estate (Shipley 1976, 459–62). There are also known commonalities between the two men with regard to strategy, to which we will return below. However, other, more contemporaneous examples are those of two bankers. Barone Giuseppe Treves de' Bonfili died in 1841, and only 45.90 % of his wealth at death consisted of real estate. Giovanni Conti, who also lived in Venice and died in 1871 (i.e. 27 years after Bogdano), had only 30 % of his wealth at death in real estate and compared to Bogdano had a much larger portion devoted to outstanding debt and shares and bonds. Our moneylender's property resembled more that of Sutton, who was not, however, a typical moneylender in his own time. On the other hand, the period Bogdano was living through was one of rapid change, especially from the 1830s onwards. Not surprisingly Bogdano was not similar in his wealth placement to that of the bankers. Giuseppe Treves de' Bonfili and Giovanni Conti were more modern and placed much greater emphasis on finance and financial instruments than did our moneylender.[19]

---

[15] *Inventario*, f. 16v., and A.E.I.B., E1, N. 129, b. 31, fasc. 58, doc. 1 (1846); Triantafyllou (1967, 207).

[16] *Inventario*, f. 14v; A.E.I.B., E1, N. 129, b. 27, fasc. 2, doc. 1–85 (1796–1871).

[17] A.E.I.B., E1, N. 129, b. 33, fasc. 87, doc. 1–42 (1852–85); b. 32, fasc. 80, doc. 1–93 (1851–9).

[18] For this as a more general process, see Clark (1996).

[19] The breakdown of Conti's estate in its major financial assets was 17.33 % in private shares and bonds issued by the Venetian state; and 40.23 % was in bills of exchange and mortgage loans (Bernardello 2002a, 587 and note 44).

To summarise, the transcription of wealth at death suggests that Bogdano acquired wealth comparable to the personal fortunes of the most prominent local bankers. This is surprising given that he was born in Patras, worked as a moneylender and arrived in Venice at a mature age. His success was not a chance outcome.

Our central question in the sections that follow are is: How did he do it? What was his strategy? How did 'business' ethics/'fairness' as a moneylender enhance his wealth?

10.5 The Contemporaneous Venetian Financial System and Bogdano's Operations

Nineteenth-century Venice was overshadowed by neighbouring Milan as a financial and business centre.[20] Nevertheless, there were some signs of progress. In 1806 the 'Banco Pignoratizio Communale' (Municipal Pawn Bank), which was modelled on the Monti di Pietà, was established, and in 1822 a savings bank, the 'Casse di Risparmio di Venezia', was founded. From the 1830s onwards there was an expansion in commercial banking, and by 1847 there were some 20 private banking houses. The two leading such banking houses, those of the Papadopoli and the Treves de' Bonfili, in addition to providing discounts and other types of private credit, played a significant role in financing new projects in industry, large commerce and infrastructure projects/utilities (Zorzi 2003, 247–8; also Bernardello 2002b, 5–66). One more indication of institutional change was the establishment in 1853 of the 'Stabilimento Mercantile di Venezia', the only bank 'authorized to issue fiduciary notes in bearer form' in the Austrian Empire apart from the Central Bank in Vienna, the so-called 'Privilegirte österreichische National-Bank' (Fratianni and Spinelli 1997, 60). This development occurred 9 years after Bogdano's death, but it is symbolic of the increasing financial sophistication of the city.

However, this was a mixed picture, and despite the aforementioned institutional steps forward the financial system remained immature throughout Bogdano's lifetime. The 'Casse di Risparmio di Venezia' could not compare with its Milanese equivalent as it 'depended upon a municipal pawnshop'. Moreover, Venice did not have a specialised discount bank, a 'Casse di Sconto', as was the case for example in Tuscany (Polsi 1996, 119–21). It may not even be far fetched to hypothesize that formal banking in Venice was not a world apart from the informal world of moneylending and that there was a (grey) area of overlap. Assuming that this was the case, Bogdano created a 'niche' as a large *scontista* (payee of promissory notes) who also provided mortgage loans and who may also have accepted deposits from at least one person: his colLabourator pawnbroker.[21] Advanced moneylender as he

[20] For nineteenth-century developments in neighbouring Milan, see Piluso (1999, 29–37, 111–115); Polsi (1996, 119–21).

[21] This was the case of Angelo Chielin, who also borrowed money on several occasions from Bogdano on a short-term basis through the *vaglia* mechanism. *Registro*, March 30 and April 12 1843.

was, he kept written documentation of transactions, but we must underline that we have no way of knowing whether there existed other transactions which were never recorded or for which no written documentation has survived. Even though gaps exist in our picture of Bogdano, it is clear that our moneylender operated in a symbiotic relationship with the formal financial institutions of Venice. Comparable to McIntosh's work on moneylending in the periphery of London, 1300–1600, we observe that Bogdano assisted in the expansion of capitalisation and also profited from growth and change in the Venetian economy (McIntosh 1988, 570–1).

When Bogdano died, 20 mortgage loans[22] and 77 promissory notes were outstanding. The oldest debt dated back to May 1811, a mortgage loan given to Luigi Alivisi. The 20 mortgage loans (see Table 10.2) were all denominated in Austrian lire and they came in all sizes: the smallest (1,771.60 AL) had been given to the widow Maria Zennaro Boscolo in March 1834, and the largest (100,000 AL) was granted to Giovanni Manerin on 25 July 1841. The length granted for the repayment of a loan was pre-specified in only eight cases and it varied from 1 to 10 years. In the remaining 12 loans we suspect the existence of a pre-agreed rollover type of agreement, i.e. open-ended loans. Only four of the eight outstanding mortgage loans at the time of death (for which termination dates were specified) were due for repayment prior to July 1844. Interestingly, for none of these four unredeemed loans is there any evidence to suggest that our moneylender took legal action against his debtors. Hence, regardless of whether there was a written termination date or not, *de facto* he seems to have practised rollovers for many of his mortgage debtors. This policy required Bogdano to have and maintain high liquidity, a theme to which we will return below.

Evidence of his high liquidity is that Bogdano seems to have acquired real estate through purchases. In one case the acquisition was made through auction: this was the landed estate in Porte Grandi del Sile in Dolo.[23] Probably he also acquired the monastery in this way, as most monastic/religious property must have been sequestrated by Napoleon in 1797. Interestingly, and not conforming to the general expectation of moneylenders, there is no evidence that Bogdano acquired real estate directly from foreclosures on the property of his defaulting borrowers. Had he done so, some trace would have survived, as such procedures, as has been noted by Shipley (albeit in another historical context), are 'universally' time-consuming and legally complicated (Shipley 1976, 468). A contextual comment on strategy is required here. This evidence on mortgage loans suggests the image of a moneylender whose main *business goal is not to obtain value through the acquisition or transfer of undervalued collat*erals but rather through expansion of lending operations to a cautiously chosen clientele. In this sense Bogdano's case is similar to that of Sutton, on whom people could rely for the provision of quick cash 'without fear of losing their property'. This is in juxtaposition to the typical case of the

[22] For mortgage loans see also A.E.I.B., E1, N. 129, b. 27, fasc. 18; b. 29, fasc. 25, 30, 39, 40; b. 30, fasc. 41; b. 31, fasc. 50; b. 32, fasc. 82; b. 33, fasc. 89, 91; b. 34, fasc. 94; b. 35, fasc. 124.

[23] Announcement for judicial auction A.E.I.B., E1, N. 129, b. 27, fasc. 13, doc. 79 (printed).

Table 10.2 Outstanding mortgage loans at death

	Austrian lire	Contract date	Duration	Interest rates
Luigi Alvisi	10,939.34	16 May 1811		
Balbi Brothers	14,115.28	10 May 1823		
Luigi Alvisi	3,000	11 August 1829	2 years	5 %
Sante Callegari	18,500	12 April 1831		
Pietro Copano	4,200	26 February 1833	1 year	5 %
Boscolo Maria Zennaro	1,771.60	8 March 1834	5 years	5 % i.
Balbi Monsignor	8,000	27 October 1835		
Antonio Negri	4,000	31 December 1835	7 years	5 %
Filippo Ruggeri	2,428	29 November 1838		5 %
Vicenzo Monaco	7,000	3 December 1838		
Vicenzo Monaco	2,095.70	3 December 1838		
Costantini Giacomo	9,001.85	20 February 1839	10 years	5 %
Giovanni Pozzati	48,000	2 January 1840		
Francesco Bonivento detto Zaniolo	8,000	23 July 1840	5 years	5 %
Giovanni Manerin	100,000	25 July 1841		5 %
Antonio Giacomelli	10,000	2 April 1842	8 years	5 %
Giuseppe Vianello detto Boscarello	18,000	12 April 1842		5 %
Guiseppe and Felice Caine	2,453	5 January 1843		5 %
Domenico and Mondaini Leoni	3,000	27 April 1843	5 years	5 %
Francesco Bonivento detto Zaniolo	3,687.52	17 June 1843		6 % i.
Total (20)	278,192.29			
Average	13,909.61			
Median	7,500			

Source: A.E.I.B., E1, N. 129, b. 25, doc. 1 (*Inventorio*), f. 14r;reg. 2 (*Quaderno della so-stanza lasciata dal fu signor Costantino Bogdano fu Paolo*), 1844–8, ff. 43v-57r

moneylender-usurer in economic theory.[24] An open question is whether his strategy was something typical in the environment of Venice at the time.

Interest rates on mortgage loans were paid bi-annually. In six cases interest was not mentioned at all, and again this suggests some type of oral agreement. In the remaining 14 loans it was 5 % per annum, with the exception of one loan which had a 4 % interest rate and another which had a 6 % interest rate. What were the interest rates given by formal institutions in the surrounding area at the time? They could reach as high as 6 %, but this was not always the case. Bartolomeo Ponti, one of the most important bankers in neighbouring Milan, charged an interest rate of just under 5 %. Occasionally, the Milan-based 'Cassa di Risparmio per le Provincie

[24] See, for example, Bhaduri (1983).

Lombarde' offered a slightly lower rate of about 4–4.5 %.[25] It is also known that the interest rate paid by the revolutionary provisional government of the City of Venice for an emergency 10,000,000 Italian lire loan on 14 May 1848 was 5 % (Papaioannou 1986, 102). Hence, Bogdano was no Shylock, but rather charged 'competitive' rates. His sense of 'good practice' is consistent with his 'good character' and his ability to choose reliable clients. It also suggests an increasingly competitive market in Venice and the fact that he was in a position to choose dependable people as clients.[26]

We can now turn to promissory notes, the bread and butter of Bogdano's credit operations, but let us start with two introductory remarks. Firstly, during his time mortgage/long-term lending and the provision of short-term credit were not two totally separate activities, as there was an interface between them. When a customer did not repay/redeem a promissory note, his obligation would sometimes be transformed into a long-term loan (Polsi 1996, 127). In the case of Bogdano this practice was realised in some cases. Moreover, there were instances in which a borrower who would receive a mortgage loan from Bogdano would offer him a promissory note, usually a dry bill of exchange (*vaglia cambiara*), in order to pay his instalments for the mortgage loan.[27] An example of this was Giovanni Pozzati, who had concluded a mortgage loan on 2 January 1840 and who largely paid the instalments for this 10-year loan through the issuing of a *vaglia cambiara* in his name.[28]

Secondly, Bogdano—given his identity as a proper moneylender and hence as a person operating in the informal economy—was in an advantageous position as a discounter of promissory notes. During Bogdano's lifetime, while of course banking houses offered the service of commercial discounting, business people would more likely have preferred an unofficial and discreet venue for this practice if they could find one at a fair rate, for 'a merchant who signed a bill was regarded as a man in difficulty'.[29]

It is not surprising that at the time of Bogdano's death the bulk of outstanding loans was in the form of short-term credit (see Tables 10.3 and 10.4). He granted short-term credits in Austrian lire, and in only one-fourth of the cases (mostly early transactions) did he use other currencies (coins), a mixture of Venti franchi, Luigi d'oro, talleri bavere or 'bavaresi' of Munich (Bavaria), and Italian lire. However, in

[25] Notably, Conca Messina (2004, 119, 139–141 and Appendix, Tables 11–14); Galli (1991, 83–5 and *passim*); also of related interest is Piluso (1999, 38–111, 156–245).

[26] See also Section V below.

[27] Bills of exchange drawn only to grant credit were called dry bills of exchange. These served solely as instruments of credit and were unconnected to purchase or sale of merchandise (Allen 2001, 146–7).

[28] Inventario, f. 10r and reg. 2 (Quaderno della sostanza lasciata dal fu signor Costantino Bogdano fu Paolo), 1844–48 (hereafter reg. 2).

[29] Polsi (1996, 126–7). Comparably, in early modern England, where it has been noted that when bills of exchange were not paid on time, the reputation of a man would be damaged (Muldrew 1998, 192, note 92).

Table 10.3 Outstanding dry bills of exchange and other promissory notes at death. Summary according to year granted

Year credit granted	Number	Total value in Austrian lire
1844	43	320,749.97
1843	16	185,143.37
1842	1	565
1841	3	4,106.65
1840	2	1,000
1829	1	578.68
1828	3	6,558
1820	7	1,609.16
1815	1	541.95
Total (1815–1844)	77	520,852.78

Source: Compiled from A.E.I.B., E1, N. 129, b. 25, doc. 1 (*Inventario*) ff. 10r-12r and 13v-14r

all instances Bogdano recorded the sums owed in Austrian lire. Whether he expected repayment in Austrian lire or whether this was an accounting practice cannot be established.

The outstanding short-term credits consisted of 77 promissory notes owed to him. Of these, 72 were described as *vaglie* (by this obviously meaning *vaglie cambiare*), two as *cambiare*, two as *lettere confessionali*, and one as a *pagherò*. The bulk of the outstanding promissory notes originated from 1843 and 1844 and concerned paper with a repayment date after the death of Bogdano. Unredeemed debt, i.e. short-term credits that had a repayment date prior to the death of Bogdano, amounted to only 15 promissory notes (see Table 10.5), i.e. 3.6 % of the total outstanding debt from the provision of short-term credit. Almost half of this unredeemed debt concerned paper issued between 1815 and 1829, namely the early days of the Second Austrian Occupation.

No mention of interest rates is made for any of the promissory notes. This was the common custom during Bogdano's time, and commission charges were included in the paper, i.e. the original *vaglia cambiaria* (henceforth, *vaglia*, following our moneylender's practice). On the basis of Bogdano's acknowledged fairness towards his clients with regard to interest rates for mortgage loans, it is difficult to imagine that he transformed into a shark in the field of promissory notes.

On average the individual *vaglie* provided by Bogdano would each have a value of over 1,000 AL. However, there was a larger variation in sizes compared to mortgage loans. The highest promissory note was the 55,000 AL *vaglia* issued for Angelo Chielin in December 1843, and the lowest outstanding short-term 'paper' was the 200 AL *lettera confessionale* of Giacomo Mola 1 month earlier.[30] Even this was not a small sum. Let us compare it with the estimated value of some of the objects in Bogdano's home: his desk with seven drawers had an estimated value of 14 AL, and the 27 of his shirts that were made of costanza had an estimated value of

[30] Inventario, ff. 10r, 11r.

Table 10.4 Outstanding dry bills of exchange and other promissory notes at death in detail

Type of transaction	Date credit granted	Specified date for repayment	Debtor	Amount due in Austrian lire
Vaglia	30-6-1844	31-12-1844	Giovanni Pozzati	6,000
Vaglia	28-6-1844	28-12-1844	Giuseppe Regazzi	2,000
Vaglia	28-6-1844	31-12-1844	Natale A. Vianello	9,217
Vaglia	27-6-1844	31-12-1844	Antonio Giacomelli	4,000
Vaglia	24-6-1844	31-12-1844	Salomon Piran	1,000
Lettera confessionale	23-6-1844	8-7-1844	Giuseppe Regazzi	800
Vaglia	22-6-1844	22-11-1844	Giuseppe Traine Lucia Padella Traine for 50 Venti franchi	Abusive 1,200
Vaglia	21-6-1844	21-12-1844	Natale A. Vianello	36,343
Vaglia	17-6-1844	1-7-1844	Samuel Dalla Vida for 1,000 Venti franchi	Abusive 24,000
Vaglia	6-6-1844	1-12-1844	Natale A. Vianello	11,000
Vaglia	2-6-1844	20-12-1844	Giovanni Manerin	4,800
Vaglia	26-5-1844	26-11-1844	Giuseppe Regazzi *con giro* di Pasqua Scandiani Regazzi	800
Vaglia	13-5-1844	16-11-1844	Giuseppe Regazzi *con giro* di Natale A. Vianello	2,000
Vaglia	7-5-1844	8-12-1844	Antonio Giacomelli	6,000
Vaglia	7-5-1844	7-11-1844	Natale A. Vianello	6,000
Vaglia	30-4-1844	31-8-1844	Giovanni Pozzati	6,000
Vaglia	30-4-1844	31-10-1844	Antonio Giacomelli	3,000
Vaglia	29-4-1844	29-10-1844	Pasqua Scandiani Regazzi	4,000
Vaglia	29-4-1844	29-10-1844	Natale A. Vianello	3,000
Vaglia	27-4-1844	31-12-1844	Giovanni Manerin for 250 Venti franchi	Abusive 6,000
Vaglia	20-4-1844	20-10-1844	Natale A. Vianello	2,863
Vaglia	5-4-1844	5-10-1844	Natale A. Vianello	37,000
Vaglia	1-4-1844	31-12-1844	Giovanni Manerin for 400 Venti franchi	Abusive 9,600
Vaglia	30-3-1844	30-3-1845	Antonio Giacomelli	6,000

(continued)

Table 10.4 (continued)

Type of transaction	Date credit granted	Specified date for repayment	Debtor	Amount due in Austrian lire
Vaglia	13-3-1844	1-11-1844	Samuel Dalla Vida	12,000
Vaglia	13-3-1844	1-12-1844	Samuel Dalla Vida	12,000
Vaglia	13-3-1844	1-2-1845	Samuel Dalla Vida	12,000
Vaglia	1-3-1844	31-8-1844	Pasqua Scandiani Regazzi	1,096.97
Vaglia	26-2-1844	20-2-1845	Lorenzo Scarpa	6,000
Vaglia	11-2-1844	31-1-1847	Nicol? Esdrin	5,600
Vaglia	1-2-1844	31-1-1845	Nicol? Esdrin	4,080
Vaglia	1-2-1844	31-1-1846	Nicol? Esdrin	5,900
Vaglia	1-2-1844	31-1-1848	Nicol? Esdrin	5,300
Vaglia	30-1-1844	31-7-1844	Carlo Anconetta	300
Vaglia	28-1-1844	31-7-1844	Eliodoro Radaelli *con giro* di Nicol? Esdrin	8,000
Vaglia	25-1-1844	30-9-1844	Salomon Piran for 75 Venti Franghi	Abusive 1,800
Vaglia	24-1-1844	1-9-1844	Samuel Dalla Vida	15,000
Vaglia	24-1-1844	24-1-1845	Lorenzo Vianello	1,300
Vaglia	20-1-1844	20-1-1845	Lorenzo Vianello	14,170
Vaglia	18-1-1844	18-7-1844	Giuseppe Traine for 70 Venti Franchi	Abusive 1,680
Vaglia	18-1-1844	18-9-1844	Natale A. Vianello *con giro* di Lorenzo Vianello	1,900
Vaglia	7-1-1844	30-11-1844	Giovanni Manerin	10,000
Vaglia	2-1-1844	1-8-1844	Samuel Dalla Vida	10,000
Vaglia	31-12-1843	31-12-1844	Antonio Giacomelli	6,000
Vaglia	30-12-1843	31-1-1845	Francesco Fossati	2,000
Vaglia	30-12-1843	30-6-1845	Francesco Fossati	2,000
Vaglia	29-12-1843	20-11-1844	Natale A. Vianello *con giro* di Lorenzo Vianello	6,000
Vaglia	27-12-1843	31-12-1844	Angelo Chielin	55,000
Vaglia	24-12-1843	31-12-1844	Giovanni Maffei-Giuseppe Valarelli *con giro* di Giovanni Chielin	5,000

(continued)

Table 10.4 (continued)

Type of transaction	Date credit granted	Specified date for repayment	Debtor	Amount due in Austrian lire
Vaglia	24-12-1843	31-12-1844	Giovanni Maffei-Giuseppe Valarelli *con giro* di Giovanni Chielin	5,000
Vaglia	8-12-1843	8-12-1844	Antonio Vianello *con giro* di Lorenzo Vianello	6,000
Vaglia	7-12-1843	10-8-1843	Samuel Dalla Vida for 700 Venti franchi	Abusive 16,800
Vaglia	27-11-1843	30-11-1844	Lorenzo Vianello	17,163.37
Lettera confessionale	19-11-1843	15-1-1844	Giacomo Mola	200
Cambiale	19-10-1843	19-4-1845	Carlo Salvodelli (di tratta) Antonio Giacomelli (di accettazione)	2,180
Cambiale	19-10-1843	19-4-1845	Antonio Giacomelli	2,300
Vaglia	27-5-1843	31-8-1844	Andrea Antonini	50,500
Vaglia	4-5-1843	4-5-1844	Lorenzo Scarpa	3,000
Vaglia	1-4-1843	31-12-1843	Antonio Lavagnin *con giro* di Natale Vianello	6,000
Vaglia	23-7-1842	1-7-1843	Biasio Bisacchia	565
Vaglia	26-8-1841	31-12-1843	Rizzardo II Roberto Balbi	1,200
Vaglia	20-8-1841	20-8-1843	Angelo Vianello *con giro* di Francesco Scarpa	1,493.33
Vaglia	20-8-1841	20-8-1843	Angelo Vianello *con giro* di Francesco Scarpa	1,413.32
Vaglia	2-2-1840	31-8-1844	Giovanni Pozzati	500
Vaglia	2-1-1840	31-12-1846	Giovanni Pozzati	500
Vaglia	13-1-1829	16-3-1829	Carlo Perazzolo for 200 colonati	578.68
Vaglia	27-10-1828	31-1-1829	Gemelli Brothers per nominativo Conto 100 luigi d'oro	2,900
Vaglia	30-9-1828	30-3-1829	Carlo Perazzolo for 200 colonati	1,258
Vaglia	28-8-1828	30-11-1828	Gemelli Brothers for 400 talleri bavere	2,400
Vaglia	26-10-1820	1-9-1821	Giovanni Battista Tassadio for 200 Italian Lirae	229.88
Vaglia	26-10-1820	1-8-1821	Giovanni Battista Tassadio for 200 Italian Lirae	229.88

(continued)

Table 10.4 (continued)

Type of transaction	Date credit granted	Specified date for repayment	Debtor	Amount due in Austrian lire
Vaglia	26-10-1820	1-7-1821	Giovanni Battista Tassadio for 200 Italian Lirae	229.88
Vaglia	26-10-1820	1-12-1821	Giovanni Battista Tassadio for 200 Italian Lirae	229.88
Vaglia	26-10-1820	1-6-1821	Giovanni Battista Tassadio for 200 Italian Lirae	229.88
Vaglia	26-10-1820	1-10-1821	Giovanni Battista Tassadio for 200 Italian Lirae	229.88
Vaglia	26-10-1820	1-11-1821	Giovanni Battista Tassadio for 200 Italian Lirae	229.88
Pagherò	3-7-1815		Angelo Marchi for 471,501 Italian Lirae	541.95
Total (77)				520,852.78
Average				6,764.32
Median				3,000

Source: Compiled from A.E.I.B., E1, N. 129, b. 25, doc. 1 (*Inventario*) ff. 10r-12r and 13v-14r

135 AL.[31] Mola's *lettera confessionale* was also larger than an annual rent of a typical small house and four times the price of 100 kilos of wheat. As a further measure of comparison, the grand prize of Bingo played in the foyer of the Fenice Theatre was 500 AL![32] As was the case with the provision of mortgage loans, our moneylender was not driven by rapaciousness as there is no evidence that he took legal action against his bad debtors.[33]

10.6 Registro Libro Crediti (1843/1844): Insights into His Vaglie Business and Other Sources of Income

We now turn our attention to the sole surviving copy of a *Registro* (*Libro creditori*), that for the last 18 months of Bogdano's life (January 1843 to July 1844) This document provides important insights into the dynamics of his *vaglie* business,

[31] Values taken from the Inventario.

[32] Venice Research, http://www.veniceresearch.com/fenice2.htm.

[33] Inventario, f. 11r: lettere onde evitare il protesto in caso di scadenza.

Table 10.5 Unredeemed dry bills of exchange and promissory notes

Date granted	Amount in Austrian lire	Year	Number of unredeemed paper	Total value in Austrian lire
19-11-1843	200	1843	3	9,200
4-5-1843	3,000			
1-4-1843	6,000			
26-8-1841	1,200	1841	1	1,200
13-1-1829	578.68	1829	1	578.68
27-10-1828	2,900	1828	3	6,558
30-9-1828	1,258			
28-8-1828	2,400			
26-10-1820	229.88	1820	7	1,609.16
26-10-1820	229.88			
26-10-1820	229.88			
26-10-1820	229.88			
26-10-1820	229.88			
26-10-1820	229.88			
26-10-1820	229.88			
Total	19,145.84	Total	15	19,145.84

i.e. remittance, delivery and rollover mechanisms (see Appendix, Table 10.8). That Bogdano kept a *Registro* for *vaglie* transactions attests to the size of his operations and his sophistication as a moneylender.[34] His relatively large number of clients and the extensive *con giro* and rollover operations he engaged in, required, as was the case for banks, careful book-keeping and not simply oral contracts as was usual with moneylenders (Goetzmann and Rouwenhorst 2005, 4–5). We have focused solely on 1843 and have left out the period after January 1844, as Bogdano was ill for some months before his death in July 1844.

The *Registro* entries total 92 *vaglie*. For some *vaglie* there was more than one transaction, i.e. a *vaglia* could be issued or rolled over in 1843 as well as paid back in the same year. It is clear that nearly half of the *vaglie* entered in the *Registro* were issued prior to 1843. For the remaining *vaglie*, which in total amounted to over 350,000 AL, it is not clear which ones were issued and accepted by Bogdano in 1843 and which were rollovers from previous issues which had a termination date in

[34] A.E.I.B., E1, N. 129, reg. 1 (Libro creditori 1843, 1844, 1845. Copia fedele tratta dall' originale dal fu signor Costantino Bogdano), 1843–4.

1843. Thus we are in the dark regarding the exact number and value of new issues. However, precise information is given concerning a total of 19 *vaglie* amounting to 145,905.00 AL which were rolled over during that year, and for 23 *vaglie* of a total value of 113,090.97 AL which were paid back (from individuals who had received cash from him either in 1843 or earlier).

In his *vaglie* operations, as was the case with mortgage loans (and, as shown below, the leasing of property), Bogdano was lenient and not only because he practised rollovers. In quite a few instances the initial specified time length for payment of a *vaglia* could be more than 6 months and up to 1 year. This was indeed a longer continual time horizon for *vaglie* compared to formal banks (Bernardello 2002a, 588).

Usually a debtor would make a payment directly to Bogdano. However, there would often be a *con giro*, and the payee would be a business colLabourator or a relative of the indebted person. Giovanni Chielin, for instance, owed 5,000 to Bogdano for a *vaglia* issued in December 1843 and paid the debt back to Bogdano's estate 1 year later through Giovanni Maffei and Giuseppe Valarelli, who made a *con giro* as they in turn were indebted to Chielin.[35] Moreover, there was the possibility of repayment not in cash but through barter exchange, as exemplified by the case of Angelo Chielin, who settled a 10,000 AL *vaglia* debt to Bogdano by giving him shares of an equivalent value in the 'Strada Ferrata'.[36]

At this point let us return to the mystery of how many new *vaglie* our money-lender accepted in 1843. Perhaps the best approach is to estimate the incomes Bogdano received during the year and use this figure as a basis for understanding how much money he had available to provide for the acceptance of new *vaglie* issued. As mentioned above and exhibited in table 10.6, in 1843 Bogdano received 113,090.97 AL as income from *vaglie* paid back to him. In addition, the imputed incomes received from the fees for *vaglie* rollovers known to us and the annual interest rate on outstanding mortgage loans amounted to a total of 6,974.17 AL. Extra money was obviously available from other sources.

Real estate was an important source of income (see Table 10.7 in the Appendix). At the time of his death he was leasing 26 of his 38 properties in his adopted land (known annual rent at the time amounted to 9,304.97 AL). Before looking into other sources of income, let us note here that as with moneylending Bogdano was no Shylock with his lessees. He seems to have charged low rents. The ratio between annual rents and total value of most of his rented real estate property seems to have been less than 1 %! Even if we assume that this low ratio may be due to a deliberate over-inflation of the value of his properties by the authorities, one fact is undisputed: after his death the administrators of his estate raised rents by a large margin. The shop at San Marco (Canonica) 311, for example, which had been leased to Francesco Nicoletti in 1840 for an annual rent of 232 AL, had its rent increased by the Community to 288 AL; likewise, the charge for the shop at San

[35] For con giro see also A.E.I.B., E1, N. 129, reg. 2 (11–20 March and 26 May 1843).

[36] A.E.I.B., E1, N. 129, reg. 2 (1 May 1843), b. 32, fasc. 80, doc. 1–93 (1851–9).

Table 10.6 Observed and imputed cash inflow for 1843

Austrian lire	
1. *Vaglie* paid in	113,090.97
2. Imputed incomes from rollovers and interest credit	
2a. Commissions from *vaglie* rollovers	1,459.05[a]
2b. Imputed interest on outstanding mortgage loans	4,125.1
Total	5,584.15
3. Other sources of income	
3a. Known rents	9,304.97[b]
3b. *Livello*	1,781.35
Total	11,086,32
Grand total	129,761.44

Source: Compiled from information in the *Inventario*, A.E.I.B., E1, N. 129, reg. 1 and reg. 2
[a]This income has been calculated on the basis of the known average commission for rollovers at the time
[b]This figure is given to us posthumously for 1844, but it is legitimate for us to make the assumption that it was not much different for the calendar year 1843

Maria Zobenigo 2060, rented in 1839 to Marco Mescalchi for 120 AL, was raised to 192 by the same authority.

Obviously, Bogdano could afford to show such largesse because he had other sources of income, such as the *livello*; and we can hypothesize that he may have had some income from the brigantine and that he must have had a relatively large income from his landed estates and deposits held in Corfu. Moreover, we can suggest that speculative profits made from selling real estate properties may have been an important source of income. We do not know what other properties he owned during his lifetime and whether he sold any: we know only what properties were in his hands at the time of his death. Given the large rise in the values of properties during his long residence there, we can surmise that over the years he may have sold at a good profit properties acquired during his early days in Venice: to quote Greenfield, "After 1830 the value of rents and real estate increased on average in most of the city of Venice about 80 % and even doubled in central Venice." (Greenfield 1939, 325, ref. 46). We know the price at which he acquired his real estate in one instance, that in Porte Grandi del Sile. This property appears to have been purchased in 1828 for some 68,000 AL, and it is known that at his death the value was 500,000![37] Since he did not sell it, the surplus value (windfall profit) is hypothetical—though it is a measure of what profits he may have gained from other real estate deals. In a nutshell, the known and imputed income allowed him to accept *vaglie* of a value of over 130,000 AL in 1843; though in reality, on the basis of the above hypotheses, it is highly likely that he was in a position to grant more funds than that, without operating at a deficit.

[37] A.E.I.B., E1, N. 129, b. 27, fasc. 13, doc. 79 (printed).

We would like to close this discussion with the comment that whatever may have been the sources of his hidden income, the picture of a competitive and just moneylender remains unscathed. Moreover, the hypothesis that Bogdano had diverse incomes from a variety of sources, some hidden to us, strengthens our argument that he was a careful, professional moneylender who operated within the framework of solid relations of trust. Indeed, it was the development of that trust that provided the key to his success: the ability to offer extensive rollovers and the low default rate on loans he granted.

10.7 The Key to Success and 'Fair Practice'

How did Bogdano succeed in having such a low ratio of unredeemed to outstanding debt? The clue to solving this puzzle lies in his choice of colLabourators and clients. Although a late arrival to Venice, our moneylender cultivated founts of good information and built strong bonds of trust with colLabourators and clients. Bogdano operated within the framework of multiple transactions with the same person. The number of clients was lower than the number of loans granted. Also some clients would purchase diverse products from our moneylender. For example, Monsignor Rizzardo II Roberto Balbi borrowed both short and long term from him.[38] In addition, among the recipients of loans were individuals who also rented property from him. His share of the Valle L'Averto in Dolo was rented out to his borrowers Francesco and Antonio Bonivento 'detti' Zaniolo,[39] while the estate in Porte Grandi del Sile was let to his borrower Antonio Giacomelli.[40]

Family capitalism was fundamental to Bogdano's operations. He did not rely solely on the reputation of an individual with whom he would do business, but also on that of his family. One family member would be granted short-term credit from Bogdano, while another might borrow on mortgage. Mortgage loans, whether large or small, involved complicated arrangements and were often family affairs. There is evidence that in the circle within which Bogdano operated it was customary for claims and loan obligations to be transferred among individuals. An example is that of Cecilia Moro Lin who passed an 1842 mortgage loan on to Bogdano in 1843 which was originally owed to her from Moisè Pinkerle, who in the meanwhile had passed his debt on to Felice and Giuseppe Caine.[41] Transactions could become even more complex as a husband would mortgage the dowry of his wife in order to obtain credit. One relative would provide the guarantee for another member of the household to receive a loan (often a parent or a spouse), or one would pay back the loan of another. The recipient of a mortgage loan would often be not one person

[38] See A.E.I.B., E1, N. 129, b. 27, fasc. 13, doc. 1–79 (1810–93).

[39] See A.E.I.B., E1, N. 129, b. 28, fasc. 24.

[40] A.E.I.B., E1, N. 129, b. 27, fasc. 13; b. 28, fasc. 20, doc. 1–527 (1827–94).

[41] A.E.I.B., E1, N. 129, b. 33, fasc. 89, doc. 1–115 (1852–96).

but two relatives. Perhaps because times were hard, resources (collaterals) had to be pooled, either because the borrowers could not do otherwise or because Bogdano demanded this, as increased securities enhanced his ability to charge decent rates.

Bogdano's clients were citizens from both within the city of Venice and its rural hinterland, and in this sense we may argue that he is an example of an urban-based moneylender who as a creditor and an investor in land acted as a link between the urban and rural economies and the finance-land circuit in Venice.[42] His clients lived in both worlds, sometimes simultaneously. One example is Antonio Negri, a shopkeeper, who also held some farm land and property in Mestre and Treviso.[43] He was indebted to a few merchant houses, among them Nomviller et Campagnia, before turning to Bogdano for financial assistance. His clients also came from many walks of life. The titled Balbi brothers borrowed money from him, as did Samuele della Vida, from a prominent family of the Jewish elite in Venice.

The *livello* in Padua was leased to the important Vendramin Callergi Valmarana, whose family[44] were of Byzantine-Cretan origins and owners of a palazzo in the Canal Grande (now the municipal casino).[45] Among his clients were also a lawyer (Vicenzo Monaco), a captain (Antonio Mondaini) and one Francesco Scarpa, possibly a notary based in San Dona di Piave. The aforementioned *cambiavulante/cambiavalule* Angelo Chielin placed pawned items on the market for Bogdano. However, the bulk of his clients consisted of merchants, shopkeepers, rentiers and *possidenti* (such as Pietro Coppano, Giovanni Pozzati, Giovanni Manerin and Maria Zennaro). Apparently Bogdano's clients were basically locals. However, at least two, Francesco Fossati and Eliodoro Radaelli, who did a *con giro* for Nicolò Esdrin, had typically Lombard surnames.[46] Bogdano did not rent out property or lend money to Greeks. At the time the Greek Community was indeed small, but it is incredulous that none were in need of ready cash. It could possibly be that our moneylender preferred not to have compatriot clients, rather as with Jews, who could legitimately lend at interest only to Christians and not to other Jews (Ferguson 2009, 37).

In contrast, regarding business colLabourators Bogdano turned only to the 'aristocracy' and was not averse to Greeks. The co-owner of his *livello* seems to have been Aurelio Venier Fonte of the renowned noble family of the Republic of Venice.[47] Moreover, Angelo Papadopoli (a member of the prominent Venetian

---

[42] For other such examples in history, see Tittler (1994, 259).

[43] For information on him and his financial relationship with Bogdano, see A.E.I.B., E1, N. 129, b. 33, fasc. 91, doc. 1–231 (1853–96).

[44] For *livelli*, see Corazzol (1986, 13–41, 109–24G).

[45] *Inventario*, f. 14v. See also A.E.I.B., E1, N. 129, b. 27, fasc. 2. Also, Brusegan (2005) and Vincent (2001).

[46] We wish to thank Giandomenico Piluso for this piece of information.

[47] *Inventario*, f. 14v. See also A.E.I.B., E1, N. 129, b. 27, fasc. 2, doc. 1–85 (1796–1871). For Papadopoli, see Zorzi (2003, 298).

banking family and elder brother of Giovanni, the Greek benefactor mentioned above) helped our financier to acquire from the Reale Demanio three houses, a storehouse and four shops on Campo SS. Filippo e Giacomo. He did this by making the direct purchase of these assets on 21 April 1814 by paying the Reale Demanio the amount of 16,943.43 Italian lire. Perhaps Angelo, with his powerful connections and social status, acted for Bogdano, to whom these properties were transferred soon afterwards.[48] The other elite Greco-Venetian from whom our financier sought support was his lawyer and executor, Calucci.[49] He was the husband of Cecilia Moro Lin, a Venetian aristocrat whom we have already mentioned.

This difference between the choice of clients (Venetians from all walks of life) and associates (highly placed (Greco)-Venetians) made sense. Bogdano could thus combine a diverse but family-based clientele (and hence, by not putting all his eggs in one basket, remain secure at the same time). It was also logical for him to draw his colLabourators from a narrow elite and be active in the governing body of the Greek Community. In this manner, he could attain both social sanction and have an important advantage: privileged access to information.

At the core of all of Bogdano's business operations lay relationships of trust, something which is well known to have been the case with successful moneylenders of previous centuries from the evidence of English examples (Muldrew 1998, 252). This was a two-way street: he trusted his web of business colLabourators and clients, and they in turn could trust him. Bogdano had confidence that clients would not default either because of their wealth, and/or because of their personal ties with him and/or because they were backed up by better-placed relatives. Bogdano's ultimate feat was his low incidence of defaulting clients.

Conclusion

What then are the significant points of Bogdano's story? What do we learn about the role of the money lender in Venetian finance at a time of transition?

Though a latecomer to Venice, our moneylender succeeded in making a fortune which placed him in high standing with a personal wealth similar to that of long-established local elite merchant bankers.

Even during a time of fast transition in the financial system, a traditional actor such as a moneylender could fulfil needs and exploit new opportunities. Bogdano's example supports the wider argument that economic change is an evolutionary process and that within the course of change there linger remnants of the previous epoch and hence continuities. Our moneylender acted as a facilitator who supplied cash in a cash-strapped environment and enhanced the amount of credit in circulation. His clients had their own property, but

(continued)

[48] See A.E.I.B., E1, N. 129, b. 27, fasc. 4, doc. 1–19 (1808–30).

[49] Will and *Inventario*.

they still came from diverse social groups and were driven to borrow from him for a variety of reasons. Some turned to him in order to gain credit for a business transaction. Others sought cash from him in order to maintain their standard of living or even attain higher levels of consumption or to acquire new property. We cannot preclude the possibility that some of his clients were at the brink of poverty and only postponed their inevitable decline into destitution by resorting to Bogdano. However, the evidence at hand suggests that many improved their position in the long run by turning to him for a temporary cash injection. Hence, our versatile moneylender was part of the scene of economic growth and facilitated the demand for cash of an economy in which there was expansion in important areas.

As part of the finance-land circuit in Venice, our moneylender maintained a specialization in the traditional business of short-term commercial credit and real estate mortgages. Venetian merchant banks at the time appeared to be moving towards the emerging business of investment banking. But though a traditional moneylender and not an innovator, Bogdano was *au fait* with contemporary methods. He kept accounting books, invested in new products—such as company shares—and participated in formal partnerships, although he ran his core business as a one-man show. Moreover, he did business deals with professionals and members of the financial elite and came to resemble a quasi-banker by charging fair prices.

Bogdano was a capable but cautious provider of credit. He had a wide social circle of clients, with many of whom he made repeat transactions. He would ask for guarantees of mortgages and jewels, but simultaneously he would prudently solicit implicit guarantees from family members. It was these assurances that lowered his risk of default and allowed him to offer a fair rate of interest and good terms to his clients, such as rollovers, and they did not fear losing their property when turning to him for loan capital. He did not prosecute bad clients. Thus, he contests the standard perception of the avaricious moneylender and could maintain a Christian/Ethical conscience both within the private world of his home, his business, and in society.

Appendix

Table 10.7 Breakdown of real estate property in Venice at death

Parish	Number	Type of property	Annual rent	Lessee	Date of contract for the lease	Value a.p.	% rent of total value
S. Zaccaria (circond. SS. Filippo e Giacomo)	4,047	Shop	155.16	Filippo Cattani	1-4-1815	99,934.00	0.155
S. Maria Zobenigo	2,069	House	364.64	Giovanni Pittoni	1-1-1818	197,253.00	0.184
S. Maria Zobenigo	2,068	House	291.72	Raffaele Todeschini	23-7-1819	187,659.00	0.155
S. Zaccaria (circond. SS. Filippo e Giacomo)	4,058	Shop	289.68	Widow of Antonio Stefani	14-9-1823		
S. Maria Zobenigo	2,072	House	144	Bortolo De Col	23-2-1827	175,762.00	0.081
S. Maria Formosa	4,785	House	360	Giuseppe Traine	1-7-1834	237,931.00	0.151
S. Marco (circond. S. Giuliano)	247	House	230	Francesco Fornasier	20-7-1837	317,241.00	0.072
S. Maria Zobenigo	2,065	Shop	228	Giuseppe Beccari	1-3-1838	128,453.00	0.177
SS. Giovanni e Paolo (circond. S. Giustina)	3,110	Warehouse	283.43	Giovanni Battista Coletti	1-9-1838	309.31	91.63
S. Maria Zobenigo	2,075	House	144	Tomaso Battaglini	1-1-1839	101,313.00	0.142
S. Maria Zobenigo	2,060	Shop	120	Marco Mescalchi	25-3-1839	90,414.00	0.132
S. Trinità	2,854	House	205.44	Giuseppe Stecchetti	4-8-1839	142,759.00	0.143
S. Maria Zobenigo	2,060–2,061	Shop	228.6	Giuseppe Gagrizia	28-9-1839	128,483.00	0.177
S. Marco (Canonica)	312	Shop	326.84	Luigi Ventura	1-7-1840	214,138.00	0.152
S. Salvatore (calle di mezzo)	4,277	House	708	Luigi Bontempelli	27-5-1843	507,585.00	0.139
S. Zaccaria (circond. SS. Filippo e Giacomo)	4,048	Shop	168	Filippo Miletta	1-8-1843	95,172.00	0.176
S. Marco (Canonica)	311	Shop	232	Francesco Nicoletti	11-3-1844	157,035.00	0.147

(continued)

Table 10.7 (continued)

Parish	Number	Type of property	Annual rent	Lessee	Date of contract for the lease	Value a.p.	% rent of total value
S. Maria Zobenigo	2,076	House	82.32	Angelica Rado	31-4-1844	57,103.00	0.144
S. Zaccaria (circond. SS. Filippo e Giacomo)	4,057	House	144	Giacomo Moro	Cannot be read		
S. Maria Zobenigo	2,073	Warehouse		(?) Gitti	Oral agreement	33,310.00	
S. Maria Zobenigo	2,074	Warehouse		Giovanni Pittoni	Oral agreement	47,663.00	
S. Geremia (circond. ai Scalzi)	102	House with garden		House of Bogdano			
S. Geremia (circond. ai Scalzi)	54 rosso	Monastery				Sold 60,000[a]	
S. Zaccaria (circond. SS. Filippo e Giacomo)	4,046	House		House of Bogdano		244,839.00	
S. Zaccaria (circond. SS. Filippo e Giacomo)	4,049	Warehouse		Warehouse of Bogdano			
S. Zaccaria (circond. SS. Filippo e Giacomo)	4,056	Warehouse				16,882.00	
S. Zaccaria (circond. SS. Filippo e Giacomo)	4,059	Shop	Together with the previous				
S. Zaccaria (circond. SS. Filippo e Giacomo)	4,060	House					
S. Marco (Campo della guerra)	530	Half house	1,492	Antonio Missiaglia		951,722.00	0.156
S. Marco (Campo della guerra)	531	Shop	Together with the previous				
S. Stefano	2,590	House					
circond. S. Gregorio	519	Half house					
circond. S. Gregorio	242	House					
circond. S. Gregorio	249	Half house					

SS. Filippo e Giacomo	4,354	Shop					
SS. Filippo e Giacomo	4,355	Shop					
Porte grandi del Sile-campagna detta Granza		House, meadows, camp	1,050	Antonio Giacomelli		541,561.00	0.193
Lugo fraz. a distretto di Dolo-Valle L'Averto		Valley for chase and fishery	2,057.14	Francesco and Antonio Bonivento detti Zaniolo			
Total			9,304.97			4,734,521.31	
Average			422.95			197,271.72	4.508
Median			231			135,621.00	0.152

Source: Compiled from *Inventario* and reg. 2 *Quaderno della sostanza lasciata dal fu signor Costantino Bogdano fu Paolo*), 1844–8, ff. 43v-57r
[a]A.E.I.B., E1, N. 129, b. 33, fasc. 87, doc. 1–42 (1852–85)

Table 10.8 *Vaglie* listed in the 1843 *registro*

Name of borrower (in whose name a *vaglia* was issued)[a]	Value of *vaglia* AL	Date in margin of *registro* entry[b]	Termination date	Name of borrower (in whose name a *vaglia* was issued)	Amount in AL	Date in margin of *registro* entry	Termination date
Carlo Capeler	600.00		31-1-1843	Antonio Giacomelli	5,000.00	29-4-1843	29-10-1843
Giuseppe Traine	1,680.00		18-1-1843	Lorenzo Vianello di Francesco	5,159.35	2-10-1842	30-11-1843
Fortunato Gorin[a]	206.00		31-1-1843	Lorenzo Vianello di Francesco	5,000.00	2-10-1842	30-11-1843
Benedetto Bortolini[a]	2,030.00	16-10-1842	16-1-1843	Samuele dalla Vida	7,531.71	6-1-1843	30-11-1843
Lorenzo Vianello di Francesco[a]	540.00		15-1-1843	Antonio Giacomelli[a]	5,000.00	20-5-1843	27-11-1843
Lorenzo Scarpa	6,000.00		8-2-1843	Eleonora Balbiani[a]	4,800.00	29-5-1843	29-11-1843
Francesco Fossati[a]	2,000.00		8-2-1843	Giuseppe Regazzi	800.00	27-5-1843	26-11-1843
Nadalin Vianello	2,099.50		24-2-1843	Antonio Giacomelli	6,000.00	31-12-1843	31-12-1844
Antonio Giacomelli[a]	2,173.50		24-2-1843	monsignor Balbi	1,200.00	26-8-1843	31-12-1843
Lorenzo Vianello di Francesco	6,000.00		20-2-1843	Lorenzo Vianello di Francesco	6,000.00		8-12-1843
Giovanni Pozzati[a]	500.00		28-2-1843	Lorenzo Vianello di Francesco	6,000.00		19-12-1843
Giovanni Chielin	5,000.00		11-3-1843	Lorenzo Vianello di Francesco	1,000.00		19-12-1843
Eleonora Bolbiani[a]	3,340.50	21-2-1843	11-3-1843	Lorenzo Vianello di Francesco	1,424.00		29-12-1843
Samuele dalla Vida	12,500.00		30-4-1843	Nadalin Vianello	36,343.00	1-4-1843	31-12-1843
Nadalin Vianello	6,000.00	5-10-1842	5-4-1843	Nadalin Vianello	6,000.00	1-4-1843	
Nadalin Vianello	37,000.00	5-10-1842	5-4-1843	Giovanni Manerin[a]	12,000.00	13-4-1843	15-12-1843
Giovanni Pozzati	8,000.00	13-12-1842	16-4-1843	Giovanni Manerin[a]	4,800.00	13-4-1843	23-12-1843
Eleonora Bolbiani[a]	5,725.80	8-2-1843	7-4-1843	Giovanni Manerin[a]	4,200.00	10-5-1843	10-12-1843

Nadalin Vianello	1,500.00	3-10-1842	13-4-1843	Giovanni Manerin[a]	6,000.00	21-6-1843	20-12-1843
Andrea Antonini	50,500.00		31-5-1843	Samuele dalla Vida	19,200.00	10-5-1843	10-12-1843
Lorenzo Scarpa	3,000.00	4-5-1842	4-5-1843	Salamon Piran[a]	800.00	16-5-1843	31-12-1843
Samuele dalla Vida	14,500.00	5-10-1842	31-5-1843	Nadalin Vianello	800.00	13-7-1843	13-1-1844
Giovanni Pozzati	3,000+ 3,000	26-10-1842	31-5-1843	Eleonora Balbiani	7,200.00	8-7-1843	8-1-1844
Nadalin Vianello	6,000.00	7-11-1842	7-5-1843	Giovanni Manerin	4,200.00	9-11-1843	8-1-1844
Nadalin Vianello	11,295.00	2-12-1842	6-6-1843	Samuele dalla Vida	9,888.00	7-12-1843	31-1-1844
Nadalin Vianello	28,000+ 6,000	21/27-12-1842	21/27-6-1843	Francesco Fossati	2,000.00		8-2-1844
Giuseppe Traine	1,200.00	22-12-1842	22-12-1843	Giovanni Manerin	2,920.85		29-2-1844
Pasqua Regazzi	2,000.00	31-12-1842	30-6-1843	Pasqua Regazzi	3,000.00	1-9-1843	18-2-1844
Antonio Giacomelli	4,000.00	31-12-1842	30-6-1843	Benedetto Bortolini	1,000.00	18-12-1843	18-3-1844
Angelo Chielin	24,000.00	2-1-1843	31-12-1843 (55000)				15-3-1844
Angelo Chielin	13,500.00	2-2-1843	P (15000)	Francesco Sartori	600.00	22-10-1843	30-4-1844
Angelo Chielin	22,500.00	30-3-1843		Antonio Giacomelli	2,180.00	19-10-1843	19-4-1844
Angelo Chielin	10,000.00	12-4-1843		Antonio Giacomelli	2,300.00	19-10-1843	19-4-1844
Biagio Bisacchia	565.00		31-7-1843	Salamon Piran	670.72		15-4-1844
Samuele dalla Vida	12,000.00	1-12-1842	31-3-1844	Giuseppe Regazzi	500.00		15-4-1844
Giovanni BattistaSerboloni[a] Alvise Manzato	4,000.00	28-1-1843	31-10-1843 (2000) (2000)	Lorenzo Scarpa	3,000.00	4-5-1843	4-5-1844
Francesco Vianello[a]	1,685.32	14-3-1843	14-7-1843	Nadalin Vianello	800.00	26-11-1843	26-5-1844
Nicolò Rossi[a]	700.00		31-7-1843	Nadalin Vianello	2,000.00	11-11-1843	13-5-1844
Francesco Fossati[a]	2,000.00		8-8-1843	Giuseppe Traine	1,200.00	22-12-1843	22-6-1844
Antonio Giacomelli[a]	2,230.50		20-8-1843	Giovanni Pozzati	6,000.00	31-12-1843	30-6-1844
Francesco Scarpa	1,493.33		20-8-1843	Samuele dalla Vida	16,800.00	7-12-1843	10-8-1844

(continued)

Table 10.8 (continued)

Name of borrower (in whose name a *vaglia* was issued)[a]	Value of *vaglia* AL	Date in margin of *registro entry*[b]	Termination date	Name of borrower (in whose name a *vaglia* was issued)	Amount in AL	Date in margin of *registro* entry	Termination date
Pasqua Regazzi	1,096.97	1-3-1843	31-8-1843	Giovanni Chielin	5,000.00	1-6-1843	31-8-1844
Giovanni Chielin[a]	3,000.00	1-3-1843	31-8-1843	Lorenzo Vianello di Francesco	17,163.37	27-12-1843	30-11-1844
Lorenzo Scarpa[a]	3,000.00		3-9-1843	Angelo Chielin	55,000.00	27-12-1843	31-12-1844
Giovanni Pozzati[a]	4,500.00		30-9-1843	Lorenzo Vianello di Francesco	6,000.00	8-12-1843	8-12-1844
Nadalin Vianello	2,863.11	20-4-1843	20-10-1843	Francesco Fossati	2,000.00	30-12-1843	31-1-1845

Source Compiled from: A.E.I.B., E1, N. 129, reg. 1

[a]Denotes the *vaglie* which were paid back in 1843

[b]Not clear whether it is date of issue or previous termination date of a *vaglia*

References

A'Hearn B (2003) Anthropometric evidence on living standards in Northern Italy, 1730–1860. J Econ Hist 63:351–381

Allen L (2001) The global financial system, 1750–2000. Reaktion Books, London, pp 146–147

Angelou A, Chatziioannou MC (eds) (1997) Introduction to A. Syngros, Apomnimonevmata (Reminiscences). Estia, Athens, in Greek

Bernardello A (1996) La prima ferrovia fra Venezia e Milano. Storia della imperial-regia privilegiata strada ferrata Ferdinandea lombardo-veneta (1835–1852). Istituto Veneto di Scienze, Lettere ed Arti, Venice

Bernardello A (2002a) Iniziative economiche, accumulazione e investimenti di capitale (1830–1866). In: Isnenghi M, Woolf S (eds) Storia di Venezia. L'Ottocento e il Novecento, vol 14. Istituto Italiano della Enciclopedia Italiana, Rome, pp 1991–2002

Bernardello A (2002b) Venezia, 1830–1866. Iniziative economiche, accumulazione e investimenti di capitale. Il Risorgimento 1:5–66

Bhaduri A (1983) The economic structure of backward agriculture. Academic Press, London, Chap. 5

Brusegan M (2005) La grande guida dei monumenti di Venezia. Newton & Compton, Rome

Cafagna L (1973) The industrial revolution in Italy, 1830–1914. In: Cipolla CM (ed) The Fontana economic history of Europe: the emergence of industrial societies, Part 1, vol 1. Fontana, London, pp 279–328

Cameron R, Bovykin VI (eds) (1991) International banking, 1870–1914. Oxford University Press, Oxford

Cipolla CM (1970) The economic decline of Italy. In: Cipolla CM (ed) The economic decline of empires. Methuen, London, pp 196–214, esp. 202–14

Clark M (1996) Modern Italy, 1871–1995. Longman, New Jersey

Conca Messina SA (2004) Cotone e imprese. Credito, commerci e tecnologie nell' età dei mercanti industriali. Valle Olona, 1815–1860. Marsilio, Venice

Corazzol G (1986) Livelli stipulati a Venezia nel 1591. Giardini Editori e Stampatori. Studio storico, Pisa

Ferguson N (2009) The ascent of money: a financial history of the world. Penguin, New York, NY

Fratianni M, Spinelli F (1997) A monetary history of Italy. Cambridge University Press, Cambridge

Galli AM (1991) L' Ottocento. In: Cova A, Galli AM (eds) La Cassa di Risparmio delle Provincie Lombarde dalla fondazione al 1940, vol 1. Cariplo-Laterza, Milan, 4 vols

Gilmour D (2011) The pursuit of Italy: a history of its land, its regions and their peoples. Allen Lane, London

Ginsborg P (1979) Daniele Manin and the Venetian revolution of 1848–49. Cambridge University Press, Cambridge, Chap. 1

Goetzmann WN, Rouwenhorst KG (2005) The origins of value: the financial innovations that created modern capital markets. Oxford University Press, Oxford

Greenfield KR (1939) Commerce and new enterprise at Venice, 1830–1848. J Mod Hist 11:313–333

Gritsopoulos TA (1967) The Orlov Rebellion: the revolution in the Peloponnese in 1770 and its consequences (in Greek)

Katsiardi-Hering O (2004) From the Greek Communities abroad to the historiography of the phenomenon of migration, 15th–19th centuries. In: Historiography of modern and contemporary Greece, 1833–2002, vol 2. Centre of Neohellenic Research, Hellenic National Research Foundation, Athens, pp 223–250

Kindleberger CP (1993) A financial history of Western Europe. Oxford University Press, Oxford

Kindleberger CP (1996) World economic primacy: 1500 to1990. Oxford University Press, New York, NY

Lane FC (1937) Venetian bankers, 1496–1533: a study in the early stages of deposit banking. J Polit Econ XLV:187–206
Maltezou C (1999) The Venice of the Greeks. Militos, Athens, in Greek
Maltezou C (2008) A guide to the archive. Athens–Venice. Istituto Ellenico di Studi Bizantini e Postbizantini di Venezia, Library number 26 (in Greek)
Mcintosh MK (1988) Money lending on the periphery of London, 1300–1600. Albion 20:557–571
Mertzios KD (1939) Thomas Flanginis, Studies of the academy of Athens, vol 8. Academy of Athens, Athens, pp 1–165, in Greek
MuldrEw C (1998) The economy of obligation. Macmillan, Basingstoke
Papaioannou AP (1986) The Greeks of Venice and the Venetian revolution of 1848–9. University of Ioannina, Ioannina
Pepelasis Minoglou I (2002) Ethnic minority groups in international banking: Greek diaspora bankers of Constantinople and Ottoman state finances, c. 1840–81. Financ Hist Rev 9:125–146
Pezzolo L (2007) Venice and Doppler. In: Hiebel E, Musso M (eds) Christian Doppler, life and work: principles and application. Living Edition, Pöllauberg
Piluso G (1999) L'arte dei banchieri. Moneta e credito a Milano da Napoleone all'Unità. Franco Angeli, Milan
Polsi A (1996) Financial institutions in nineteenth-century Italy: the rise of a banking system. Financ Hist Rev 3:117–137
Shipley NR (1976) Thomas Sutton: Tudor-Stuart money lender. Bus Hist Rev 50:456–476
Tittler R (1994) Money-lending in the West Midlands: the activities of Joyce Jefferies, 1638–49. Hist Res 67:249–263
Triantafyllou KN (1967) Konstantinos Bogdanos from Patras in Venice, national benefactor. Thesaurismata 4:192–195, in Greek
Triantafyllou KN (1980) Historical Lexicon of Patras 3rd edn. Koulis, Patras, 1995 (in Greek)
Vincent AL (2001) The Callergi case: crime and politics in western Crete under Venetian rule. Thesaurismata 31:211–292, in Greek
Xanthopoulou-Kyriakou A (1977) The Greek community of Venice (1797–1866). Aristotle University of Thessaloniki, Thessaloniki, in Greek
Zorzi A (2003) Venezia austriaca. Libreria Editrice Goriziana, Gorizia

Sources

Istituto Ellenico di Studi Bizantini e Postbizantini di Venezia: The Bogdano Archive, no. 129 of the archival series: Archeio Ellinikou Institoutou Benetias (Archive of the Hellenic Institute in Venice), E'.Oikonomiki Diaheirisi (Economic management) 1. Diathikes (Wills), Klirotodimata (Foundations), Dorees (Donations).

Part IV
Insights for Today from Ancient Greece

Chapter 11
The Qualities and Workings of Direct Democracy: Lessons from Classical Athens

Paschalis A. Arvanitidis and Nicholas C. Kyriazis

11.1 Introduction

In recent years we have seen a renewed interest among scholars in the operation and effects of direct democracy (see *inter alia* Frey 1994; Feld and Savioz 1997; Matsusaka 2004, 2005; Pallinger et al. 2007; Blume et al. 2009; Kaufmann et al. 2010; Altman 2011; Shrivastava 2012; Bitros and Karayiannis 2013). One reason of this has been the general dissatisfaction with representative politics and the growing desire among people for genuine involvement in the decision-making processes, expressed in many cases with the introduction and implementation of direct democracy by an increasing number of communities around the world (Kaufmann et al. 2010). Thus, in the last 20 years more than a 100 countries have established mechanisms of direct citizen participation, whereas the number of referendums and plebiscites held at a national level was increased by about 62 % (as compared to the previous two decades).

All these developments have given a new impetus to the analysis of the first democracy, developed in Greece more than 2,500 years ago. Democracy was established in the city-state (*polis*) of Athens during 510–507 BC (henceforth all dates are BC unless otherwise stated) with the constitutional reforms of Kleisthenes and lasted until 322 (with few-months-long interruptions in 411–410 and in 404–403) when Athens was defeated by Macedon.[1] Classical Athens constitutes a

We wish to thank Prof. Josiah Ober and Prof. George Bitros for their useful comments. The usual disclaimer applies.

[1] It seems that democracy was practiced again in Athens during the third and second centuries, until the Roman conquest of Greece, but sufficient evidence on its detailed workings over this period is missing.

P.A. Arvanitidis (✉) • N.C. Kyriazis
Department of Economics, University of Thessaly, 43 Korai Street, 38333 Volos, Greece
e-mail: parvanit@uth.gr; Nkyr@uth.gr

G.C. Bitros, N.C. Kyriazis (eds.), *Essays in Contemporary Economics*,
DOI 10.1007/978-3-319-10043-2_11

prototype of direct, participatory, democracy, where all issues of public interest (including public finance, taxation, foreign policy, etc.) were debated and voted in the Assembly (*Ekklesia*) of citizens,[2] consisted of all free adult males of Athenian parentage.[3] Thus, the Assembly was the supreme decision-making body, holding not only legislative, but also executive, auditing and judicial powers (it elected magistrates, including the generals and chief financial officers, and tried public officers for corruption and treason).[4] Any ordinary citizen was free to speak, to propose motions or amendments in the Assembly[5] and to prosecute illegal behaviour on another's behalf. There were no political parties[6] or elections in the modern sense and appointment to legislative, executive and judicial boards was made by lot and for a limited term (ensuring significant office rotation). Moreover, all public officials were subject to strict accountability procedures (they were reviewed by special examiners, called *euthynoi*, and auditors, called *logistai*) and liable to juridical prosecution for any misdeed or even for misleading the *Ekklesia* (so, too, were all public speakers).

Over the years, a substantial amount of literature has been published, where scholars, including economists, economic historians and political scientists, have analysed direct democracy as practiced in classical Greece and especially in Athens (for which most extant information is available), and its effects on the polity, society and economy. Thus, some of the most recent studies have explored the

---

[2] There is no consensus as to the actual number of Athenian citizens (and Athenian population consequently). Most scholars, such as Jones (1958), Hansen (1999) and Rhodes (2006), accept the established view that citizens were about 30,000 people. Others, such as Hansen (2006) and Arvanitidis and Kyriazis (2012) argue for a figure that lies well above the general consensus, estimating that Athenian citizens were about 50,000–60,000 people.

[3] It should be noted that participation in the Assembly was not compulsory. In addition, high opportunity costs (i.e. the time and income lost due to attendance) and decision-making costs (i.e. the costs of getting properly informed on the matter under discussion) would have made attendance less attractive to some citizens. This is probably why Athenians of the fifth century instituted a fine for those caught abstaining, with a squad of public slaves policing and marking with red color those citizens not being in the meeting place (*Pnyx*) (Aristophanes 1911) After the restoration of the democracy in 403, pay for Assembly attendance was introduced, promoting a new enthusiasm for Assembly meetings. However, only the first 6,000 to arrive (constituted, according to Hansen (1999) the required quorum) were admitted and paid, with the red squad now used to keep latecomers at bay (Aristophanes 2004).

[4] In the fourth century, however, some of these judicial powers were transferred to the courts.

[5] Although in principle all citizens could address the Assembly, in practice much (but not all) of the debate was carried out by a cadre of skilled statesmen known as rhetors or demagogues. However, the mass of ordinary citizens rule the *Ekklesia* through its control of public speech achieved by the hegemony of democratic ideology (or, as we term it, 'public identity', cf. below) and other formal and informal mechanisms (Ober 1993). Thus, in simple terms, the statesman "had to conform to his audience's ideology or face the consequences: losing votes or being ignored" (Ober 1989: 43–44).

[6] The absence of parties and party platforms meant that there were nothing like party discipline in public votes on matters of policy. Athenian citizens were free to attend to and to follow or ignore the advice of a diverse range of would-be leaders of the moment.

workings of democracy in general, and the development of political, legal, and economic institutions (see Ober 1989, 1993, 2000, 2008a, b, 2010; Hansen 1999, 2006; Cartledge et al. 2002; Manning and Morris 2005; Harris 2006; Amemiya 2007; Bitros and Karayiannis 2010, 2013; Tridimas 2011). Yet, others have focused their analysis on specific economic aspects in classical Greece, such as public finance (Lyttkens 1994, 2010; Kyriazis 2009; Burke 2010), public goods (Lyttkens 1997; Wilson 2000; Kaiser 2007) credit and banking (Thompson 1979; Cohen 1990, 1992; Millett 1991; Shipton 1997, 2000), money and coinage (von Reden 1997; Figueira 1998; Schaps 2004), entrepreneurship (Thompson 1983; Karayiannis 1992; Bitros and Karayiannis 2006, 2008, 2012), the structure of economy and market functioning (French 1991; Morris 1994, 2004; Manning and Morris 2005), even real estate leases and mortgages (Finley 1985; Harris 1988, 1993; Nevett 2000), to name but a few.

In the present study we address an aspect of direct democracy which has not been explored yet in detail: public choice in policy-making, approached from the point of view of the individual citizens who were the voters and thus the ultimate decision makers. The paper is organized as follows: drawing on the experience of classical Athens the next section discusses the structural underpinnings of direct democracy, whereas the following ones analyze the qualities and workings of direct democracy to provide a simple model of public choice in policy-making. The last section concludes the paper summarizing the key points drawn.

11.2 The Underpinnings of Direct Democracy

We conceive direct democracy as an institution in itself,[7] comprising a set of institutional and organizational arrangements that place the power to effect change in the public realm (and thus, to reconstitute it) directly and exclusively in the hands of the people. Direct democracy, according to our definition, is not simply a form of government. It is rather a complex politico-socio-economic system, where citizens as a whole, dialectically and recursively develop (create anew, abolish, transform, modify or maintain) policies, strategies, mechanisms, processes, organizational arrangements, etc., in the public domain, in order to successfully cope with the changing conditions and circumstances they face, while remain committed to prevalent social values. On these grounds, the supremacy of ‘public discourse’ and ‘public identity’ is the basis of the system’s endurance and power. Let us now explore these two in more detail, before we move to discuss the qualities and workings of direct democracy.

[7] Institution defies easy definition; even within the school of Institutional Economics the word has never enjoyed a precise meaning. For the purposes of this research we define institution as a set of related rules, conventions, norms and habits in specific domains, which shape human agency and interaction.

Public discourse refers to the reciprocal, interactive and dialectical communication of citizens, making possible the integration of the (compartmentalized) knowledge each individual possesses and its diffusion to the community. By doing so, public discourse moulds the beliefs and identity of the individual, while at the same time forges the consolidation of a common identity, that enables the alignment of interests within citizenry (sometimes under the thread of legal, political or social sanctions[8]) and the coordination of collective action (by reference to the shared body of knowledge and the common identity). Knowledge in this context comprises information, views, experiences, technical knowledge, social knowledge (i.e. knowledge of people, attitudes, habits, practices, etc., which is possessed by many people but at different degrees), and latent and tacit knowledge[9] (i.e. hidden, not-explicitly-known, difficult-to-expresses knowledge), organized in ways that can be reproduced and shared within collectivities. This sort of knowledge, Ober (2008a) states, is capable of producing, when put to appropriate use through reutilization and innovative deployment, substantial political and economic effects that lead to the flourishing of the community. Aggregation, distribution and (through integration) anew creation of such knowledge is achieved through the intense interaction people have in political fora (e.g. in the Assembly, magisterial boards, etc.), but also in other occasions, such as economic (in the *agora*), social (e.g. in public festivals and theatrical performances), religious and athletic (e.g. Panathenaea, Dionysia, etc.), which were quite common in classical Athens (Ober 2000, 2008a).

In sum, public discourse is of paramount importance for effective decision-making in matters of public policy, since it enables diverse sorts of knowledge to be taken into account by the citizenry, while simultaneously aligns private interests across a common identity. We argue that public discourse is beneficial not only to the community but to the individual as well. As regards the community, the accumulation of knowledge due to public discourse would mean fewer costly mistakes in decision-making,[10] as well as lower implementation costs (since, a more informed assessment of the situation, rationalizes sacrifices and reduces social resistance). In turn, for the individual the benefits lie on the knowledge gained, enabling the pursuit of self-interest in line with the prevalent social and political values.

Public identity (or 'public culture', or 'public ideology'), in turn, refers to a pragmatic (in the philosophical meaning) set of social and political values held by

---

[8] Which are possible due to intervisibility among citizens, offered by public discourse under direct democracy.

[9] Given the high potential value of latent and tacit knowledge, and the difficulty of bringing it to the surface in a systematic way, this constitutes a major advantage of direct democracy over other regimes.

[10] This resembles the application of the Condorcet jury theorem to politics, stating simply that "non-specialist" voters come to correct decisions under simple majority rule.

the citizenry.[11] This set of values has no metaphysical or universal existence outside the ongoing collective experience. In these terms, public identity is essentially: operative (aiming to confront real problems faced by the collectivity), contingent (in the sense that it is the outcome of the conscious and unconscious behaviour of the agents of the past), and dynamic (recursively evolving by current agents in their daily lives as a response to external and internal conditions). With specific reference to the classical Athens, scholars (e.g. Ober 1989, 1993, 2000, 2008b; Bitros and Karayiannis 2008; Karayiannis and Hatzis 2012) acknowledge that, since the beginning of the fifth century, ordinary citizens had developed a fairly cohesive and engrained democratic public identity[12] capable of aligning individual behaviour and eliminating many of the collective action problems associated with individuals seeking their own interest. This identity was based on the values of 'freedom', 'equality', 'security' and 'loyalty'.

Freedom (*qua* lack of dependency) of speech and behaviour signified that all citizens were free to attend and participate in public fora, to express and adhere to their own opinion with regard to matters of public concern, as well as to pursue their own interests in the economic life (within the boundaries of legal and moral norms), by owning property, being employed as they pleased, engaging in voluntary transactions, even setting up business partnerships. Equality of opportunity and action signified that all citizens independent of their class, education or wealth had an equal standing before the law and the state (in terms of public obligations) an equal access to, and voice (vote) in, collective decision-making. Security of human and property rights signified that all people were legally protected against unfair treatment and assault, and the rights of private property (use, usufruct, alteration, transfer, etc.) were clearly defined and credibly respected[13] (and enforced) by the state, even in times of national emergency (such as this followed the Peloponnesian War). Finally, loyalty to the *polis* signified commitment for the defense of the

[11] Of course we do not mean here by *all* citizens. A public identity should be embraced and performed by a lot of people, but not necessarily by *all* of them or *all* the time (Ober 2008a). In these terms its strength lies on its ability to be open enough for the development and voicing of honestly dissident opinions and the incorporation of different viewpoints and mentalities that naturally exist within any community.

[12] That such a strongly embedded and stable public identity did exist in Athens (during the fifth and fourth centuries) can be inferred from the fact that it survived the catastrophic aftermath of the Peloponnesian War. In 404, an aristocratic regime (the so-called Thirty Tyrants) was imposed by Sparta which abolished democracy. This regime was brusquely ended a few months later (in 403) by a popular revolt (with the active participation of the aristocratic elite), and Athens returned to democracy until its defeat by Macedon.

[13] Despite the fears of certain members of the wealthy elite (i.e. aristocratic or rich citizens), in democratic Athens no attempt was ever made to coercively redefine property rights, redistribute private property, or to cancel debts (Jones 1958; Ober 1993; Bitros and Karayiannis 2008; Karayiannis and Hatzis 2012). The fact that the state was 'credibly committed' to the security of private property rights helps to explain why the regime, in contrast to others, was at once so cohesive and so stable. Yet, public identity had found other (non-coercive, moral) ways to encourage voluntary redistribution of wealth and to limit wealth inequality (cf. below).

fatherland, respect for the institutions and principles of the democratic state, and duty towards the good and the prosperity of the community.

Before closing with public identity it is important to highlight two points. First, the aforementioned values were engrained (internalized) in the behaviour of the citizenry through education[14] and enforcement by social and legal sanctions (since misbehaviour was relatively ease to observe), enabling to eliminate individuals' free riding on others' cooperative behaviour (Ober 2000). Second, despite ordinary citizens' ideological hegemony, elite mentality was not completely eliminated in Athens. Rather, specific attributes of it had been channelled to serve the public benefit. For instance, 'conspicuous consumption', *a la* Veblen (1899), and elite generosity (*kalokagathia*) were directed into voluntary contributions to impoverish fellows and to the state (for the provision of public goods), using public honours, inter-elite competition, and judgment by the mass of ordinary citizens (Ober 1993).

11.3 The Qualities and Workings of Direct Democracy

On the basis of the above qualifications let us now discuss the qualities of direct democracy as an institution. A key feature of direct democracy is that it enables the internalization of externalities in at least two occasions. First, the costs and benefits of decision-making are internalized, since each citizen-voter is himself directly accountable for the policies undertaken (in contrast to other regimes where policies are decided and imposed on citizens by an external authority). On these grounds, each decision-maker bears directly on his welfare the result of his personal decisions. Given the continuous nature of policy-making under direct democracy, this gives citizens a pecuniary incentive[15] (besides ideological and social dictates[16]) to invest on knowledge necessary for decision-making, to actively engage in the political and policy-making process, and to seek to overcome problems of political coordination and collective action.[17] As such, citizens of direct democracy are expected to be more knowledgeable, more motivated and mobilized, more politically mature and active and to show an inclination toward cooperation and

[14] In classical Athens public education was provided in the form of subsidized theatrical performances (Kyriazis 2009). These performances taught to Athenians social values, ethical norms, mores and morals, history and religion.

[15] Supported, in the case of Athens, by mechanisms of reinforcement and punishment, such as pay for participation and fines for abstaining (see Aristophanes 1911, 2004).

[16] It must be stressed again that Athenian citizens did not participate in political activity solely driven by economic motives (i.e. to increase or to safeguard their personal wealth). Rather, the public identity values of freedom, equality and loyalty (cf. above) were deeply ingrained in their identity, dictating their behavior and providing a measure of meaning to their life.

[17] A behavior which should have been enhanced by the accumulated educational experience of participating in public fora, teaming up with others in public ventures, and serving in the public offices.

conciliation. All these, *inter alia*, account for the mitigation, if not elimination, of the well-known problems of shirking, free-riding and principal-agent (Lyttkens 1994; Ober 1989, 2008a), which are apparent in other regimes.

This brings us to the second instance of internalization of externalities under direct democracy, which concerns learning and knowledge. As mentioned, citizens, due to their dual status as decision-makers and directly decision-bearers and the repetitive character of policy-making, have high incentives to acquire information to enhance their learning, and to increase their knowledgebase. Moreover, the (relative) social normalization achieved by the equitable allocation of political powers, the alignment of interests forged by both public discourse and public identity, and the overall stability of the system (enhanced by the security of property rights), come to ensure that, individual knowledge will be spread in and shared within the citizenry, that the accumulated public knowledge will be applied in solving the problems the collectivity encounters, and that the same collective knowledge may be employed again to innovatively confront other problems that come across. In a sense, in this continuous course of policy-making and welfare pursuit, knowledge accumulation and learning are being built into the system (i.e. internalized), whereas both the individual and the collectivity as a whole become more expert.[18] On these grounds, it can be asserted that the knowledge accumulation and learning are greater in direct democracy as compared to other regimes, simply because the net gains (benefits minus costs) accruing to both the individual and the society are positive and higher (Ober 2008a). This is despite the fact that the overall learning and knowledge costs incurred to the individuals (known as decision-making costs) would be higher in direct democracy as compared to other regimes (Buchanan and Tullock 1962).

Given these qualities let us now outline the workings and effects of direct democracy on public policy making. A unique characteristic of direct democracy is that any citizen may come out as an initiator of a policy, in the sense that he[19] can put forward a motion, which can be adopted or rejected by the citizenry through direct voting. At any time, the set of available policy options is expected to be richer, as compared with all other regimes, simply because those which are allowed to initiate a motion are relatively more (in fact, all citizens and not just political parties, oligarchies, kings, etc.), more motivated, and more informed and knowledgeable (since both individual and collective knowledge is increased and refined as a result of public discourse and public identity). As such, direct democracy, in contrast to other regimes, exhibits a variety of options, and as a consequence, is characterized by considerable flexibility and adaptability, along with relative consistency and stability afforded by the existing (democratic) public identity and

[18] Keep in mind that knowledge is possessed by individuals, but is nurtured in social networks and reproduced by institutionalized processes, both of which were strong in the Athenian democracy (Ober 2008a).

[19] The pronoun "he" applies literally in the Athenian democracy (and so it is used here instead of the politically connect form "she"), because, as mentioned, citizens were only (native, adult) males.

institutional apparatus.[20] The high number of available options, of course, does not necessarily mean that the best choices would always be adopted (i.e. those which indeed maximize utility). This is because citizens are bounded-rational,[21] and therefore they may adopt a policy proposal which ex-ante is deemed to suit their interests, but they may be proven wrong ex-post (at least, simply because conditions have changed). The same, of course, is the case with the other regimes, which, in addition, lack such flexibility and plurality in choices.

The agent of policy choice is the individual citizen-voter (and therefore, the ultimate decision maker), which is characterized by self-interested, utility-maximizing, bounded rationality (Lyttkens 1997, 2010; Christensen 2003; Farenga 2006; Ober 2008a; Kyriazis 2009). Such a rational voter applies economic calculus to reach his decision (under information and cognitive constraints, and in line with the prevailing public identity), assessing all alternative public-policy options on the basis of the net gains they offer. The enlargement of knowledgebase enables voters to be more confident of their choices; due to the more accurate assessment of the risks and prospective results. In turn, the security and stability of political and property rights they enjoy ensure that the results will be fully attributed to them, and equitably shared among the citizenry.

Through a process of trial and error and the continuous calculation of welfare at each point in time by every citizen-voter, new policies can be adopted, while less successful ones are set aside. This may well lead to the alteration of the institutional apparatus: obsolete and ill-suited institutions may be abolished, others may be transformed and adapted, and new ones may be introduced, to serve better the emerging situation. These institutional changes are functions of, or linked to, the new set of policies that is put in force. In this continuous process, rigid path dependence and institutional lock-in (associated with declining efficiency) can also be broken (as a result of public discourse and the enhanced knowledgebase/expertise of both the individual and the community) setting the conditions for economic growth and the prosperity of the *polis* (Kyriazis and Zouboulakis 2004; Kyriazis 2007; Kyriazis and Karayiannis 2011). Scholars who have explored these issues in classical Greece have highlighted the important role played towards this end by institutional changes that lowered transaction costs and delivered secure and

[20] It was been acknowledged that these qualities are reflected not only in the political but also in the economic and the legal processes and outcomes (Ober 2008a; Karayiannis and Hatzis 2012).

[21] Agency is bounded by informational constraints, structural uncertainty, the limited cognitive capacity of the human mind, and the structure of the social environment within which it functions (Simon 1956, 1959). The latter indicates that agents are self-consciously reflexive about their preferences and sensitive to societal norms, values and morals. Interestingly, Lanni (2009: 725) provides an excellent discussion of the Athenian legal system where compliance to society's norms, values, etc. might be seen as a rational response, since Athenians "...could be sanctioned again and again for the same legal or extra-statutory norm violation in every future lawsuit". On these grounds it was in one's own interest to adhere to the societal norms throughout his life rather than risk that a violation would be (sooner or later) brought up in court.

credible (on the part of the state) property rights (see Cohen 1992; Morris 2004; Ober 2008a, 2010; Lyttkens 2010; Karayiannis and Hatzis 2012).

Once the voting and policy-making procedures go on for some time, and direct democracy works its wonder to deliver economic prosperity to citizens, the regime entrenches and reinforces itself (by building up credibility and trust). It can be argued that this constitutes a kind of "fundamental transformation" (*a la* Williamson 1979) of the polity, since specific investments (sunk costs) have been made and specialized assets have been developed by both the individual and the society (capital, knowledge, skills), which deter return to previous regimes (tyranny, oligarchy or aristocracy). This is because such a reversion would, *inter alia*, entail depreciation of the assets developed, and a consequent welfare loss for the society.

Summing up our discussion up to this point we can argue that direct democracy supports equitable allocation of political powers, clear specification and protection of property rights, relative alignment of interests, successful generation and diffusion of knowledge (i.e. relatively symmetric information), and easiness in interaction and cooperation (i.e. low transaction costs), all of which are essential for collective action towards growth and prosperity, as classical Athens clearly testifies (Ober 2008a, 2010). The key agent of the system is the individual (voter/decision-maker) who freely, directly and continuously expresses his preferences on matters of public policy to incur in person its effects, internalizing in this way the benefits and costs of decision-making. On these grounds, the costs of individual participation are overbalanced in the long term by the higher returns of collective action accrued by (vital) public knowledge accumulation and its innovative (re-) deployment in appropriate policy-making. If these arguments hold, then direct democracy can be seen as a continuous, dynamic, cooperative "game", capable of producing substantial political and economic effects relevant to the flourishing of an organized community.

11.4 A Simple Model of Public Choice Under Direct Democracy

Moving to the formulation of a simple public-choice model in Athenian democracy policy-making, let us assume that at the time when the "game" begins there is a set of policy options available to the citizenry. Then, someone (i.e. the initiator) may come with a fresh idea proposing a new policy, which enriches the available choice set at the next period of the game. As argued, this is an essential function of direct democracy (and constitutes the necessary condition of our model), and we expect this to continue as long as the regime runs effectively. For the sake of simplicity we suppose that only one motion is put forward each time, although, as noticed, more options can be proposed at the same time by one or more initiators. Moreover, although the introduction of a new policy option may require alterations to the existing policy set (e.g. some existing practices may need to be adjusted or simply to fall into disuse), this is to take place in subsequent steps and periods of the game.

In order to cast his vote on the option put forward, and given the existing conditions at the time, each decision-maker makes an ex-ante calculation of the prospective personal costs and benefits (in a rather forward-looking manner—see Nordhaus et al. 1989). When he concludes that the proposed policy is going to increase his welfare more than the existing ones, then he votes for it. If it gets a simple majority vote, it is then adopted and implemented by the Assembly (sufficient condition of our model). This means that the proposal put to the vote as a single option should get more than half of positive ('yes') votes, whereas in choosing between alternatives (two at a time) it should get the plurality of them.

During the next period of time each voter compares his ex-ante expected welfare situation under the new policy with his actual ex-post situation after its implementation. If he is satisfied[22] with the results, he will continue to support the new policy. If not, he will vote against it during one of the next periods; an option available in direct democracy.

Moreover, as the game continues, another option might come into play, that of some citizens offering compensation to others for their eventual loss caused by the new policy (i.e. 'logrolling').[23] Thus, even some voters whose initial cost-benefit calculation may be unfavourable to the new policy might be induced to vote for it, if some others which are in favour offer them sufficient compensation out of their own welfare gains (a situation resembling the Kaldor-Hicks approach to economic efficiency). Or, stated somewhat differently, the voters in favour of the proposed policy will commit themselves that in a future period will vote (even though this goes against their own interests) for a policy favouring those voters who are now against, in return of the latter's present support for it. These cases increase the efficiency of the system and boost network ties among voters, turning the game into a cooperative one.[24]

Conclusions

Drawing on classical Athens the paper explored the attributes and mechanisms of direct democracy as an institution and developed a simple model of public choice to analyze policy-making. On its grounds, it looked into the motives, processes and consequences of decision-making in classical Athens,

(continued)

[22] "Satisfied" means here that his ex-post welfare is the same as calculated ex-ante, or even higher, which are clear cases of the voter sticking with the new strategy. If the ex-post welfare is less than that expected ex-ante, the voter may still support the strategy, if he still regards that this welfare is superior to the welfare of the alternative strategies or if he expects some gains in the future (e.g. due to logrolling).

[23] Although there are good reasons to question its expedience (see Basu 2007).

[24] This has been recognized by Buchanan and Tullock (1962) and Greif (2006), among others.

ascertaining that under direct democracy individuals embrace policies which further both their own interests and the overall welfare of the community.

The paper started by outlining the qualities and workings of direct democracy based on the concepts of public discourse and public identity. The former refers to the reciprocal communication among citizens enabling, *inter alia*, the integration of diverse knowledge they possess and the coordination of collective action. The latter refers to a pragmatic set of collective values (i.e. emerged dialectically as a result of ongoing collective experiences) enabling to reduce diversity of thought and behaviour and with it many of the collective action problems that communities encounter. With public discourse and public identity as cornerstones, direct democracy as an institution is able to exhibit flexibility and adaptability along with relative stability and security. Flexibility is achieved through plurality in knowledge and agency options, whereas stability is afforded by the relative fixity and hegemony of the democratic public identity and the institutional apparatus.

Overall we have argued that the system of direct democracy is characterized by equitable distribution of political powers, credible protection of property rights, innovative creation and dissemination of knowledge (i.e. fairly symmetric information), expediency in interaction and cooperation (i.e. low transaction costs), and effective coordination and alignment of interests, all of which are essential for collective action towards growth and prosperity, as the case of classical Athens clearly testifies. This is because the costs of individual participation are overbalanced by the higher returns of collective action accrued by (vital) public knowledge accumulation and its innovative (re-)deployment in the formation of problem-solving, growth-promoting institutions. The key mechanism of the system is the ability of the individual voter/decision-maker to freely, directly and continuously express his preferences on matters of public policy, and as such to incur personally the effect of his choice, internalizing in this way the benefits and costs of decision-making.

References

Altman D (2011) Direct democracy worldwide. Cambridge University Press, Cambridge
Amemiya T (2007) Economy and economics of ancient Greece. Routledge, London
Aristophanes (1911) Acharnians of Aristophanes. Blackwell, Oxford
Aristophanes (2004) The Ecclesiazusae. Kessinger, Kila
Arvanitidis AP, Kyriazis N (2012) Public choice, economy and war in classical Athens. In: 16th Annual international conference on economics and security, Cairo, June 2012
Basu K (2007) Coercion, contract and the limits of the market. Social Choice Welfare 29:559–579
Bitros GC, Karayiannis AD (2006) The liberating power of entrepreneurship in ancient Athens. In: Cassis Y, Pepelasis-Minoglou I (eds) Country studies in entrepreneurship: a historical perspective. Palgrave, London, pp 11–24

Bitros GC, Karayiannis AD (2008) Values and institutions as determinants of entrepreneurship in ancient Athens. J Inst Econ 4(2):205–230
Bitros GC, Karayiannis AD (2010) Morality, institutions and the wealth of nations: some lessons from ancient Greece. Eur J Polit Econ 26:68–81
Bitros GC, Karayiannis AD (2012) The city-state of Athens as a prototype for an entrepreneurial and managerial society. In: Prastacos GP, Wang F, Soderquist KE (eds) Leadership and management in a changing world: lessons from Ancient east and west philosophy. Springer, Heidelberg, pp 289–304
Bitros GC, Karayiannis AD (2013) Creative crisis in democracy and economy. Springer, Berlin
Blume L, Müller J, Voigt S (2009) The economic effects of direct democracy—a first global assessment. Public Choice 140:431–461
Buchanan J, Tullock G (1962) The calculus of consent: logical foundations of constitutional democracy. University of Michigan Press, Ann Arbor, MI
Burke EM (2010) Finances and the operation of the Athenian democracy in the 'Lycurgan Era'. Am J Philol 131:393–423
Cartledge P, Cohen EE, Foxhall L (eds) (2002) Money, labour, and land: approaches to the economies of ancient Greece. Routledge, London
Christensen P (2003) Economic rationalism in fourth-century BCE Athens. Greece Rome 50:31–56
Cohen EE (1990) Commercial lending by Athenian Banks: cliometric fallacies and forensic methodology. Class Philol 85:177–190
Cohen EE (1992) Athenian economy and society: a banking perspective. Princeton University Press, Princeton, NJ
Farenga V (2006) Citizens and self in ancient Greece: performing justice and the law. Cambridge University Press, Cambridge
Feld LP, Savioz MR (1997) Direct democracy matters for economic performance: an empirical investigation. Kyklos 50:507–538
Figueira TJ (1998) The power of money: coinage and politics in the Athenian Empire. University of Pennsylvania Press, Philadelphia, PA
Finley MI (1985) Studies in land and credit in ancient Athens, 500–200 BC: The horos inscriptions, 2nd edn. Transaction, New Brunswick
French A (1991) Economic conditions in fourth-century Athens. Greece Rome 38:24–40
Frey B (1994) Direct democracy: politico-economic lessons from Swiss experience. Am Econ Rev 84:338–342
Greif A (2006) Institutions and the path to the modern economy: lessons from medieval trade. Cambridge University Press, Cambridge
Hansen MH (1999) The Athenian democracy in the age of demosthenes: structures, principles, and ideology, 2nd edn. Bristol Classical Press, Bristol
Hansen MH (2006) Polis: an introduction to the ancient Greek City-state. Oxford University Press, Oxford
Harris EM (1988) When is a sale not a sale? The riddle of Athenian terminology for real security revisited. Classical Q 38:351–381
Harris EM (1993) Apotimema: Athenian terminology for real security in leases and dowry agreements. Classical Q 43:73–95
Harris EM (2006) Democracy and the rule of law in classical Athens: essays on law, society, and politics. Cambridge University Press, Cambridge
Jones AHM (1958) Athenian democracy. Frederick Praeger, New York, NY
Kaiser BA (2007) The Athenian trierarchy: mechanism design for the private provision of public goods. J Econ Hist 67:445–480
Karayiannis AD (1992) Entrepreneurship in classical Greek literature. S Afr J Econ 60:67–93
Karayiannis AD, Hatzis AN (2012) Morality, social norms and the rule of law as transaction cost-saving devices: the case of ancient Athens. Eur J Law Econ 33:621–643

Kaufmann B, Büchi R, Braun N (2010) Guidebook to direct democracy, in Switzerland and beyond. The Initiative and Referendum Institute Europe, Marburg
Kyriazis N (2007) Democracy and institutional change. Eur Res Stud 10:65–82
Kyriazis N (2009) Financing the Athenian State: public choice in the age of demosthenes. Eur J Law Econ 27:109–127
Kyriazis N, Karayiannis A (2011) Democracy, institutional changes and economic development the case of ancient Athens. J Econ Asymmetries 8:61–92
Kyriazis N, Zouboulakis M (2004) Democracy, sea power and institutional change: an economic analysis of the Athenian Naval Law. Eur J Law Econ 17:117–132
Lanni A (2009) Social norms in the courts of ancient Athens. J Legal Anal 1:691–736
Lyttkens CH (1994) A predatory democracy: an essay on taxation in classical Athens. Explor Econ Hist 31:62–90
Lyttkens CH (1997) A rational-actor perspective on the origin of liturgies in ancient Greece. J Inst Theor Econ 153:462–483
Lyttkens CH (2010) Institutions, taxation, and market relationships in ancient Athens. J Inst Econ 6(4):505–527
Manning JG, Morris I (eds) (2005) The ancient economy, evidence and models. Stanford University Press, Stanford
Matsusaka J (2004) For the many or the few: the initiative, public policy, and American democracy. University of Chicago Press, Chicago, IL
Matsusaka J (2005) Direct democracy works. J Econ Persp 19:185–206
Millett P (1991) Lending and borrowing in ancient Athens. Cambridge University Press, Cambridge
Morris I (1994) The Athenian economy twenty years after the ancient economy. Classical Philol 89:351–366
Morris I (2004) Economic growth in ancient Greece. J Inst Theor Econ 160:709–742
Nevett LC (2000) A real estate 'market' in classical Greece? The example of town housing. Ann Br School Athens 95:329–343
Nordhaus WD, Alesina A, Schultze CL (1989) Alternative approaches to the political business cycle. Brookings Pap Econ Act 1989:1–68
Ober J (1989) Mass and elite in democratic Athens: rhetoric, ideology, and the power of the people. Princeton University Press, Princeton, NJ
Ober J (1993) Public speech and the power of the people in democratic Athens. Polit Sci Politics 26:481–486
Ober J (2000) Quasi-rights: participatory citizenship and negative liberties in democratic Athens. Soc Philos Policy 17:27–61
Ober J (2008a) Democracy and knowledge: innovation and learning in classical Athens. Harvard University Press, Harvard
Ober J (2008b) What the ancient Greeks can tell us about democracy. Ann Rev Polit Sci 11:67–91
Ober J (2010) Wealthy Hellas. Trans Am Philol Assoc 140:241–286
Pallinger ZT, Kaufmann B, Marxer W, Schiller T (eds) (2007) Direct democracy in Europe: developments and prospects. VS Verlag, Wiesbaden
Rhodes PJ (2006) A history of the classical Greek world: 478–323 B.C. Blackwell, Oxford
Schaps DM (2004) The invention of coinage and the monetization of ancient Greece. University of Michigan Press, Ann Arbor, MI
Shipton KMW (1997) The private banks in fourth-century BC Athens: a reappraisal. Classical Q 47:396–422
Shipton KMW (2000) Leasing and lending: the cash-economy in fourth-century BC Athens. Institute of Classical Studies, London
Shrivastava M (2012) Relevance of direct democracy in the contemporary world. Res J Human Soc Sci 3:100–106
Simon HA (1956) Rational choice and the structure of environments. Psychol Rev 63 129–138

Simon HA (1959) Theories of decision-making in economics and behavioural science. Am Econ Rev 49:253–283

Thompson WE (1979) A view of Athenian banking. Museum Helveticum 36:224–241

Thompson WE (1983) The Athenian entrepreneur. Antiquite Classique 51:53–85

Tridimas G (2011) A political economy perspective of direct democracy in ancient Athens. Const Polit Econ 22:58–82

Veblen T (1899) The theory of the leisure class: an economic study of institutions. Macmillan, New York, NY

von Reden S (1997) Money, law and exchange: coinage in the Greek polis. J Hellenic Stud 117:154–176

Williamson OE (1979) Transaction-cost economics: the governance of contractual relations. J Law Econ 22:233–261

Wilson P (2000) The Athenian Institution of the Khoregia: the chorus, the city, and the stage. Cambridge University Press, Cambridge

Chapter 12
The Glue of Democracy: Economics, Warfare and Values in Classical Greece

Nicholas C. Kyriazis, Xenophon Paparrigopoulos, and Emmanouil-Marios L. Economou

12.1 Introduction

A fourth century Athenian orator, Demades, said that the *theorika* (payments out of the Athenian budget to the poorer citizens, to allow them to participate at the main Assembly days (40 per year) and to watch the 4 days theatrical contests, was the "glue of democracy" (Plutarch *Moralia* 1011b)), sought to establish a community of interests in favour of democracy. The *theorika* made the majority of poorer citizens to have a stake in democracy.

Rich citizens on the other hand were also satisfied in general with democracy in the classical Athenian period (fifth–fourth centuries) although they were taxed through the system of *liturgies*, which had (again for the first time in history) a redistributive function (Hansen 1983, 1999). Rich and medium income citizens profited also from the general economic development in Athens, and apparently also in other maritime city-states (for which we have only fragmented information) such as the islands of Naxos, Samos and Chios in the Aegean sea, Megara in the northern section of the Isthmus of Corinth or Akragas and the major city of Syracuse in Sicily, or Croton in today's south Italy etc. (Robinson 1997; Raauflaub and Wallace 2008) and so were willing to support (or at least accept) direct democracy.

But direct democracy as a political institution is much older than the introduction of the first *theorika* at the time of Pericles (after 450 BC). One of the preconditions for the emergence of democracy was the new type of warrior, the *hoplites* and the new tactics that were developed as the most suitable form to accommodate the hoplites. The new battle tactical formation, the *phalanx*, led to the development of new values and ideals in the field of battle, which, once established, became widely

N.C. Kyriazis • X. Paparrigopoulos • E.-M.L. Economou (✉)
Department of Economics, University of Thessaly, Korai 43 Street, PC 38333 Volos, Greece
e-mail: Nkyr@uth.gr; emmoikon@uth.gr

G.C. Bitros, N.C. Kyriazis (eds.), *Essays in Contemporary Economics*,
DOI 10.1007/978-3-319-10043-2_12

accepted, and thus were introduced also in the political field. These were the values on which direct democracy rested.

We maintain that no democracies developed without the existence of hoplites and phalanxes. But, in some cases, like Sparta, hoplites and phalanxes did not lead to full democracy, while in others it did. So, the emergence of the hoplites and the phalanx seems to be a necessary but not a sufficient condition for the emergence of democracy. A further analysis of the ancient Greek city-states shows that those that transformed themselves into seapowers and maritime states, tended to be also democracies. Apart from Athens, the relationship between seapower and democracy finds its most clear example with the case of the island of Rhodes. Since 395 BC and then, democratic reforms became deeper and went hand in hand with the existence of strong navy and the rise of maritime commerce (Robinson 2011). Thus, seapower seems to be an almost sufficient condition for the emergence and endurance of democracy in classical times, and we explain this as being due to the establishment of a community of mainly economic interests.

Although the *hoplite* and the phalanx were the main elements in the establishment in the new mind-set ideas and values, it was not the only one. Other elements were the city-state environment, leading in most case to face to face cultures, religion and sports. Greek religion was "democratic" in its working, as portrayed by the Assembly of the gods were women goddess had equal speaking and voting rights, as well as the absence of an established caste of priests (Kyriazis and Economou 2012a). Sports also, as institutionalised in various athletic games as the Olympics, Nemean, Pythian, Panathenean, Isthmian, Heraean etc. contributed to an egalitarian set of values and ideas (Kyriazis and Economou 2012b, 2013a).

The essay is organised as follows: In the first section, we trace the development of the hoplites, the introduction of the phalanx as a battle formation, and its economic basis. In the second, we discuss the emergence of new values and how these values were transferred to the political field, and led to the introduction of democracy and to democratic values. In the third, we analyse the emergence of Athens as a maritime power, the link between seapower and democratic values and the community of interests on which the durability of democracy was based. This is followed by our conclusions.

12.2 The Hoplites, the Phalanx and the Emergence of New Values

"The connection between democracy and the militia principle has long been recognized; it takes little insight to perceive that those who vote for war also commit themselves to fight in it".[1] That this is not universally true is demonstrated

[1] See John Keegan, Introduction to Victor Davis Hanson, *The Western Way of War* (Berkeley and Los Angeles: University of California Press, 2009) xii.

by the fact that during the fourth century BC, Athens and many other city-states voted for war, but used mainly mercenaries. So, the commitment was for financial resources first, and for military service sometimes as a second. A particularly strong example is the Phoceans, who decided on war, plundered the treasure of the oracle at Delphi, and used the proceeds to buy the services of mercenaries (Sakellariou 1972). What has been not sufficiently analysed, as far as we know, is that the emergence of the hoplites and the phalanx led to particular values on which democracy was based. These values that emerged on the battlefield became democratic values.

The hoplite, the heavily armed infantryman emerged during the late geometric age (during the eighth century BC and later). He was armed with a heavy round shield, the *hoplon* (from which he took his name) that covered the body up to the upper legs, greaves, a bronze or leather armour for his torso and back, and a bronze helmet at the time usually of the Corinthian type which enclosed his head, leaving only slits for his eyes (Despotopoulos 1972; Sekunda 1986). Offensive weapons were a spear with an iron tip on a 2–3 m wooden shaft and a short sword (Kyriazis and Paparrigopoulos 2012).

This equipment was new, and unique, developing only in central and southern Greece, linked both to economic and geographic factors. The economic one was the establishment of independent farmers, who owned the land they cultivated and were not tenants or slaves. The most prosperous of them could afford the hoplites equipment, which was financed and owned by them. The geographic factor was the morphology of the area, which did not favour the development of large bodies of cavalry, as in eastern countries, but also the area of Thessaly in central Greece. The areas were hoplites developed lacked adequate pasturelands for large herds of horses. Lighter types of infantry like archers, javelin throwers and slingers could have developed, and were used, but only in small numbers, their use not being a battle deciding factor. We believe that this was due to the fact that the new hoplites defensive armour offered adequate protection against the offensive power of the light infantry's weapons. Also, even when the hoplites confronted cavalry, either Greek (Thessalians) or foreign (Persians) they usually emerged victorious, partly also because ancient cavalry (at least to the second half of the fourth century) lacked offensive power against the phalanx formation.[2] Ancient cavalrymen were inhibited in their stability on horseback because they lacked stirrups and adequate saddles (in contrast to e.g., medieval knights).

In order to be effective, the hoplites had to be used in new efficient formations. So, the phalanx emerged, a new and revolutionary formation. Up to then, both in Greece and in the east, battles were decided in individual "melées", where aristocrats battled usually each other and also mixed in battle against each other, as

---

[2] The first indications that the phalanx formation could intercept a cavalry formation became obvious as early as 510 BC, before the Greek-Persian wars of 490–479 BC, when the Spartan phalanx intercepted the Thessalian cavalry by using special techniques (mainly by amplifying its flanks). See Alfred S. Bradford, *Leonidas and the Kings of Sparta: Mightiest Warriors, Fairest Kingdom* (Santa Barbara, California: ABC-CLIO, 2011) p. 69.

Homer vividly portrays these combats. In the east, archery both from horsemen and infantry, was the battle-deciding weapon, and close hand-to-hand combat occurred only when one of the adversaries had been weakened. Due to this type of combat, ancient eastern armies (with the exception of very few noblemen, kings and their close relatives and bodyguards) lacked heavy defensive armament. Their shields were usually smaller and lighter than the hoplon, their body armour consisted of mainly leather with sometimes metal scales, or none at all, and their helmets covered, if carried, only the top of the head, leaving the face unprotected (Sekunda 1992; Healy 1991, 1992).

The Greek phalanx was a tight formation, usually 8–10 ranks deep, where every hoplite covered 1 m^2 of ground. Each hoplite covered, with his shield (carried on his left arm) not only himself but the right unprotected spear side of the hoplite standing to his left, while his own right side was covered by the shield of the hoplite standing on his right. During battle, the second to the last ranks (except, that is, the "front" line) trusted the external sides of their shields on the backs of the hoplite in front of them, pushing forward, and being pushed by the hoplite behind them, in a tactic called "othismos". Thus, the phalanx developed great strength in thrust, becoming a compact body that could push back in hand to hand fighting any other army type (cavalry or infantry) not being thus equipped, as demonstrated during the Greek–Persian Wars. As Xenophon (Hellenica 7.1.38) wrote there were no Asians "able to stand up to Greeks in battle", except of course other Greek phalanxes.

Victor Davis Hanson in his The Western Way of War asserts on the issue of the strength of the phalanx that "these men were the first we know of to relegate cavalry to a secondary role and thus to suppress for a thousand years to come the notion that the battlefield was the private domain of aristocratic horsemen. Nor did they have any liking for the landless poor, who were skilled only in missile attack. The hoplite class of the Greek classical age chose to ignore the low and the javelin in preference for the spear and massive bronze armour in a desire to eliminate entirely the critical "distance that elsewhere traditionally separated men in battle" (Hanson 2009, p. 17).

We do not have any extant data concerning the cost of the equipment of the hoplite, but it must have been relatively expensive. Only relatively well-off free landowners could afford it. Ancient Athens during the Persian invasions, for which we possess some information, permits us at least to estimate the number of hoplites and their percentage as to the total number of citizens. We know from Herodotus (*Histories* 6. 94–140) that the Athenian army at Marathon was 9,000–10,000 strong. Assuming that some (perhaps 2,000?) older classes of hoplites stayed behind at Athens as a reserve, we arrive at an estimate of 11,000–12,000 hoplites in 490 BC, the year of the battle.

Some additional information given by Herodotus for the year 482 BC, when Themistocles Naval Law was voted (and which as far as we know has not been used before) permits us a calculation of number of Athenian citizens. The Athenian Assembly voted for the construction of 100 warships (triremes) at a cost of a talent each, a talent being the equivalent of 6,000 drachmae. This gives a total cost for the naval shipbuilding programme of 600,000 drachmae. We also know, that another proposal was put forward to the Assembly: The total sum should have been distributed on an equalitarian basis to all Athenian citizens, each citizen due to receive 10 drachmae. A division of the two sums (total cost by individual receipt) gives a total number of citizens for 482 BC of 60,000.

Thus, during the early fifth century, only one in five citizens (or 20 %) belonged to the well-off landowning farmers' class that could afford hoplite armour. We believe that, with perhaps small variations, this proportion must have characterised all city-states, with the exception of Sparta, where one could be a citizen only if he was a hoplite, called an "equal".

In Sparta, the concepts of citizen and warrior-hoplite, merged, while in the other city-states they had, as we will demonstrate in the next section, a close link.

12.3 Values of the Phalanx and Values of Democracy

A city-state culture was not a unique Greek development. 37 such cultures in Europe, Asia, Africa and Central America have been identified (Hansen 2006). What was unique for geometric and classical Greece, was the combination of city-state culture and the emergence of the heavily armed hoplite warrior and the phalanx formation.

The hoplite and the phalanx developed together with city-state culture during the late eighth to sixth centuries, and thus preceded by at about 200 years the emergence of democracy. Evidence from pottery painting (a mid-seventh century Corinthian wine amphora called the Chigi pottery, preserved in Villa Julia, Rome) shows hoplites battling in phalanx formations. It clearly shows that phalanx formations were already battling in full development during the seventh century and even more so during the Spartan–Messenian wars of the early sixth, while the first democracies emerged only during the beginning of the sixth century, in some Greek Asia Minor city-states, on which we have only fragmentary evidence, in Athens by Solon (594–593 BC) and as a fully developed democracy only by Cleisthenes in 510–507 BC and after Themistocles Naval Law of 482 BC (Ober 2008, Chaps. 2 and 3).

Thus, historical evidence points to an influence from the phalanx to democracy and not vice-versa, not even a development in parallel. Why should this be so? We maintain that this arose because the phalanx created a particular set of ideals and values, which then where translated in political values that shaped democracy. A widely held belief today is that democracy promotes individualism. This is true in the sense of safeguarding individual rights, but it was not true for the phalanx. Homeric aristocratic warriors were supreme individualists. Lightly armed ancient warriors, fighting in loose order, and with no such close contact as the hoplites in the phalanx, fought also relatively more as individuals, as did horsemen, who required more space between them to manoeuvre their horses.

As we analysed in the previous section, the phalanx formation was very compact. The hoplites were standing very close one to another, and the middle ranks actually touching one another through their shields on front and backs (Krentz 1985). In the phalanx, the hoplites were almost literally glued together. This close fitting order gave the phalanx its great strength, but it was a strength were individuals combined their personal strength into a greater, almost "transcendental" strength of the phalanx. In the phalanx warriors did not fight mainly as individuals, but as parts of a whole. The strength of the phalanx depended on unity.

In such a formation, individual skill and courage, were subordinate to compactness and order. The phalanx moves forward and pushes as one, as a mass of shields, bodies and spears. Individuals took courage from one another, step with the same speed, the Spartans introducing even drums and fifes in order to facilitate the phalanx's movement. In the phalanx, the first value that emerges is equality: Equality in equipment (due to similar economic background) in position, in danger, in purpose.

The main purpose is to impose the phalanx's will on the enemy, to push him back, to compel him to retreat, to break and abandon the field of battle. The phalanx, through its tactic of "othismos" develops a common purpose, a common will. This equality and common purpose gave the phalanx its cohesion. A solidarity and ties of camaraderie (Hanson 2009, Chaps. 12–13) a trust to the hoplite guarding your right, to the one pressing his shield on your back, as the hoplite on your left trusted you with his life. By the seventh century BC, the hoplites had proven their superiority on the battlefield against any other type of warrior and army, be it aristocratic horsemen, or charioteers (like in Mycenaean Greece or Egypt of the New Kingdom or the Assyrian empire) or archers, javelin throwers or slingers.

Having proven their supremacy in warfare, they became conscious of their strength also in politics. We do not know exactly how the process started and developed, but by the seventh century a big political transformation had taken place: kingships did no more exist in central and southern Greece, as they were the norm during the Bronze Age. They existed only in the fringes of the Greek world where the phalanx was not yet adopted, like Macedon and Epirus, and in the mixed system of Sparta. What emerged, were oligarchies, of the relatively well-off citizens, the majority of which were of the hoplite class, and tyrannies, were some individuals seized power, but were again supported usually by a majority of the well-off citizens, hoplite-landowners.[3]

By the end of the sixth century even this sort of political arrangement was deemed to be inadequate and a new from, direct democracy, was introduced. Democracy was based on transferring to the political sphere the values that had evolved and had been tested on the battlefield in the phalanx: The fact that the phalanx formation had developed as a means of self-defence of Greek city-states made necessary the participation in it the majority of citizens of each independent city-state, without any discrimination concerning the social status (Cartledge 1977).

[3] There were a few exceptions like the mid-sixth century Athenian Peisistratos, who it seem based his power in part at least to the poorer mountain dwelling Athenians and also to mercenaries. The fact that ancient historians point this out demonstrates that in their eyes it was an exception.

Thus, the value of equality which developed in the phalanx's ranks became equality in politics, e.g. equality in rights to vote, to be elected, but also legal rights.

Solidarity, trust and camaraderie in battle were transformed in trust and solidarity in the political field. You are prepared to listen, to accept somebody's opinion if you trust him with your life in battle, and you are willing to vote for him for public office and obey him for the duration of this office, as you do if you have elected and accepted him to lead you in battle. We do not know how military leaders were chosen up to the sixth century BC, but we do know that at least by the end of this century, in Athens, the military leaders, the *10 Strategoi* (Generals), each the head of the armed contingent of each of the ten Athenian tribes, were elected democratically (Stanton 1990, p. 19–20). So, election of military leaders might have again predated the introduction of democracy.

In democracy, in parallel to the above values, one supreme ideal was developed, the ideal of common purpose, or social cohesion, which we believe again is transplanting the common purpose and the common will of the phalanx in the field of politics.[4] In democracies, this supreme ideal was called *homonoia* (Plato *Republic* 5. 432A, 433C; Lysias *Speeches*. 25.30) literally "same-mindness".[5] Based again on this, the next "revolutionary" step in politics is no longer far, to base the validation of politics and the justification of democracy on the existence of a natural right that leads to the establishment of a social contract. Ancient Athenians did actually take this step in practise by the end of the fifth century. For example, Antiphon the sophist wrote the *Peri Homonoias*, fragments of which were discovered in the nineteenth century on a papyrus. On this fragment we have the first ever formulation of the theory of natural law and *Social Contract*. Pericles also, in his *Funeral Speech* (as given by Thucydides) illustrates the concept of homonoia among the ideals of democracy.[6]

[4] Aristotle, in a famous passage (Politics 1281b. 1–8) writes: "The many out of which none is great, may, when they assemble into a body, be better than the few, not each individually, but as a whole, like in the symposia that are organised by many together. As each of the many possesses an atom of virtue and knowledge, when they come together into a body, they become concerning ethics (morals) and thinking as one human, with many hands, many legs and many sensations". We believe that there could not be a better description of the phalanx, although Aristotle uses the passage as a justification of democracy. This again, is supporting our analysis of the relation between the phalanx and democracy.

[5] Homonoia is usually being translated as concord, but Paul Cartledge in a personal communication suggested to us that a better translation could be "same-mindness" and unanimity, which is stronger than concord. Another major value was isonomia, which refers to political systems were means equality in front of the law exists, but not electoral rights, to vote and be elected.

[6] There existed two Athenians by the name of Antiphon. The first one is the so-called Antiphon the sophist, known to posterity as a discussant with Socrates, (Xenophon *Memorabilia*) the second one being one of the "ten Athenian orators" of the so-called *Canon*. See Tsatsos (1972). For analytical view of the implementation of a social contract in practise through the fiscal expansionary policy programs of Euboulos and Lykourgos during the second half of the fourth century in ancient Athens, see Kyriazis and Economou (2013b).

The influence of values developed during two centuries of phalanx warfare on the emergence of democracy can be analysed also as a case of *bounded rationality*. (Simon 1991) Instead of searching for total new solutions in a new political setting, values that have been established through "trial and error" and tested on the battlefield are introduced and adopted in politics. Finding that these values are adequate in the new political settings, agents have no longer an incentive to devote further resources (time for information, trial and error etc.) to discover new ones (Kyriazis 2012).

The historical evidence and our analysis thus indicates that phalanx warfare antedated the introduction of democracy, and that values evolved in the phalanx evolved into democratic values. Still, there were historical cases were city-states using the phalanx were not democracies such as Sparta. Sparta had a particular "constitution". It was governed by two kings, who were usually but not always the military commanders, *five ephors*, who were more or less the governing body, *30 gerousiaste* who were a kind of senate, and a popular assembly of all adult male citizens, who voted on proposals made by the ephors, but only on a yes or no basis, without having the authority to introduce or change proposals (Rhodes 2007). On Sparta's values and norms Bitros and Karayannis (2010) offer a detailed analysis. Other city-states were oscillating between democracy—oligarchy and tyranny, as e.g. Argos, Syracuse, Halkis, Eretria, Istiaia and other city-states on the island of Euboea during the fourth century, and Messina, Catanae and many other city-states in Sicily and lower Italy during the fifth and sixth century.

Historical evidence indicates thus that although the phalanx was a necessary condition for democracy, it was not a sufficient one. The hoplites-landowners class showed ambivalence between democracy, "limited democracy" (e.g. democracy according to wealth criteria, like the Solonian Athenian of 560 BC, the short-lived 411 BC in Athens and the Athenian democracy after 322 BC) and oligarchy. During the fifth and fourth century some Greek city-states took a further decisive step, taking a "turn to the sea" (Kyriazis 2006). They transformed themselves from mainly land powers into sea-maritime powers. This transformation deepened democracy and gave it strength and durability.

Most ancient maritime city-states were democracies as long as they were maritime powers (with very short-lived non democratic "intermissions" as for Athens during 404–403 BC after the end of the Peloponnesian War). Samos, Corinth, Chios, Byzance, Rhodes (during the late fourth and third centuries) and of course Athens. Already, ancient authors, such as Aristotle (*Politics* 1304a18–24; 1274a12–14) had recognized the link between democracy and seapower (Theodorakopoulos 1972). In the following section we analyse why seapower is almost a sufficient condition for democracy.

12.4 Seapower, Democracy and Community of Interests

We analyse the relation of seapower, democracy and the community of interests with the case study of Athens, which was both the prototype democracy and for which we possess sufficient information from ancient sources to enable us to trace its transformation from a land to a seapower and from a tyranny into democracy.

During the sixth century, Athenian political history was chequered: Solon introduced a limited form of democracy in 594 BC, based on wealth criteria, which was abolished by the tyrant Pisistratus and his sons during 561–510 Then, Cleisthenes introduced a more encompassing form of democracy in 510–507, but still a limited one, because seemingly the poorer Athenians (about 80 % of the total according to our previous calculations) had the right to vote, but not yet the right to be elected (Burn 1984). In 482 BC, Themistocles introduced his *Naval Law*, which was voted in the Assembly and initiated Athens' "turn to the sea" (Kyriazis and Zouboulakis 2004; Hale 2011). For the next 160 years, up to the Athenian defeat by the Macedonian fleet at Amorgos in 322 BC, Athens was the dominant seapower in the Eastern Mediterranean and the most representative democracy of the time.

The Naval Law revolutionized Athenian politics. Each warship, the trireme, required under normal conditions 180 rowers, 12 hoplites (as "marines") 15 sailors (or "deck crew") the master, the *Keleustes* (who beat the drum setting the various speeds of the ship) and the commander called *trierarchos* (Morrison et al. 2000). The about 180 Athenian ships present at Salamis required thus 32,400 rowers, and these could be provided only by the lower income class Athenians, the *thetes*, who up to then did not have political rights and did not provide military service, lacking the means to acquire the expensive hoplite equipment (each hoplite had to buy his own armour by his own means in order to participate in the phalanx formation, see Raauflaub 2008, p. 129).

We suggest that in special cases, as in Salamis, where the proximity of the land provided the necessary water and alimentation, and the narrow straights, which did not permit much manoeuvring by the ships but mainly direct confrontation, as was the tactical intention of Themistocles, the Athenian and Greek ships in general would have carried more hoplites than the usual 12. Under normal conditions, 200 ships would require 2,400 hoplites. We know from Marathon that Athens had at least 10,000 hoplites, and it seems absurd if the rest of them stood idle while the decisive battle took place!

But as rowers, they provided, for the first time in Athenian history military service, and thus, as explicitly promised by Themistocles when he brought his proposal to the Assembly, they acquired full political rights. All state positions (e.g. "government", law courts, military ones) were open to them.[7] A trireme was a microcosm of Athenian society, combining all its elements: The 170 rowers from

[7] For the financing of the Athenian fleet through *trierarchy*, which was the most expensive liturgy, see Kaiser (2007) and Gabrielsen (2010 repr., Chaps. 1 and 8). For the economic effects of the Athenian turn to the sea, see Kyriazis and Zouboulakis (2004).

the poorer class, who on land could have been less prosperous farmers, unskilled workers working for a daily wage etc., 12 hoplites of the more prosperous classes (self-employed prosperous farmers but also some skilled workers and artisans, whose proportion increased rapidly as Athens was transformed from a mainly agricultural to a mainly "industrial" and "services" economy, see Halkos and Kyriazis 2010). The sailors who belonged also probably to the middle, "skilled" class, and three "officers", specialists who belonged to the prosperous upper classes. The ship's commander, the *trierarch*, certainly belonged to the wealthy class, and had to finance out of his own means the running expenses of the ship for one operational period (about 7–8 months per year).

With the Athenian transformation into a seapower, all its citizens gave military service (and not just our estimate of the 20 % wealthier ones who fought as hoplites) and acquired full political rights. Athens (and presumably the same applied to the other Greek seapowers) was no more an "elite democracy" of the relative by wealthier citizens, but an all-encompassing one. The values evolved in the phalanx, equality, trust, common purpose and will, applied also to the trireme's crew. The different groups of men on the ship had to combine into a whole in order to have an efficient fighting ship, on which victory and the survival of everybody depended. The important point is that these common values extended now also to the poorer citizens, who before were excluded as they did not participate in the phalanx.

Figure 12.1 summarizes this argument: It shows how a set of values evolves and enforces the adoption of further related values as an iterative process. Supposing for example that in time period 1, two values that have been cultivated through the phalanxes and the trireme, such as trust (cycle 1) and will (cycle 2) affect each other, then, a new relative value such as common purpose or homonoia (cycle 3) might also be adopted in the next step (time period 2). Then, if at time period 2 this is the case, the mutual interaction of the three values (cycles 1, 2 and 3) might also lead to the adoption of a next value, say equality (cycle 4) on time period 3. This

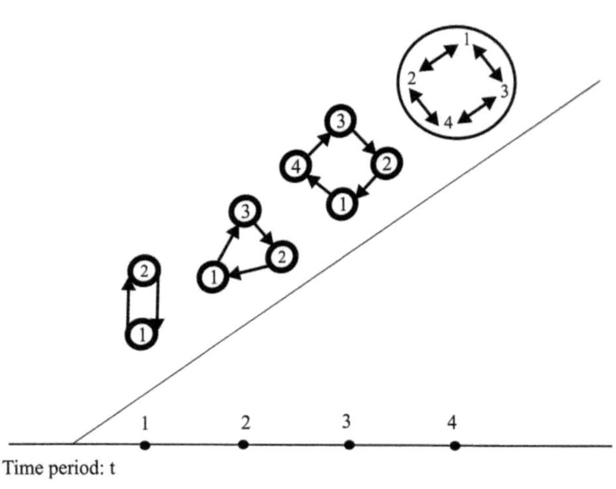

Fig. 12.1 Integration of a series of values to a new coherent whole

process might lead to an ongoing process of creating values in the next time periods (period 4 etc.).

Under this simple figure we attempted to show how values that have been cultivated through warfare may lead to a coherent system of norms and ideas. But the combination of different skills (which were not present in the phalanx were every hoplite had more or less the same equipment and the same skills) had a further great importance for the working of democracy: As on the trireme everybody listened and obeyed the expert (e.g. the rowers to the Keleustes rhythm, everybody to the sailors when sailing with sails, to the master (who was the expert on navigation and sea conditions) or to the commander in battle). It must be underlined, that since after Salamis the Athenian fleet, for all the 160 years of Athenian supremacy was always in operation (in various, but in general substantial strength) every Athenian citizen acquired this experience. As the Athenians applied their military experience to the Assembly, they learned to listen and be guided by the experts.

On the triremes the Athenians acquired two very important types of knowledge: First the nautical combination of skills into a whole, and second the general idea, that some people were the experts and it made sense to listen to them. In modern terms, we would speak of "knowledge aggregation". See Ober (2008) on Chap. 4 (networks, teams and experts) and Chap. 5 (alignment: common knowledge, commitment and coordination) on this issue but without addressing the military influence on politics, as we do here.

Thus, we suggest that this "being guided by the expert" was one of the most valuable lessons from service on ships, on which the efficient running and the duration and stability of Athenian democracy was based. Athenian political culture was thus to a great degree taken over from its naval-military culture. The shared experience, the bonds of trust and common purpose generated on board the ships worked also as a general "glue of democracy". On board a trireme, poor rowers became well acquainted with the hoplites, but also with the wealthy commanders, in a way that he would never have the opportunity to acquire in "civil" life.

We get a glimpse of how important this was for Athenian political culture from the forensic speeches of the fourth century: Defendants and accusers always mention and take pride from their military service as trierarchs, and know well that this reminder will positively influence the judges, citizens elected by lot, the majority of whom would have already served on the triremes, some even on the particular ship or ships commanded and financed by the person giving the speech at the court (see Ober 1989).

Lastly, the durability of the Athenian democracy was based on a community of economic interests. The transformation into a maritime power benefited (perhaps to different degrees) all Athenians: poor Athenians benefited from the remuneration (out of the public budget) as rowers on the triremes, but also as workers on the extended public works programmes (there were two main periods, one during 450–430 BC under Pericles and one under Lycurgus, 338–323 BC) but also as workers on the harbour services, the market place, or self-employed artisans, but also when doing remunerated public service as members of juries (courts) officials elected by lot, participating at the Assembly etc.

These exists a substantial and growing literature on the ancient Athenian economy. See for example (Cohen 1997, Chaps. 1, 5–6; Amemiya 2007, Chap. 2; Bitros and Karayannis 2010; Halkos and Kyriazis 2010). The middle (hoplite) classes benefited from higher prices for their agricultural products (which tended towards specialised high quality-high price products, some for the export markets, like honey, figs, olive oil, wool, wines, instead of bulk goods like cereals) but also as skilled artisans, artists etc. (Stone masons, shoe makers, jewellery makers, potters and in general independent manufacturers) and in the services sector, as e.g. sailors on merchant vessels. The rich benefited as entrepreneurs in manufacturing, merchants, bankers etc. *Homonoia* and social cohesion was based in the Athenian case and we believe also in the other maritime Greek states for which we lack sufficient information, on common interest and prosperity.

Table 12.1 summarizes our findings: It shows that the values that gradually developed as an entail of the functioning of the phalanx and the triremes, such as self-consciousness, cooperation, cohesion, *homonoia* (same-mindness) equality, trust, solidary etc. (Fig. 12.1) were "diffused" from warfare to the political field and became self-consciousness *isonomia* (equality to the law) *isegoria* (freedom of speech) *homomoia*, concord and patriotism. Democracy seems to have gone hand in hand with cohesion and solidarity throughout all over the Athenian society. Thus, Athenians achieved what the ancient politician Demades referred to as "the glue of democracy".

Athenians found it beneficial to entrust their future prosperity as citizens, on ambitious politicians that had already proven their capabilities in warfare, such as Themistocles, Pericles, Cimon etc. Entrusting government to former successful military men seems to have been a common practice even in recent historical cases, such as the United States (George Washington, Abraham Lincoln, Ulysses Grant, Dwight Eisenhower) and France (Napoleon Bonaparte, Charles De Gaulle) etc.

Table 12.1 Transformation and diffusion of military into political values

Warfare mechanisms	Military values	Means	Emerging political values
Hoplites and *phalanx* formation *Triremes*	Self-consciousness Cooperation Cohesion "Homonoia" (same-mindness) Equality Trust Obedience Teamwork Solidary	Bounded rationality	Self-consciousness *Isonomia* (equality) *Isegoria* (freedom of speech) *Homomoia* Concord Coordination Patriotism Abiding by Assembly's and courts decisions, obeying the law Community of interests Positive sum game

Values that have been established through "trial and error" and tested on the battlefield were democratically introduced and adopted in politics as well. Under this method, the Athenians had the aptitude to introduce ready to use solutions when complex issues seemed to have driven to stalemate by utilising the skills of their leaders. Finally, the case of the Athenian Democracy approves, that democratic procedures can lead to positive outcomes. Under concord, homonoia and coordination, cohesion, trust etc., which better emerge voluntarily through democratic procedures, a community of interests that leads to a *Pareto better* or a positive sum game situation (in economic terms) can be achieved, as the case of the recruitment of the poor Athenians in the fleet (during the fifth century) or the expanded public works programmes (during the second half of the fourth century BC) approve.

Conclusions

We have analysed the emergence of the new warrior, the *hoplite*, and the new tactical formation, the *phalanx*, and the values they created. Then, we traced the influence of these values on the emergence of democracy and its values and we suggested that the hoplite and the phalanx was a necessary, but not a sufficient condition for democracy.

We then traced the turn to the sea of some city-states, taking Athens as a case study and established it as a sufficient condition for ancient democracy. Further areas of research are the analysis of other city-state cultures (among those identified e.g. by Hansen's *Polis*) to see if similar links between military developments and democracy can be established. A particular interesting example would be the examination of the Phoenician maritime city-states like Tyre and Sidon and their form of government, or the Greek proto-federations that mainly emerged during the fourth century BC, such as the Achaean and the Aetolian Leagues (see Economou et al. 2013; Kyriazis and Economou 2013c).

Further, European late medieval and Renaissance states should be analysed to demonstrate if similar developments took place. We believe that the Swiss case does show a similar pattern: The Swiss adopted during the fourteenth and fifteenth century a phalanx formation (see Oman 1885 repr. 1968, Chap. V; Miller 1979) and developed direct democracy as a government, which they use till today.

Also, some recent studies (Kyriazis 2006) indicate that in the early modern period, sea and maritime powers, like the United Provinces (Dutch Republic) in the sixteenth and seventeenth century and England, were more democratic (although not real democracies) than any other contemporary state. In addition, other authors such as Glete (1993, vol. 1) and Rodger (1997, 2006) underline the link between sea and maritime power and the community of interests it creates. Further research into this area, including also the Italian maritime medieval and Renaissance city-states like Venice and Genoa, we believe, it will prove fruitful.

References

Ancient Authors

Antiphon "Peri Homonoias" (Ant. P.).
Aristotle "Politics" (Aristotle "Pol.).
Herodotus "Histories" (Her. Hist.).
Lysias "Speeches" (Lys. Sp.).
Thucidides "Historiai—Funeral Speech" (Thuc. F.).
Plato "Republic" (Pl. Rep.).
Plutarch "Moralia" (Plut. Mor.).
Xenophon "Hellenica" (Xen. Hel.).
Xenophon "Memorabilia" (Xen Me.)

Modern Authors

Amemiya T (2007) Economy and economics in ancient Greece. Routledge, London

Bitros GC, Karayannis A (2010) Morality, institutions and the wealth of nations: some lessons from ancient Greece. Eur J Polit Econ 26:68–81

Bradford AS (2011) Leonidas and the kings of sparta: mightiest warriors, fairest kingdom. ABC-CLIO, Santa Barbara, CA

Burn AR (1984) Persia and the Greeks. The defence of the West, C. 546–478 B.C. Stanford University Press, Stanford, reprint

Cartledge P (1977) Hoplites and heroes: Sparta's contribution to the technique of ancient warfare. J Hellenic Stud 97:11–27

Cohen E (1997) Athenian economy and society: a banking perspective. Princeton University Press, Princeton

Despotopoulos A (1972) The art of war of the Greeks, 1100-336. In: History of the Greek nation, Γ2. Ekdotiki Athinon, Athens, pp 192–235 (in Greek)

Economou EML, Kyriazis N, Metaxas T (2013) The institutional and economic foundations of regional proto-federations. Paper presented at the 53rd ERSA Congress, Regional Integration: Europe, the Mediterranean and the World Economy, Palermo, Italy, 27–31 August

Gabrielsen V, Gabrielsen V (2010) Financing the Athenian fleet. John Hopkins University Press, Baltimore, MD

Glete J (1993) Navies and nations: warships, navies and state building in Europe and America 1500–1860. Almquist and Wiksell International, Stockholm

Hale JR (2011) Lords of the sea: the triumph and tragedy of ancient Athens. Gibson Square Books, London

Halkos G, Kyriazis N (2010) The Athenian economy in the age of Demosthenes. Eur J Law Econ 29(2010):255–277

Hansen MH (1983) The Athenian Ecclesia: a collection of articles 1976–1983. Special Trykkeriet-Vyborg, Viborg

Hansen MH (1999) The Athenian democracy in the age of demosthenes. Classical Press, Bristol

Hansen MH (2006) Polis. Oxford University Press, Oxford

Hanson VD (2009) The Western way of war. University of California Press, Berkeley

Healy M (1991) The ancient Assyrians. Osprey Elite 39

Healy M (1992) New Kingdom Egypt. Osprey Elite 40

Kaiser BA (2007) The Athenian trierarchy: mechanism for the private provision of public goods. J Econ Hist 67:4445–4480

Krentz P (1985) The nature of hoplite battle. Classical Antiquity 4:50–61
Kyriazis N (2006) Seapower and socioeconomic change. Theor Soc 35:71–108
Kyriazis N (2009) Financing the Athenian state: public choice in the age of demosthenes. Eur J Law Econ 27:109–127
Kyriazis N (2012) Why ancient Greece? Psychogios Publications, Athens
Kyriazis N, Zouboulakis M (2004) Democracy, sea power and institutional change: an economic analysis of the Athenian naval law. Eur J Law Econ 17:117–132
Kyriazis N, Economou EML (2012a) Property rights and democratic values in Bronze Age and Archaic Greece. MPRA Paper No 42399. University Library of Munich, Germany
Kyriazis N, Economou EML (2012b) Macroculture, sports and democracy in Classical Greece. Paper presented at the 25th Heilbronn symposium in economics and the social sciences, Heilbronn, 21–24 June 2012
Kyriazis N, Economou EML (2013a) Macroculture, sports and democracy in Classical Greece. Eur J Law Econ. doi:10.1007/s10657-013-9390-3
Kyriazis N, Economou EML (2013b) Social contract, public choice and fiscal repercussions in the Athenian Democracy. Theor Pract Res Econ Fields 1:61–76
Kyriazis N, Economou EML (2013c) The emergence and the development of the federations: the Achaean federation, the United Provinces and the EU. MPRA Paper No 47349. University Library of Munich, Germany
Kyriazis N, Paparrigopoulos X (2012) War and democracy in ancient Greece. Eur J Law Econ. doi:10.1007/s10657-012-9352-1
Miller D (1979) The Swiss at war, 1300–1500. Osprey, Men at Arms, 94. Osprey Publishing, Oxford
Morrison J, Coates J, Rankov NB (2000) The Athenian trireme: the history and reconstruction of an ancient Greek Warship. Cambridge University Press, Cambridge
Ober J (1989) Mass and elite in democratic Athens. Princeton University Press, Princeton
Ober J (2008) Democracy and knowledge: innovation and learning in classical Athens. Princeton University Press, Princeton
Oman CW (1885) The art of war in the middle ages 378–1515. Cornell University Press, New York, Repr. 1968
Raauflaub KA (2008) The breakthrough of demokratia on mid-fifth century Athens. In: Raauflaub KA, Ober J, Wallace RW, Cartledge P, Farrar C (eds) Origins of democracy in ancient Greece. University of California Press, Berkeley
Raauflaub KA, Wallace WR (2008) Peoples power and egalitarian trends in Archaic Greece. In: Raaflaub KA, Ober RJ, Wallace W (eds) Origins of democracy in ancient Greece. University of California Press, Berkeley
Rhodes PJ (2007) The Greek city states: a source book. Cambridge University Press, Cambridge
Robinson EW (1997) The first democracies: early popular government outside Athens. Franz Steiner, Stuttgart
Robinson EW (2011) Democracy beyond Athens: popular government in the Greek classical age. Cambridge University Press, Cambridge
Rodger NAM (1997) The safeguard of the sea. Harper Collins, London
Rodger NAM (2006) The command of the ocean: a naval history of Britain, 1649–1815. Penguin Books, London
Sakellariou MB (1972) Towards Greek unity. In: History of the Greek nation, Γ2. Ekdotiki Athinon, Athens, pp 34–95 (in Greek)
Sekunda N (1986) The ancient Greeks. Osprey Elite 7
Sekunda N (1992) The Persian Army 560–330 B.C. Osprey, Elite, 42. Osprey Publishing, Oxford
Simon H (1991) Bounded rationality and organisational learning. Org Sci 2:125–134
Stanton GR (1990) Athenian politics, C. 800–500 B.C. A Sourcebook. Routledge, London
Theodorakopoulos I (1972) Aristoteles. In: History of the Greek nation, Γ2. Ekdotiki Athinon, Athens, pp 486–511 (in Greek)
Tsatsos T (1972) Rhetoric. In: History of the Greek nation, Γ2. Ekdotiki Athinon, Athens (in Greek)

Chapter 13
Civic Market and Sortition Democracy

Constantine Collmer

13.1 Introduction

The future historian will wonder how two opposite political parties in modern Greece—the 'New Democracy', applying free economy and 'Pasok', 'Socialist market'—together run the country today.

There are a lot of interpretations to this paradox but let us leave the answer to the end. What I have to remark now is a well-known rule that free economy is necessary, but not sufficient for a real democratic regime.

The third Greek parliamentary democracy (after the dictatorship 1967–1974) was a covert oligarchy of political parties, trade unions, public servants and 'charismatic' leaders like Constantine Karamanlis and Andreas Papandreou, who cancelled the above rule. It was not always like this in my country. For example, in the post-war era we had 2–3 efficient administrations (of Themistokles Sofoulis, Alexandros Papagos, and Kyriakos Varvaressos, as Governor of the Bank of Greece).

In ancient Greece, Sparta, Argos, Olympia, the Aetolian confederation, Thebes, and especially in Athens, democracy developed side by side with the freedom of the average citizen and his participation in the army and the market.

Here I will examine the relationship between the market economy and sortition democracy in ancient Athens.

C. Collmer (✉)
34 Proteos Street, 14564 N. Kifisia, Greece
e-mail: ccollmer@otenet.gr

G.C. Bitros, N.C. Kyriazis (eds.), *Essays in Contemporary Economics*,
DOI 10.1007/978-3-319-10043-2_13

13.2 Democracy and the Market

The economic crisis of seventh century BC was confronted with cancellation of debts, currency devaluation, popular assemblies and the ballot system to elect the authorities.

After the collapse of the Minoan and Mycenaean monarchies, the king's rights were curtailed and free men received property, as well flocks and herds, like Odysseus. The form of government became Timocracy i.e., only natives with certain income from their land were elected for office.

Several scholars connect the military organization of the post-Mycenaean state (Phalanx and Triremes) to the evolution of democracy through mutual trust of the soldiers-rowers but they ignore the relationship between the representative system of the masses and the market economy.

The role of the market is not so obvious unless we look at the three principles of ancient democracy:

- The equality of people before the law (Isonomia),
- The right of the citizen to address the assembly and to propose laws (Isigoria), and
- The establishment of the social accord (Omonoia).

With the ballot selection of citizens for 1 year in office (except for generals in the army) Athens created a real democratic system.

Without all of the above, which have also a correspondence in the function of the (free) market, democracy would be not have been possible in ancient Greece.

Also without democratic control, the market would become an oligopoly and the political system a "limited oligarchy" even with free elections, if we follow what Aristotle writes on the Athenians constitution.

Plato, in one of his dialogues, looks for the real concept of democracy which means the power of the people ('demos' means people and 'kratos' power in Greek).

With the word market (in Greek: 'Agora') we mean the central part of the ancient city where the peasants and the merchants used to come together to sell and buy goods.

The name Agora came from the verb: 'Agorazo', which means not only buying (as in English) but also 'I spend my time in the centre of the city, talk to the public about my products, objections, ideas. Through trading with other people, I educate myself from an exchange of ideas and knowledge. In economic terms: I put the information costs at the lowest level.'

From 'Agora' derive words like 'Demigoria', which means 'I talk in an assembly or court', the word 'Agoritis', which means orator and 'Agoracritos' who is the favourite of the people (in Aristophane' "The Knights").

13.2.1 The Evolution of the Market

At the beginning, the Agora had the form of a barter economy with a very high transaction cost. When coins were introduced circa 650 BC, not only did the transaction cost become less but also the civic Market appeared. The exchange of goods became more efficient with lower information cost (about where the equilibrium was between supply and demand). Thus the political economy was introduced.

The first to use coins in ancient Greece were the inhabitants of the island Aegina. The Aeginetans introduced a silver drachma with the sign of the turtle, not only as a local but also as an "international currency" in the Mediterranean.

Because silver was rare and imported from northern Greece and some Aegean islands, the money supply was limited, the currency overvalued, prices were low, unemployment high and debts unsustainable.

It was the Athenian traveller Solon, a legislator and a poet, who introduced the Athenian drachma (with a sign of the owl), in approximately 610 BC that solved the problem.

Solon cancelled the debts of the Athenians ('Sisachthia') and he devalued the Athenian currency by 27 % *vis a vis* the Aegina's drachma. Deposits of silver were discovered in the mines of Lavrion, and this way the Athenian economy became financially sufficient and also covered its balance of payments deficit with the transfer of silver to the foreign markets when importing grains, copper, gold etc.

With its market and democratic lifestyle, Athens became a developed economy. The welfare of the city helped the poor people. Culture, theatre and fine arts skyrocketed and the power of the citizen protected the democratic constitution from internal and external dangers.

Nevertheless, the rise of the democracy was not an immaculate conception. It started with the civil war in Athens at the beginning of the seventh century. It was followed by written legislation. The Draconian laws of 621 BC forbade the trespass of pedestrians through private property. This was the first recognition of property rights. This is when the exchange of private rights started.

After Dracon, came Solon the legislator ('thesmothetis') who arranged a tax system with four classes (Πεντακοσιομέδιμνοι, Ιππείς, Ζευγίτες and Θήτες) and transformed Athens from an agricultural to a commercial city, giving limited political rights to the poor people ('Thites') and making a compromise with the aristocrats and the landlords, who kept the office unsalaried.

Solon also took the next political step by giving to the third class ('zeugites') the right to be appointed officials and established the unique system of the Exchange Tax burden with Property (Αντίδοσις[1]).

The final stages of reforms were made by Kleisthenes. He gave compensation to the poor people with half the minimum salary ("thorika"). 'Thites' received three "ovoloi" (τριώβολον) per day, when they performed public duties as members of

[1] See Karayiannis (2007, 36) for more details on 'Antidosis'.

the assembly or in the courts and also when attending the ancient theatre with the purpose to educate themselves in collective responsibilities.

With more competition, a procedure for additional political rights began, including the ability of 'Thites' to speak in the Assembly («τίς αγορεύειν βούλεται; » in "The Acharnians" of Aristophanes). The separation of the three functions of the State (legislative, judicial and executive), became fundamental for the democracy.

Political rights were recognized with Kleisthenes, who was the first to use the word 'democracy'. An amnesty was given, 10 tribes were created, instead of the traditional four, and the municipalities of Attica were weakened. He fostered the bonds of trust between the different people of different classes, especially with the enforcement of the Counsel of 500.

But the truly revolutionary idea was of Solon, who believed in the principle of the market: that all the participants in the democracy would win. The entire fourth chapter of Solon's Laws safeguards private property, the selling and buying of real estate, the minimum wage, the export and import trade and the validity of the private contracts, which were not allowed to circumvent the existing laws. Even fishermen were not permitted to water the fish in order to present them as fresh in the market.

Commissioners were active from day to night in the Athenian market, to control the quality and profits of the wheat merchants, to prohibit the sale of ox meat and to protect animals from mistreatment. Special inspectors regulated the open area of Attica, prohibiting the plantation of fig and olive trees closer to 9 feet from foreign property. State slaves in the harbour of Piraeus controlled the imported foreign coins and sophisticated bankers were active in the money market of Athens.

I have to mention also, the monetary legislation that was made by an unknown citizen named Nicophon in 376 BC, who introduced the gold and foreign exchange standard for the first time. This was after the adoption of the Sea Law introduced by Themistocles from which starts the "Great Sea Empire of Athens", according to Thucydides.

In the period of two centuries, market ethics and a struggle for social justice in Greece brought unavoidable change. This allowed people expressing their political desire as desperate Thersitis was asking without hope in Homer's Iliad.

13.3 The Evolution of Democracy

The establishment of the people's power in ancient southern Greece occurred in all citizen assemblies like Apella in Sparta, in several committees of Olympia, in Crete, in another eight Greek city-states and in the Ekklisia of the Demos of Athens.

But how did a peasant of Messogea, the charcoal-maker Dicaiopolis of Acharnes and the 'agoracritos', sausage-maker (in the Aristophane's comedy 'The Knights') succeed in eliminating the political power of the aristocracy and consequently of the new plutocracy and to became an unavoidable part of political power?

The Spartans, without doubt, helped the Athenian people in the struggle for political rights, for they were also in favour of the majority principle in their city. That happened with the abolishment of the dictatorship of Peissistratos in Athens. But the people's Assembly (Ekklisia) and especially the Consul of the 500, was not saying a single 'yes' or 'no' on the new legislation, like the Spartans, for the proposals of the five senators (Ephoroi) in the Apella.

In Athens, the people participated in the Consul of the 500 and voted in the Ekklisia of Demos, in Pnyx, where every citizen could ask for the right to be heard according to the agenda known from the day before. That had tremendous long term consequences.

The citizen learned how to read because he had to inform himself at the Assembly of the written legislation and to prepare himself according to the agenda of the next session. In such a way, education started not only for the rich people but also for the poor citizen who studied when they had free time (from the word Σ χ ό λ η = free time, comes the word "school"). The vocal (phonetic) alphabet was invented in Greece and not by the Phoenicians.

Public education was the great achievement of democracy. In order to participate in the Assembly, citizens had to have an elementary knowledge of reading and writing in order to prepare for the agenda which was written on a wooden tablet, covered by wax.

In the Athenian market, the citizen, the legal immigrant ('metoicos') and the educated slave learned how to understand figures and use numbers.

In the vagaries of the market, the traders learned how to speak about politics. In the theatre of Athens citizen criticized politicians.

Writing on stone, wood and papyrus had unforeseen consequences for the accumulation of knowledge at least up to the time of the Monastery of Studios in Constantinople, where a monk was reading from the original and 20 monks made copies of famous work and writers. When Gutenberg produced the first moving letters, and in our times through IBM and Internet, electronic writing, knowledge and information, which means economic 'power', was transferred, to the people. The Alphabet, not 'War was father of all man's things' as Heraclitus stipulated.

The market was the first centre for collecting information, and appreciating the political outcome from the decisions of war and peace. According to Aristophanes (The 'Knights') even the price of sardines affected the Athenian parliament. The market made the future political leaders like Cleon and Nicias and ostracized them when they became dangerous for the democracy, like Themistocles and Aristides (Γραφή παρανόμων).

Beyond those incidents, there are other connections between the market and democracy: In the well-functioning market, the profit (rent) is always a positive win-win of the seller, the buyer, the producer and the consumer.

By the same token, in Democracy there is no zero-sum-game because the crowd always decides better than a few specialists on social judgment. 'In the democracy, all the people will win,' Solon said.

13.4 Election by Lot

A brief description of the workings of the Athenian democracy given by Professor Donald Kagan: "The centre of political power and action was the Assembly, which was open to all male adults who were citizens of Athens: Perhaps 40,000 men. Most Athenians lived many miles from the city, so attendance required a long walk to town. As a result, the number actually taking part on any given occasion was probably 6,000. The meetings took place, not far from the Agora, on the hill of Pnyx, where the citizens sat on the earth of a sloping hill and speakers stood on a low platform. The Assembly had four fixed meetings in each of the 10 periods into which the official year was divided. Topics included approval or disapproval of Treaties and ensuing declarations of War, assigning Generals to campaigns and deciding what forces and resources they should command. Confirmation of officials or their removal from office, whether or not to hold an ostracism and in fact every other issue of civic concern and finally all the other kinds of business. After a full debate, they made a decision by simple majority. The same happened with the Counsel of 500 which prepared the different bills".

Prof. Kagan (2009) adds: "Athens had no executive, no Prime Minister, no Cabinet or any elected official, except the generals, and no administration. On the other hand, the city had the Examiners, sitting the regular market hours at the statue of Eponymous hero of each tribe. If any citizen wishes to refer a charge against any official, within 3 days he must write on a board his own name and the accusers. The Examiner decided if the charge had any merit and he passed it onto the appropriate popular court for the final judgment. All the other officials were chosen by lot. The vendors who farmed out public contracts to work the state mines and to collect the taxes, were also chosen by lot. So too were the accountants and the city commissioners, who, according to Aristotle, examined the price even of lira-girls and cast lots, in case of higher demand in symposia".

All the above reminds us of the functions of the Market. Inspectors examined the purity of articles for sale, the honesty of the merchants, the price and quality of imported grains and the weight of a loaf of bread.

In modern terms, the Athenians kept the management of their public life in the hands of ordinary citizens away from professional judges, bureaucrats, politicians and parties. That was the first direct democracy and not the Swiss.

Direct democracy, according to macroeconomists solves the problems of 'the principal agency', real preference of the voter and accountability of failed politicians.

Markets are better suited in solving allocation of resources. The average people are a better "principal agency" for managing public affairs compared with the professional politician who avoids political cost and gets political rent.

Last but not least, a Market Decree (Μεγαρεικόν ψήφισμα) barring the city of Megara, a member of the Peloponnesian League, from the use of the Athenian Agora and the harbour of Piraeus, proved to be the most significant cause of the Peloponnesian war. It was the first embargo in peace time (ibid., Kagan).

I will read now in ancient Greek what Dikaiopolis said in the comedy 'The Acharnians' (v.719) when he made his own personal peace with the Spartans. [I'm reading this to not only emphasize the importance of the Market in democratic life but also to show how close modern Greek is to the ancient language.

Όροι μέν αγοράς εισίν οίδε τής εμής ενταύθ'αγοράζειν πάσι Πελοποννησίοις εφ'ώτε πωλείν πρός εμέ, Λαμάχω δέ μή.[2]

I left open the question of what happens to Greece now. Two different parties are governing the country. Is that coming back to the abolition of different political ideologies? 'Omonia' returns to the Greek people as in ancient Athens? Unfortunately, the only explanation I can give to this paradox is that both parties are more or less the same and trying to save the political establishment from the consequences of a general default that was created by them.

This is exactly was happened when Pericles and Cleon in the Peloponnesian war acted against the true interest of the Athenians. The third parliamentary 'failed state' of modern Greece is now harming not only the people but also business and the markets.

But those two forces, the people and markets, will sooner or later abolish the office of failed parties exactly as it happened in the Athenian democracy after its defeat in the Peloponnesian War.

To paraphrase Thucydides, this is a useful reminder for all of us.

References

Kagan D (2009) Thucydides. The reinvention of history. Viking Press, New York, NY

Karayiannis AD (2007) *Αρχαιοελληνική Πρωτοπορ(ε)ία στα Οικονομικά*, Αθήνα: Εκδόσεις Παπαζήσης

[2] The frontiers of mine market are these. Here to the Peloponnesians and Beotians and the Megarians Permit to sell and to buy with me, except of Lamachos.

Chapter 14
Fair Distribution of Wealth: From the Greek Syssitia to the Dinners of Love

Christos P. Baloglou

14.1 Introduction

A thorough understanding of the socio-economic views of the Disciples and of the construct of the primeval Church of Christ can better be achieved if they are examined and compared to the works of ancient Greek literature. Indeed, a comparative retrospective co-examination of both the New Testament and the Greco-Roman letters have become fundamental in the biblical, theological and philological research not only for the historic data they provide but also for their rich theological content.

Quite many comparative studies between the biblical and the Greco-Roman literature have been put forward so far on the subject of credit and lending at interest,[1] political philosophy,[2] Household-economics and organization and administration of an economic unit.[3] This study considers the institution of *syssitia*, as it is described in specific constitutions (politeumata) in ancient Greek city states, and attempts its comparison to the institution of communal meals, an institution which is pivotal in primeval Apostolic Church. In this respect, it is essential to analyse the historic, anthropological and social background of the biblical texts.

A detailed research of the institution of syssitia in «prosperous» societies as described by Aristotle is presented in Sect. 14.2 of this study in order to effectively

The present paper has been translated into English by Mrs. Marion Kavallieros. I would like to express my gratitude and thanks for her help. I'm responsible for any errors that might be found.

[1] Maloney (1971, 79–109), Gordon (1982, 406–426). Especially for the Old Testament see Oikonomou (1973), Patras (2007, 3–11).

[2] Antonopoulos and Terezis (2009, 129–192).

[3] Lehmeier (2006), Baloglou (2013, 43–80).

C.P. Baloglou (✉)
Chomatianou 30, 15123 Amaroussion Attikis, Greece
e-mail: cbaloglou@ote.gr

G.C. Bitros, N.C. Kyriazis (eds.), *Essays in Contemporary Economics*,
DOI 10.1007/978-3-319-10043-2_14

co examine the institution of ancient Greek syssitia and the construction of the vital components of the Primeval Church as well as the problems that entailed from its organization. The institution of the ancient Greek syssitia is viewed in the scope of a fair distribution of wealth, the accomplishment of which would bring «unity» (homonoia) among citizens and would eliminate discord and rivolts in the state that implemented it.

One of the major concerns of the Disciples was to guarantee a unified Church, free of rivalry among its members. Section 14.3 analyzes the crucial role of the communal meals of love for the integrity of the Church. This institution reflected the socio-economic status of the particular community and determined the way goods were distributed among its members. Given the available data, the most characteristic example is the Church of Corinth. The problems among the scholars and the painful problem of «schisms» or «discords» that emerged in the Church of Corinth all derive from the uneven distribution of wealth.

Section 14.4 compares the similarities and differences between ancient Greek syssitia and communal meals. The Conclusions summarize the outcome of this research.

14.2 The Institution of Syssitia

According to Aristotle, there were two prosperous («εὐδοκιμοῦσες») city-states (poleis)[4] in antiquity that developed the institution of syssitia within a broad context of socio-economic institutions that were essential for their smooth function: Crete and Sparta.

The institution of syssitia appears to be the evolutionary form of *symposia*, a basic component of aristocratic life style that dates back to Homeric ages (*Iliad* IV 257; XVII 248–250; XXII 492–495; *Odysseia* iv 621–625; xi 184–188) and was observed by a large number of areas in Greece, Asia Minor and Italy such as Megara (Theognis, *Elegeiai* I 33–36; Plutarch, *Aetia Graecia* 18(=*Ethica* 295d)), Boeotia, Macedonia (Athenaios, *Deipnosophistai* I 17–18), Miletus, and Thourioi (Plato, *Laws* I 636b). It was later abandoned except for the cases of Crete and Sparta. Other than Homer, the only reference about syssitia as an integral part of the organization of their social life but without much detail is made by Diodorus Siculus (hereafter Diod. Sic.) concerning the people living on the complex of Lipari Islands in the Tyrrhenian Sea, off the northeastern coast of Sicily.

In their effort to colonize Sicily around 580 BC, Greek colonists from Knidos (Diod. Sic. V 7–9) were defeated by the locals and their leader, Pentathlos, was killed. On their way back home, their vessels were driven ashore Lipari, the largest of the Aetolian Islands, where they settled and organized their life anew on the site of the village now known as Castello. The colony successfully fought the Etruscans who tried to take over the islands and control the Tyrrhenian Sea. The inhabitants

[4] Cf. Microyannakis (1972–1973, 402–415); Idem 2002–2003, 49. Baloglou (2011a).

organized their defense in a way that would allow them to efficiently repel «the thieves». For this reason, they shared the tasks, they provided the division of labour, such as the «building of ships» and «farming the islands». They lived their life together, worked together and ate common meals at the syssitia (Diod. Sic. V 9_{4-5}). It is interesting to note that although there is scanty information about them, the life style of the inhabitants of Lipari consists «a small but interesting corner of Greek history» (Buck 1959, 35–39), a case study of a society based on joint ownership and collective farming (Stephanidis 1948/2003, 183–185).

14.2.1 The Organization and Operation of Syssitia in Crete

The institution of the syssitia[5] was considered extremely important for the maintenance of the social system and the security of social peace in the Doric society of the Cretan cities where it was observed until the Hellenistic Ages. The Cretan syssitia and their organization, called *andreia* according to Aristotle (*Politics* II 1272 a1–4) and Ephorus (FGrHist. 70 F. 149(=Strabo, *Geographica* X IV 18 (C. 481))), attracted the interest of many writers among whom are Plato (*Laws* I 625d–626b;633a;636b;VI 780a–c;780d–781c; VIII 842b), Ephorus (FGrHist. 70F. 149(=Strabo, *Geographica* X V 16–21 (C. 480–484))), Plutarch and the Cretan historians Dosiadas (FGrHist. 458 F.2(=Athenaios, *Deipnosophistai* IV 143a–d)) and Pyrgion (FGrHist. 467 F.1(=Athenaios, *Deipnosophistai* IV 143e–f)).

Aristotle, who is concerned mostly with the physical and social aspect of the institution, after comparing the Spartan syssitia versus the Cretan, openly states his preference of the Cretan version of the institution (Aristotle, *Politics* II 10, 1272 a14–15). He briefly describes the operation of the syssitia: «In Crete they were even more communal. Of all the ripe fruit, livestock and income tax that the citizens brought in, a part was put aside for the gods and the communal ceremonies while the rest was offered to the communal meals so that everybody would eat, women, children and men together» (Aristotle, *Politics* II 10, 1272 a17–23).

The citizens' exact contribution to the syssitia has been debated by many so in order to interpret the above citation accurately, we need to examine the inscriptions found in some Cretan cities, as for example in Gortyn[6] Littos or Lyktos[7] and Datala.[8] Following are some conclusions ensuing from the critical examination of the available data.

Firstly, the communal meals aimed at ensuring the equality and similar treatment of the citizens as far as provisioning was concerned by enabling the poor to eat on public funds. However, we should not overlook the fact that there existed a certain

[5] Cf. Mandalakis (2004, 189–220).

[6] Koerner 1993, No. 152; Efféntere and Ruzé (1994).

[7] Dosiadas in FGrHist. 458 F.2. For the problems of the critical presentation of the text cf. Latte (1968, 299), not. 13; Link (1991, 123).

[8] Efféntere and Ruzé (1994), I, No. 22 A1–10. For the problematic presentation and analysis of this text see Mandalakis (2004, 205–207).

degree of socio-economic inequality as attested by an inscription found in Gortyn.[9] Inequality was already evident in the fifth century BC and is reflected in Aristotle's texts as well as in Ephorus' texts. Aristotle (*Politics* II 1272 a33–34) mentions a handful of powerful families who retained the privilege of passing power into alternative family stock, while Ephorus sees two distinct «classes», the wealthy and the poor (cf. Strabo, *Geographica* XV 16–21 (C. 480)), when he refers to the socio-economic reality of Crete.

Secondly, the syssitia burdened the community economically, especially those of Crete.[10] Each participant was to contribute to the syssitia by offering part of his yield. The citizens' contribution was the primary supply of the syssitia. In Crete contributions equalled 1/10 of the annual yield and therefore the danger of losing one's civil rights for not complying was essentially lower compared to that in other cities where citizens had to contribute to the syssitia equally regardless of the quantity of their yield.[11]

Thirdly, nourishment in communal meals under the auspices of the polis created in the citizens the sense of belonging and of being equally treated. And so political tensions were vented out which in other cities of the time would ultimately lead to the fall of aristocratic regimes.[12]

Fourthly, the plenary participation of the population in the syssitia-women, children, teenagers and men-outlines the democratic nature of the institution. Women are in charge of the syssitia, take the best quality food portions and offer them to those whose deeds in the war or in the community have been acknowledged (cf. Dosiadas, in Athenaios, *Deipnosophistai* IV 143d).

Fifthly, the physical environment of the operation of the syssitia, the *syssitikos oikos* (cf. Dosiadas, in Athenaios, *Deipnosophistai* IV 143b–c) functioned also as a forum, a place where serious public affairs—«περὶ τῶν κοινῶν»—, were discussed (Athenaios, *Deipnosophistai* IV 143d). It is during these discussions that the junior members of the syssitia were given the opportunity to become initiated in politics, learn the value of bravery and shape their character.

Sixthly, noteworthy is the term «koinoteros» (meaning that the cost of the syssitia should mostly burden the state) used by Aristotle (*Politics* II 5, 1263 a40; II 9, 1271 a28; 1329 b5) as well as by other writers (cf. Plato, *Laws* 842b; 847e. Strabo, G*eographica* X IV 16;20), regarding his vision of the ideal polis. Aristotle's objective is to ensure the minimum standards of living for all the citizens in his ideal polis so that none faces destitution (*Politics* 1330 a2). In the Athenian Democracy, the much sought public funds that would allow all the Athenians to eat at communal meals (Xenophon, *Poroi (Revenues)* IV 33) were a vital issue. They were an issue that troubled fourth century BC financial policies and practices.[13]

---

[9] Fiorakis (1973).

[10] Cf. Aristotle, *Politics* II 10, 1272 a17–18: «ἐν δὲ Κρήτῃ κοινοτέρως».

[11] Link (1994, 14–20).

[12] Austin and Vidal-Naquet (1977, 70–75), Mossé (1984/1987) 151–155.

[13] Schütrumpf (1991, 338). For an extensive analysis of Aristotle's financial program see Baloglou (1998).

14.2.2 The Regulation and Organization of the Spartan Syssitia

The comparative examination of the Cretan and the Spartan syssitia results in important findings about their operational differences. In Sparta each male citizen undertook the responsibility of rendering an established amount of goods that made him eligible for participation in the syssitia. Failing to meet this obligation would automatically entail his exclusion from the syssitia and loss of civil rights. In Crete, however, the cost of the syssitia burdened mostly the city. All the citizens had to bring in the ripe fruit, livestock and taxes part of which was put aside for the gods and the public ceremonies, while the rest was given to the syssitia to feed everyone in common meals (Aristotle, *Politics* II 10, 1272 a15–22).

Aristotle makes an unobjectionable statement here. The state functions as the supplier of the syssitia to a bigger extent in Crete than it does in Sparta.[14] In Crete the citizens' contributions came from their private property and constituted a regular source of replenishment for the syssitia. Although the Cretan syssitia are not explicitly stated in Aristotle's texts, their existence is considered certain, since common ownership characterizes the Cretan institution more than it characterizes the Spartan.[15] Consequently, the citation «from public funds» most probably refers to the income, produce and cattle that Cretan cities yielded from public and private land and pasture. The Cretan syssitia were supplied from the total amount of products that came from private or public land, from cattle that grazed in public land and from the fees paid by commissioned farmers. In this respect, it becomes easier to comprehend Aristotle's reference that in Sparta and in Crete the legislator had established through the institution of syssitia a form of communism at least as far as nourishment is concerned.[16]

Aristotle points out that in Sparta the institution of syssitia had developed quite differently from the legislator's initial intention (Aristotle, *Politics* II 9, 1271 a26–28). The citizens were to render the agreed upon contribution—«τὸ τεταγμένον»—, which was the same for everybody regardless of one's productive potential. Those who failed to meet this obligation could no longer participate in the syssitia and lost their civil rights. There was a «requirement by the polis», a «paternal» one, according to which the one «who did not redeem the fee» was not allowed to be part of the community, that is of the polis, resulting in loss of civil rights (Aristotle, *Politics* II 9, 1271 a34–37). Therefore, the «democratic nature» of the syssitia ends up being «less democratic» (Arist., *Politics* II 9, 1271 a33–34).

In conclusion, Sparta virtually applied economic criteria that had to do with the assets of her citizens in order to grant them civil rights and citizenship eventually

---

[14] Link (1991, 119, not. 71), Talamo (1987, 17).

[15] Cf. Aristotle, *Politics* II 9, 1271 a28–29: «Ἔδει γὰρ ἀπὸ κοινοῦ μᾶλλον είναι τὴν σύνοδον, καθάπερ ἐν Κρήτῃ». Cf. Mandalakis (2004, 195).

[16] Cf. Aristotle, *Politics* II 5, 1263 b40–1264 a1: «τὰ περὶ τὰς κτήσεις ἐν Λακεδαίμονι καὶ Κρήτῃ τοῖς συσσιτίοις ὁ νομοθέτης ἐκοίνωσε».

resulting in the gradual decrease of their number (Arist., *Politics* II 9, 1271 a33). That became the cause of Aristotle's criticism (Arist., *Politics* II 9, 1271 a26–27. Cf. *Politics* II 10, 1272 a16–17; 26–27).

It is interestingly enough, to point out, Saint Great Basil (330-1.1.379), Bishop of Caesareia in Cappadocia, who had classical Greek influences[17] remembered on the organization of the Spartan syssitia. It is noteworthy that he delivered a speech,[18] during the famine of AD 368 in Asia Minor, where there have been echoed the Spartan polity wrapped in Christian veil praising the system of common ownership so that people will be able to enjoy earthly goods. He reminisces both the ancient Spartan and Cretan customs as well as the life of the first Christians. «Let us enjoy what the charitable Greeks bequeathed to us», notes Saint Great Basil, since «their humanitarian laws designated one common dining table, common meals under a common roof for the populous citizens» (PG 31, col. 305). And so he urges his fellow people to imitate the example of the first «three thousand Christians as they shared everything, their life, their soul, opinion and dinner table» (PG 31, col. 305).

The above statement coming from a prominent priest of Christendom is of significant historic importance considering that it compares institutions of two very different ages.

14.2.3 The Institution of the Syssitia in Aristotle's «Best Polis»

It is noteworthy that through his writing Aristotle reveals to us that the institution of syssitia is age old, the beginning of which is lost in the mists of myth. He states that the practice of syssitia is ancient; the ones in Crete took place around the ages of King Minos' reign, while the syssitia in Italy long before those (Aristotle, *Politics* 1329 b6–8). In his effort to identify the first one to initiate the institution, Aristotle mentions the «Italus», who turned the citizens of Oinotroi from nomads to farmers (Aristotle, *Politics* 1329 b14–15), established laws and was the first one to found the syssitia (Aristotle, *Politics* 1329 b16). This reference by Aristotle leads to the following conclusions.

Firstly, the institution of syssitia appears in organized societies and follows a special law order. With this statement, Aristotle implies that nomads are not law-abiding people (For example Herodotus, *Histories* IV 106). Secondly, the institution of syssitia derives from the peaceful co-existence of the citizens and

[17] Schoinas (2006, 263–279).

[18] St. Great Basil «Homily (Ομιλία) ρηθείσα εν λιμώ και αυχμώ», PG 31, cols. 303–328.

does not have war-like origins, as Plato (*Laws* I 625e–f; I 633 a4) supports and is apparent in the constitution of his *Republic* (III 416 e3).[19]

The above information is consistent with Aristotle's «best polis»[20] both in terms of its components and its type. Similarly, he seizes the opportunity to emphasize that it is useful (*Politics* VIII 9, 1330 a4) for the well-organized cities (*Politics* VII 9, 1330 a5) to provide syssitia. Furthermore, he suggests that the buildings in which the syssitia are offered be conveniently (*Politics* VIII 12, 1331 a25–26) located near the ones that are dedicated to the gods (*Politics* VIII 12, 1331 a24) and near those in which the city keeps its most important archives (*Politics* VIII 12, 1331 a25).

Evidently, what Aristotle bears in mind when he plans out his «best polis» that should be founded around the syssitia is the organization of the Cretan syssitia. A comparison between the two passages, the first one *Politics* II 10, 1272 a17–21 and the second one VIII 10, 1330 a9–14 may as well be convincing. Their only difference is that in the passage that discusses land distribution and syssitia supplying in the best polis-state (*Politics* VIII 10, 1330 a9–11) there is no provision for communal operations that apparently burdened the state-budget in Crete,[21] which Aristotle did not favor anyway (*Politics* VII 5, 1320 b3–4). «Many of which he would be glad to abolish», as Newman (1887/2000) remarks.

14.3 The Creation and Constitution of «Common Meals»

The social dynamics of the theology of the New Testament focus firstly on the problem of gender equality, secondly on the issue of slavery, thirdly on wealth management and fourthly on dealing with fringe groups (Oikonomou 2010, 17–43).

From its early days already, the social organization of welfare was a matter of great importance for the Apostolic Church, the organization of which was gradually imposed by the Apostles on all the newly established Churches. Besides, the Apostles' mission was to meet both the material and spiritual needs of their followers as it is witnessed by the two miracles of feeding the multitudes that Jesus worked in Bethsaida. The first miracle, the feeding of the 5,000 is present in all canonical Gospels: Matthew 14:13–21, Mark 6:31–44, Luke 9:10–17 and John 6:5–15. The second miracle, the feeding of the 4,000 is reported by Mark 8:1–9 and Matthew 15:32–39 and is also known as the miracle of the seven loaves and fish.

The organization of social welfare does not only present the Church as a systematically integrated society but is also vital for illustrating the pastoral activity of the Disciples and of all those who were authorized to do so since providing for the people was a task absolutely intertwined with the spiritual hypostasis

[19] Cf. Schütrumpf (2005, 397–398).

[20] Aristotle, *Politics* VIII 1, 1332 a14. This term has been used also in other passages. Cf. *Politics* 1324 a17–18; 1334 a23–25.

[21] Newman (1887/2000, 353), Cf. Latte (1968, 299).

(existence) and promotion of the members of the Church (Voulgaris 2012, 59). This is clearly depicted in the New Testament by the term «society», which refers both to the mystical and spiritual life and also to the creation of a spirit of understanding among the members of the Church regarding the various needs that their fellow people faced.[22] In the first Church of Jerusalem the organization of welfare began so dynamically that the system of common ownership was established almost immediately. «They shared everything, the farms and the property and made division of it among them all, as they had need» (Acts 2:44–45). This is clearly a form of common ownership of commodities which took place in Palestine. It was dynamic in nature and constituted an act of love of the first, primeval Church.[23]

In the primeval Apostolic Church social organization is evident already from the first days after Pentecost (Acts II: 42; 44–47; IV 23–37; V1; VI 1), especially after the establishment of joint ownership. Consequently, the conventional form of ownership which classifies people into wealthy and poor[24] was abolished by the Apostolic Church and was turned into an element of unity, an expression of equal participation of all its members in these goods, a true «society» (Acts 4:32–5:11). In short, because «the multitude of the believers was one heart and one soul, no one claimed that their possessions were their own but rather that everything they had was common» (Acts 4:32) and so there was none among them who was needy (Acts 4:34).

The existence of similar institutions in the community of Qumran[25] among the Healers of Egypt (Egyptian priest-physicians)[26] and in Roman Collegia[27] does not diminish the value of the institution in the Primeval Church.[28] The members of the community shared their assets willingly and voluntarily, those who owned lands or houses sold them in order to put the proceeds at the feet of the Apostles for distribution to everyone as needed (Acts 4:35).

This is not a random incident and neither is the term at his feet a figure of speech. It is the result of an age old procedure that began in the ages of the prophets Michaeas and Isaiah, when the practice of accumulating wealth was criticized as being the cause of destitution of farmers. It continues with the teaching of Jesus Christ who equated the practice of accumulating wealth to theft in accordance with the prophetic tradition and asked that the young and rich landowner sell the assets

[22] Acts 2:42. Rom. 15:26; II Cor. 8:4; Hebr. 13:16. 1 Ioan. 3:6–7.

[23] Cf. Hadjimichalis (1972, 113).

[24] Theodorakopoulos (1974, 354–360).

[25] The communism established by the Essaeans as it has been described by Eusebius, Bishop of Caesareia in Palestine, was almost absolute. Eusebius, *Evangelica* VIII XII 114–6. Idem VIII XII 125. This information about the common ownership of goods is found also by Plinius, *Historia Naturalis E 34*:97 and Josephus, *Judaean War* II 7, 3 and 4.

[26] Philon, *De vita contemplativa* 10–13 (473). Cf. Taylor (1998).

[27] Tacitus, *Annales* XIV 17. Plinius, *E 34*:97. Minucius Felix, *Octavius* 8–9.

[28] Philippidis (1958, 480–488), Agouridis (1963, 177–206) (=1971, 251–276).

he had accumulated in order to give it to the poor who had lost their land through the mechanisms of land ownership, borrowing at interest and debt (Mark 11:17–22).

The procedure of selling property in order to give the money to the poor found a worthy imitator in the face of Barnabas, a Levite born in Cyprus. Barnabas sold a field he owned in the outskirts of Jerusalem and turned over its price to the Apostles to give it to the members of the Church (Acts 4:36–37).[29] However, the case of Ananias and Sappheira (Acts 5:1–11) was a warning to others. They also sold a piece of property but kept back part of the money for themselves and brought the rest to put it at the Apostle's feet (Acts 5:2) saying that it was the whole fee. Ananias was punished with death by the Holy Spirit. «Upon hearing Peter, Ananias fell down and died» (Acts 5:5) and so did his wife «at that moment she fell down at his feet and died» (Acts 5:7–10).[30]

The way commodities were distributed among the first Christians and the way they were fed added another 3,000 believers to their number on that day as Luke states (Acts 2:41). This number is so large that St. John Chrysostom (PG 60, cols. 65–66) exclaims: «If we could apply joint ownership in our days, both rich and poor would lead a better life. In fact, this would please the rich more than it would please the poor». And then he used some hypothetical numerical data to prove that to redistribute the rich people's wealth for the benefit of the poor would be in the best interest of the rich (PG 60, cols. 65–66).

St. John Chrysostom addressed the questions of wealth and poverty and described the voluntary nature of giving founded in indissoluble spiritual bonds among Christians. He pointed out that «they noticed that the spiritual assets are common and that nobody possessed more than the other and so they soon ended up giving away their material possessions. Their feeling was that they were under the paternal roof where there were no cold words as «mine» or «yours». So they felt comfortable to be able to sit at the dinner table together. Neither were the poor embarrassed nor did the wealthy brag about their riches. And that's exactly what made them feel graced. The poor felt that they were well taken care of and probably enjoyed themselves. And the rich also felt that they were praised and so they united with the poor» (PG 60 (1860), cols. 65–66).

St. John Chrysostom emphatically praised the voluntary efforts of the Christians to establish unity and made a great mark of honor «they were so generous that there was not any among them that lacked because they did not give away only part of their property saving some of it for themselves, neither did they offer everything and yet they considered it to be common property. When they ridded themselves of this (social and psychological) anomaly, they lived in abundance and mutual respect. And they did not dare place their possessions in the hands of the Apostles, neither did they hand in their property with pride but laid it at the Apostles' feet and asked them to distribute it and gave them the power to spend it as if it were

[29] See Baloglou (2011b, 247–298).

[30] Ruef (1960), Brown (1969), All this scene and the description in the *Acts* has been characterized by Robbins (1998, 24), as the only event of economic interest in the New Testament.

common, not as if it were their own. This freed them of vanity. If this took place now, we would all be living happily, both the wealthy and the poor...» (PG 60 (1860), col. 96).

14.3.1 The Institution of Deaconship

The institution of deaconship should be examined in the context of a fair distribution of the harvest. The reason is that there arose complaints on the part of Grecian or Hellenistic Jews of Diaspora (those whose ancestors had been dispersed from the land in Israel's captivities) against native Hebrews (those who were born and raised in the land of Israel) because their widows were discriminated against in the daily serving of food. The Hellenistic Jews of Diaspora most likely did not speak Aramaic but spoke Greek or the language of the nation from which they had come and so they had their own Synagogue (Acts 6:1; cf. also Acts 9:29;11:20).

According to the established practice of philanthropy and almsgiving of the Great Jewish Assembly, every poor Hebrew was to receive money for 14 portions of food on Fridays, while a non-Hebrew (stranger) would receive the benefit only for 1 day (Voulgaris 2012, 62). The Apostles noticed the murmuring of the Hellenes against the native Hebrews, gathered the believers together and asked them to find seven men to care for the meals as the needs of the growing Church kept them too busy to deal with all the responsibilities. The Apostolic Church then extended the system of daily distribution of food to all the Judean widows regardless of being native Hebrews or Hellenistic Jews. It is noteworthy here that this incident marked the beginning of ecclesiastical hierarchy since until then the handling of money and food and the evaluation of each one's needs had been undertaken exclusively by the Apostles, though not by order of the believers. From then onward, the seven deacons (see Tsitsigkos 1993, 450–454) would be handling these tasks as preachers (Acts 6:10) and as missionaries (Acts 8:5) in a fashion that was similar to the traditions of the Judaic cities in Palestine that applied strictly socio-economic[31] criteria in handling public affairs[32] except that now they would be social workers acting by order of the believers as the verse indicates : «Brothers and sisters, choose seven men from among you who are known to be full of the Spirit and wisdom» (Acts 6:3).

[31] Cf. the 15th Canon of the Local Synod of Neocaesareia (315) and the 16th Canon of the Oecumenical Synod (680). Agapios (Leonardos) and Nikodemos (1864/2003, 233–234, 395).

[32] Strack and Billerbeck (1992–1998, vol. 3, 641); Meyer (1921, 155).

14.3.2 *The Organization of the «Common Meals» and the Institution of «Logeia»*

The practice of offering «common meals», as described by Luke in the *Acts (of) Apostles*, concerns the Church of Jerusalem, however not exclusively, and reflects the prevailing socio-economic conditions in the area.[33] Jerusalem was built in a mountainous area that did not have water resources or any other resources. The cost of living was high and the city relied economically on its Temple that attracted pilgrims from all the Diaspora. In this sense, it became a pole of attraction for beggars to such an extent that it was righteously called «the city of idlers» (Jeremias 1969, 115–116). Therefore, the «Love Feasts» were instituted in consonance with contemporary attitudes and were the natural thing to do under the circumstances.

At the time, economic recess was accentuated by population explosion as well as heavy state and religious taxation imposed by Herod the Great (Josephus, *Judaean Archaeology* I XXI (1) 401–(13) 430), who wanted to meet the immense expenditures for the construction of cities and grandiose edifices (Grant 1926, 81–87). This resulted in having poor unemployed and landless peasantry, but also big landowners and rich bankers all in one place, Palestine. The poor farmers became increasingly poorer swamped in debt and despair. Many ended up begging piously in the city streets or in the villages only hoping for a miracle that would save them. Others resorted to robbery and pillaging of those using connecting streets. These people took to caves and rocks for protection.[34]

As far as the organization of the «common meals» in other communities is concerned, the case of the Church of Corinth is the most known because of the volume of information we have through Saint Paul's detailed descriptions. His *Second Letter to the Corinthians* (hereafter II Cor.) is the most important source of information regarding the kind of problems that Christianity faced. The Apostle of Nations faced problems that had to do with the Sunday Dinner disorder and those who opposed him. Indeed, the «disorder» (Ioannidis 2008a, 211–236) that took place during the common meals after Liturgy and Holy Communion in the First Church of Corinth was initiated by the members of the upper economic class and targeted the brothers of the lower economic class. Saint Paul's deep concerns about this vital problem[35] influenced his Eucharist Theology in the issue of the socio-economic effects. At least four «factions» (parts) of the Christians in Corinth are mentioned by name (1 Corinthians (hereafter 1 Cor.) 1:10–12, 3:3–5, 10:18–19). Moreover, the Church of Corinth consisted mainly of members, who came from the lower social and economic strata-the so-called «infants, diseased, non-born,

---

[33] Cf. the useful information given by Jeremias (1969). See also Agouridis (1989, 161–162).

[34] Klausner (1926, 174–190). Cf. Agouridis (2005, 145–149).

[35] The problem of St. Paul's opponents as it has been described in His Two Letters to the Corinthians is one of the most distinguished and provocative issue in the modern literature. The reference—work for this problem is Georgi (1964).

non-existing»,—but also included some members who were educated,—«wise»,—«powerful» and of noble ancestry (1 Cor. 1:26).

St. Paul wrote *His First Epistle* to correct what he saw as erroneous in the Church of Corinth. He had been informed about incidents of deviation from and distortion of true Christian life. Some had made factions (1 Cor., Chaps. 1–4), some had appealed to pagan courts (1 Cor. 6:1–11), others had been eating pagan food (1 Cor. Chaps. 8–10), while some groups had been fighting one another regarding Sunday Dinner (1 Cor. 11:17–34). There was also fighting over power among those who prophesied and those who spoke foreign languages (1 Cor. Chaps. 12–14). In his effort to restore social peace and uniformity of belief, St. Paul referred to three main points in his 1 Cor. 11:17–12:31. Firstly, St. Paul referred to Eucharist, secondly to the distribution of offers and benefits and to the division deaconship and thirdly to the concept of the Church as congregation where each member is called to perform a specific and special task depending on merit (1 Cor. 7:20)[36] by cooperating with other members of the society in order for them to become useful and integral members of their community.[37] The Holy Eucharist depicts the unity of the Apostolic Church of Corinth participation in which does not assume a personal character but a collective one since «as there is one bread, the multitudes of us are one body, because we are all parts of the same bread» (1 Cor. 10:17). Therefore, any discrimination among the congregation is ruled out since the characterization of the Church as «the body of Christ» (Coloss.1:24; Ephes. 1:23) is depicted and expressed in all social events and in all aspects of life of its members. St. Paul considered that dining together on Sunday (1 Cor. 11:10) would be the believers' main manifestation of anticipation and an early savoring of God's reign (Vasileiadis 2009, 64). In addition, the Eucharistic Theory of Deaconship or Christian solidarity dates back to the Apostolic ages and to the first Christian ages when it was closely linked to the Eucharistic gatherings. And such being the nature of the institution of the common meals «of love», St. Paul makes persistent efforts for «the Collection for the Lord's People» (1 Cor. 16:1),[38] the selection of the seven deacons (Acts 6:1–6) and the ordination of deacons and deaconesses during the Holy Sacrament.[39]

St. Paul became aware of the socio-economic differences among the members of the Corinthian congregation because when they gathered to worship God, they lacked the spirit of love, self-sacrifice and community of Christ: «So when you get together, it's not the Lord's Supper that you eat, for as you are eating, each of you continues with your own meal. As a result, one goes hungry and another gets drunk» remarked he in 1 Cor. 11:20–21.

The second problem he encountered in the Church of Corinth was its division into «factions». Usually, besides the underlying theological controversies, there is

---

[36] See also Rom. 11:29. Ephes. 4:1.

[37] Ioannidis (2008b), Chap. 2.

[38] Eckert (1981, 65–80), Betz (1993), Georgi (1994).

[39] Theodorou (2009, 74).

also the socio-economic dimension of the phenomenon, which is based on the differential conceptualization of the ways and methods used by the charismatic touring missionary community organizers. St. Paul's adversaries represent the type of charismatic touring missionary of the early ages of Christianity originating in Palestine and fitting the moral bill of having no home, family, property or security. On the contrary, the Disciple of Nations represents a type of missionary lawfulness, a form of «functional» legitimacy. So, while the charismatic touring missionaries depended on the community's financial support, St. Paul developed a new theological ethos that was oecumenical and at the same time social and moral. St. Paul took particular pride (II Cor. 11:10–12) in being able to sustain himself and not becoming a burden for anyone (II Cor. 11:9). He had his own reasons for doing so, merely to shake off any suspicion on the part of his enemies that he profited from his mission. In his *First Epistle to the Thessalonians* 2:5 he wrote «You know that we have never used flattery, nor have we put on a mask to cover up greed, God is our witness» and reassured that as far as this was possible he did not exercise the right[40] his doctrine gave him to receive support from the community he served (1 Cor. 9:4–14). Given that St. Paul's opponents in the Corinthian camp were members of the higher social strata (Vasileiadis 2006, 301), it is easy to understand the reason why they reacted against the program of collection for the poor people and also why St. Paul found it necessary to bring this matter up anew (*Logeia,* II Cor. Chaps. 8 and 9), analyze it in detail, and expound his positions in the austere letter he wrote to them (II Cor. 12:14–15).

A thorough examination of Chaps. 8 and 9 of II Corinthians[41] leads us to the conclusion that the program of collecting for the poor was founded after the Lord's example of a fair distribution of material goods. In this sense, he praised the Macedonian attitude—«Brothers, we want you to know that the grace of God was given to the Church of Macedonia» (II Cor. 8:1)—for setting the standards of evaluating the true love of Corinthians. He reminded them of the "grace" of the Lord who «became poor for our sake although he was rich, so that we would become rich through his poverty» (II Cor. 8:9).

All this gave St. Paul the opportunity to repeat his urge to the Corinthian Christians to volunteer their generous contribution to the fund raising program (*logeia*, II Cor. 8:10). Moreover, he pointed out to them that «it doesn't matter how much you have. What matters is how much you are willing to share from what you have» (II Cor. 8:12). This was to mean that he would be pleased with just a symbolic act of giving on their part, while he had praised the Macedonians before for having contributed to the relief program far beyond their power. There is certainly some explanation for this differentiation. The Christian community in Corinth was of lower economic status, as it has been already stated, which St. Paul felt obliged to respect by asking that they offer only whatever they could (Vasileiadis 2006, 356).

[40] Weiss (2001, 423).

[41] For a detailed analysis see Vasileiadis (2002). Idem (2006), 305–400, 401–448.

According to the sociologist of the Age of the New Testament G. Theissen, «the primeval Hellenistic Christianity was not a proletarian movement of the lower classes, nor did it originate from the upper social strata. On the contrary, remarkable for its social structure is the fact that it consisted of several social classes of various attitudes, traditions and conditions» (Weiss 1974, 267). This view explains any possible conflict that may have arisen, indication of which is found in 1 Corinthians 11:20–2. «The Christians, who gather to eat on Sunday, do not eat the Lord's Supper but each one eats his own meal. So, one goes hungry while another gets drunk». This verse reveals the presence of heresies that led to deplorable incidents.

Pivotal in comprehending the relief program and, consequently, the policy of redistributing wealth that the Disciple proposes to Christians is the definition of the term «equality» used by St. Paul in verses 8:13–14. The term «equality» is used only twice in the Septuagint; the first is in Iob 36:29 and the second in Zechariah 4:7—in fact, without a Hebrew equivalent (Vasileiadis 2002, 366). The term is also seen in St. Paul's *Epistle to the Colossians* 4:1 in which he reminds the masters of servants of what is right behavior towards them: «Masters grant your servants that which is fair and equal, knowing that you also have a Master in Heaven». This verse belongs to a duty list (Colossians 3:18–4:1). The term «equality» here does not refer to parity between masters and servants before Christ but to the fact that masters should take proper care of their servants, according Theodoretus of Cyrrhus (PG 82 (1859), col. 621D).

Oecumenius' commentary interprets the issue in a similar fashion: «Justice and equality is the reward of the laboring servants and also abundance of the necessary goods» (PG 119 (1864), col. 24C). Even more understandable and sharp is John Chrysostom who raises the question: «What is the fair thing to do? What is equality?» only to provide his own answer: «Give them everything in abundance not only what they need, but reward them for their hard work» (PG 62 (1860), col. 398). In this way John Chrysostom approaches St. Paul's interpretation of alms-giving. St. Paul does not recommend that the masters free their servants in the name of the new faith, but urges that masters be fair and always meet their obligations towards them.[42]

If we co-examine the passages in Colossians 4:1 and II Cor. 8:13–14, then the term «equality» is defined according to Hellenistic standards. In particular, the concept of equality bore a rather legal meaning in ancient Greek literature. Although in *Gorgias* (507ff.) Plato presumes that equality stems from cosmic equality or is part of it, and at the same time Euripides personifies it (*Phoinissai* v.536), equality in ancient Greece defines legal relationships. Equality was a basic principle in Athenian Democracy. Aristotle spoke of «freedom and equality» (Aristotle, *Politics* IV 4 1291 b34–36), «political equality» (Aristotle, *Politics* VI), and also of «a polis established on the equality of citizens» (Aristotle, *Politics* III 6, 1279 a10). Consequently, while initially the term «equality» differed from the term «similarity» in that the former pertained to legal relationships and the latter to

[42] Karavidopoulos (1981/2007), 522.

physical, gradually both terms came to mean the same thing: «A polis for the equals and similars» according to Xenophon (*Hellenica* VII I 45), «equalities and similarities» according to Isocrates (*Areopagiticus* 7,61). Aristotle puts it very eloquently: «what is fair is what is equal» (Arist., *Ethica Nicomachea* I 1) and so «equality» results in including the idea of justice: «An fair judge» according to Plato (Law XII 957), «equal and fair judges» according to Polybius (*Histories* XVI 15_3). The Stoics, who lived in the New Testament ages and identified equality with integrity, stress that «equality and gratefulness follow justice» (Diog. Laert. VII 125), while to Philon this relation is exactly the opposite as «Equality is the mother of Justice» (*Περί φυτουργίας Νώε* 122).

Paul traces the notion of equality in ancient Greek literature and adds to it new content that is based on the idea of Christian love arising from Jesus Christ's teachings about the Kingdom of Heaven (Matthew 10:1–16). In II Cor. 8:14 Paul takes it even further. Equality becomes the objective of social behavior—as «Christian behavior should be». However, this attitude contrasts the ideal of joint ownership of the early Christians, as it is expressed in the verses of Acts 2 44 ff. 4:36 ff. 5:16ff.

In the effort to resolve its social problems and release tension to some acceptable degree the Roman society of the New Testament ages perceived equality as the extension of Roman citizenship to as many social strata as possible with the exception of some groups such as servants and foreigners. Christianity, though, conferred the state of freedom on all people without exception. According to Paul's statement «there is no difference between Jews and Greeks, between slaves and free people, between men and women, for you are all one in Christ Jesus» (Galatians 3:28). Compared to the growing social pressures and demands of the Roman Empire, Paul's perception of equality offered a new, successful form of social integration at a time when all efforts for reform by the Roman Imperium failed—as in the case of Gracchi for example—and led to a vicious cycle of alternating enlightened monarchy (second century AD) with absolute monarchy (fourth century AD).

The social context of Paul's argumentative, as this materializes in the program of collection for the poor (*logeia*, II Cor. 8:13–15), brings forward the ideal of a fair distribution of wealth through the prospect of Christian brotherhood among all of Father's children and through Providence.

Wealthy Corinthians were not to keep for themselves more goods than necessary to get by. Therefore, it should be their duty to offer the rest of their belongings to the poor brothers of Jerusalem (Cf. II Cor. 8:13–14). If Christians perceive material possessions as God's gifts and not as human accomplishment, then they will contribute to reaching a state of equality where private property will be abolished, not through violence but through the power of love. St. John Chrysostom aptly remarks that if «we all have one stomach to fill and one life to live and one body to cover», then rich people won't have any reason to prosper in order to give their surplus to the poor.

In his effort to convince Corinthians to be generous and well-disposed in almsgiving, he urges them to regard it as a «blessing», as a «gift», a bounteous collection that is given largely and liberally rather than as something that is redundant, an act of covetousness of men who usually do what they do sparingly, tenaciously, keeping their money as long as they can, loathing to part with (II Cor. 9:5). «Superfluity» in the Septuagint and also in the New Testament implies someone's continual tendency to acquire more possessions disregarding others, in fact at their expense. Particularly in the Old Testament acquisitiveness is directly opposite to love for fellow people and especially for the poor who the (Hebraic) Law is to protect against (Exodus 20, 17–22, 14ff.; Deuteronomy 24, 10ff). St. Paul uses the term with various connotations in his Epistles to the (Romans 1:29, 1 Cor. 5:19–21; 6:9; Colossians 3:5; 1 Thessalonians 4:6) to refer to sins of sexual nature and paganism. In any case, whether material greed or sensual greed, the result is the same i.e. a greedy person takes advantage of his fellow man instead of serving him (Vasileiadis 2002, 418–419).

The Corinthian people's generosity, which is an imperative characteristic for them, leads them to self-sufficiency (II Cor. 9:8). Self-sufficiency (1Tim. 6:7, content Philippians 4:11), a Stoic term, is a wise person's principle virtue.[43] In the Cynic and Stoic Philosophy this term describes the person whose willpower makes him do with very little so that he can be independent and therefore content (Diogenes Laertius VI 105; Epictetus, *Diatribai* III 13,10). Although for the Stoics self-sufficiency is resultant of all virtues, its essential characteristic is that it derives from human powers and limits itself—or rather exhausts itself—to the individual alone. On the contrary, Paul says that the source of self-sufficiency is God. Adequacy is God's gift, the result of God's grace. As a consequence, it is not exhausted exclusively in the narrow context of the individual. Its most important specification is caring for the others. Self-sufficiency is a virtue as long as it is accompanied by social welfare and as long as it is conducive to all that is virtuous.

The social aspect of Paul's relief program is attested in the reference he makes in his 2Corinthians 9:9 to the Old Testament and especially to Psalm 111:9 «As the scripture says, He gives generously to the needy; his kindness lasts forever». The word «needy» appears only once in the Old Testament compared to the word «poor» that is widely used in the Gospels and scarcely used in the long Paul's Epistles (Romans15:26; Galatians 2:10, 4:9), «needy» sounds weaker as it describes the one who is in socially and financial difficulties and generally the one who is in need. However, the word «poor» is used in its religious connotation, describing the one who has no possessions, relies on his fellow people's charity and as a result, has confided his existence in God. God will reward the work and philanthropic disposal of Corinthians in almsgiving righteously, that is by granting them prosperity and well-being.

[43] Pohlenz (1949, 69–104), Ioannidis (1934/2001, 188–189), Oikonomou (1980, 17–34).

14.4 Syssitia and Common Meals: A Unity in the Polis and in the Church

The whole effort to organize the syssitia and institute the relief program aims at a single thing: the unity of the Church, as this is reflected in the «Church in the house» (Rom. 16:5; 1Cor. 16:19; Colossians 14:15; Philemon 2), whose representative is its bishop.[44] Indeed, as «Head of the Eucharist», the bishop is the person around whom the Church is united (Ignatius of Antiocheia, *To Magnesians* 6), meets the credentials, sees to the salvation of his sheep and also to the fair management of the Christian members of the Church. Therefore, the bishop must divide wisely among the orphans, the weeping widows and the poor strangers the money that is «voluntarily» offered for the less fortunate members of the Church. Management of the money has to be distributed fairly among those who need it and not misused. This is how all discord, conflict and contention will be avoided in the body of the Church. The warrantor of the Church's unity is the bishop.

The magistrates in an ancient polis have the obligation to keep the people united. Consequently, it would not be far-fetched to compare the Bishop of the Church to the magistrates of a polis. For both of them have a common goal which is the eradication of rebellions, the persistence in keeping the Church as well as the city united as a whole.

Final Conclusions

Crete and Sparta, two «prosperous» poleis according to Aristotle which are also extremely important to Greek people's historic awareness, had instituted and implemented the syssitia aiming at a fair re-distribution of wealth. In spite of the Spartan institution drawbacks, as it grew to be in practice, the institution of syssitia satisfied the citizens' need for «equality», «equal rights», «justice» and state integration.

Aristotle, as a critical assessor of constitutions and of the political theories of various scholars analyses the institution of syssitia and accepts it in his «best polis», because it is in accordance to the basic principle of self-sufficiency, conduces to smoothing out any social tension that might arise among citizens and also conduces to maintaining social unity and harmony.

All sources attest that, implicitly or explicitly, Jesus strongly opposed the mechanisms that disrupted social peace. The Oral Tradition of the Early Church known as the Q source (Luke 6:20–22), the teachings of prospering in Heavens (Luke 12:33–34 = Matthew 6:19–21) versus prospering on earth (Luke 12:22–32 = Matthew 6:25–34) and especially those regarding the incompatibility of worshipping both God and mammon, the demon of

(continued)

[44] Cf. the extensive analysis by Zizioulas (1965/2009).

gluttony, riches and injustice (Luke 16:13 = Matthew 6:24) in St. Mark's Gospel, the identification of usurers as «thieves» (Mark 11:15–17), St. Luke's special teachings, Jesus' teaching in Nazareth (Luke 4:16–18), the intriguing Parable of Lazarus and the Rich Man (Luke 16:19ff, Matthew 13:24–30) and the excerpt on Final Judgment (Matthew 25:30–46), all is consistent with the fact that Jesus followed the Prophets' tradition[45] (143) of demonstrating that daily sustenance—and not the unfair accumulation of wealth—is a better economic system. And so the Lord urged His followers to pray «Give us each day our daily bread» (Luke 11:3) same as Matthew's 6:11 «Give us our daily bread».

The institution of syssitia falls into line with the aforementioned New Testament testimonies. It can be described as a supreme institution of the early Church, one that conveys to the participating Christian the sense of belonging to the one and unified Church regardless of one's socio-economic background. At the same time, *logeia*, Paul's pioneer program of collecting for the poor, in the form that it is postulated in *II Corinthians* Chaps. 8–9 and also the radical ethics of *The Epistle* of James aimed at «equality» and «equal distribution of wealth» which both describe a society beyond the bipolar system of capitalism and socialism. On the contrary, this system does not focus on the production and division techniques and processes but rather on the very source of material affluence as «The earth is the Lord's and everything in it, the world, and all who live in it» (David's Psalm 24:11).

References

Agapios (Leonardos), Nikodemos (eds) (1864/2003) Πηδάλιον της νοητής νηόςς της Μίας, Αγίας, Καθολικής και Αποστολικής Εκκλησίας (3rd edn). Raftanis, Zante (reprinted 13th edn. Athens: Papadimitriou)

Agouridis S (1963) Η κοινοκτημοσύνη εν τῇ πρώτῃ Εκκλησίᾳ. In: Αθωνική Πολιτεία επί τῇ χιλιετηρίδι του Αγίου Όρους. Thessalonikē, pp 177–206 (reprinted Idem, Βιβλικά Μελετή--ματα, vol II. Thessalonikē 1971, 251–276)

Agouridis S (1989) Αρα γε γινώσκεις ά αναγινώσκεις; Ερμηνευτικές και Ιστορικές μελέτες σε ζητήματα των αρχών του Χριστιανισμού. Artos Zoes, Athens

Agouridis S (2005) Δοκίμια στις ρίζες του Χριστιανισμού. Ennoia, Athens

Antonopoulos A, Terezis Chr (2009) Διάλογος βιβλικής και φιλοσοφικής ερμηνείας : Αποστόλου Παύλου Α' προς Κορινθίους και Αριστοτέλους Πολιτικά. In: Απόστολος Παύλος και Κόρινθος (Apostle Paul and Corinth). Proceedings of the International Scientific Congress (Corinth, 23–25 September 2007). Editor-in-chief: St. Papadopoulos, edited by K. Belezos with the assistance by S. Despotis and Christos Karakolis, vol 1. Psychogios, Athens, pp 129–192

[45] It is worth noting that the Prophets in Israel criticized the unequal distribution of wealth, but they do not propose any social changes, but the internal change of men (Gordon 1975, 76–78; Oikonomou 2006, 444–447; Idem 2003, 235–247).

Austin MM, Vidal-Naquet P (1977) Economic and social history of ancient Greece: an introduction, transl. by M. M. Austin. Berkeley, Los Angeles
Baloglou Chr P (1998) Το πρόγραμμα δημοσιονομικής και κοινωνικής πολιτικής του Αριστοτέλη (Συμβολή στην οικονομική σκέψη και πρακτική των μέσων του 4ου π.Χ. αιώνα). Eleftheri Skepsis, Athens
Baloglou Chr P (2011a) Η κριτική ανάλυση των πολιτειακών θεσμών «ευδοκιμουσῶν πολιτειῶν» από τον Αριστοτέλη. Athens, Unpublished paper available from the author
Baloglou Chr P (2011b) Η οικονομική και επιχειρηματική δραστηριότητα του Αποστόλου Βαρνάβα. Ekklesiastikos Pharos 82:247–298
Baloglou Chr P (2013) Διάλογος βιβλικής και φιλοσοφικής ερμηνείας: Η διοίκηση και οργάνωση του Οίκου και της οικονομικής μονάδος κατά τον Ξενοφώντα και τους Αποστόλους Πέτρο και Παύλο. Celestia Nova 4:43–80
Betz HD (1993) 2. Korinther 8 und 9. Gutersloh
Brown B (1969) The Meaning and function of Acts 5, 1–11 in the purpose of Luke-Acts. Dissertation, Boston University Press
Buck RJ (1959) «Communalism on the Lipari Islands (Diod 5.9.4)», Classical Philology, LIV:35–59
Eckert J (1981) «Die Kollekte des Paulus für Jerusalem», Kontinuität und Einheit. Festschrift fur Mussner. Freiburg i.Br. 65–675
FGrHist: Jacoby F (1926–1958) (ed) Die Fragmente der griechischen Historiker. Brill, Leiden
Fiorakis SI (1973) Η μεγάλη δωδεκάδελτος επιγραφή της Γόρτυνος. Introduction by S. I. Fiorakis. Translation and commentary by E. E. Perakis. Herakleion
Georgi D (1964) Die Gegner des Paulus im 2.Korinterbrief. Studien zur religiösen Propaganda in der Spätantike. Vluyn, Neukirchen
Georgi D (1994) Die Geschichte der Kollekte des Paulus für Jerusalem, 2nd edn. Vluyn Neukirchen
Gordon B (1975) Economic analysis before Adam Smith: Hesiod to Lessius. Barnes & Noble, New York, NY
Gordon B (1982) Lending at interest: some Jewish, Greek, and Christian approaches, 800 B.C.—AD 100. Hist Polit Econ 14:406–426
Grant Fr (1926) Economic background of the Gospels. Oxford University Press, Oxford
Hadjimichalis, Nektarios, Archim (1972) Αι περί ιδιοκτησίας απόψεις εν τη Εκκλησία κατά τους τρεις πρώτους αιώνας. Patriarchical Foundation of the Patristic Studies, Thessalonikē
Ioannidis Bas (1934/2001) Ο Απόστολος Παύλος και οι Στωικοί φιλοσοφοι. Αι ιδέαι αυτών περί θείου προορισμού και περί αιθρωπίνης ελευθερίας. Thessalonikē (reprinted Katerini: mati)
Ioannidis T (2008a) «Αταξίες κατά την τέλεση του Κυριακού Δείπνου στην πρώτη Εκκλησία της Κορίνθου: Κοινωνιολογικές και λειτουργικές προεκτάσεις», Στα Βήματα του Αποστόλου Βαρνάβα. Χαριστήριος Τόμος προς τιμήν του Αρχιεπισκόπου Νέας Ιουστινιανής και πάσης Κύπρου κ.κ. Χρυσοστόμου Β' για τα τριάντα χρόνια αρχιερατικής του διακονίας (In the Footsteps of Apostle Barnabas Festschrift in Honour of Chrysostom II, Archbishop of New Justinianoupolis and all Cyprus). Nicosia, pp 211–236
Ioannidis T (2008b) Άνθρωπος και κόσμος κατά τον Απόστολο Παύλο. Pournaras, Thessalonike
Jeremias J (1969) Jerusalem in the Time of Jesus. An investigation into economic and social conditions during the New Testament Period. New York, SCM Press
Karavidopoulos I (1981/2007) Αποστόλου Παύλου Επιστολές προς Εφεσίους, Φιλιππησίους, Κολοσσαείς, Φιλήμονα. Pournaras, Thessalonike
Klausner J (1926) Jesus of Nazareth, transl By J. H. Dandy. New York
Koerner R (1993) Inschriftliche Gesetzestexte der frühen griechischen Polis. Aus dem Nachlass herausgegeben von K. Hallof. Böhlau, Köln (Akten der Gesellschaft für griechische und hellenistische Rechtsgeschichte 9)
Latte K (1968) «Kollektivbesitz und Staatsschatz in Griechenland», εν Idem, Kleine Schriften zu Religion, Recht, Literatur und Sprache der Griechen und Romer. C. H. Beck, München, pp 294–312

Lehmeier K (2006) Oikos und Oikonomia. Antike Konzepte der Haushaltsführung und der Bau der Gemeinde bei Paulus. N. G. Elwert, Marburg
Link S (1991) Landverteilung und sozialer Frieden im archaischen Griechenland. F. Steiner, Stuttgart (Historia Einzelschriften 69)
Link S (1994) Das griechische Kreta. Untersuchungen zu seiner staatlichen und gesellschaftlichen Entwicklung von 6. bis zum 4. Jahrhundert v. Chr. F. Steiner, Stuttgart
Maloney R (1971) Usury in Greek, Roman and Rabbinic thought. Traditio 27:79–109
Mandalakis A (2004) Κοινωνία και οικονομία στην Κρήτη κατά την αρχαϊκή και κλασική εποχή. Dissertation (1995), Bikelaian Library, Herakleion
Meyer E (1921) Ursprung und Anfänge des Christentums, 3rd edn, vol III. Stuttgart–Berlin
Microyannakis Emm (1972–1973) Ο δήμος εις «τας ευδοκιμούσας» πολιτείας κατ' Αριστοτέλη. Αθηνά 73–74:402–415
Microyannakis Emm (2002–2003) «(Αρκυς) web of views». Επιστημονική Επετηρίδα Φιλοσοφικής Σχολής Πανεπιστημίου Αθηνών 34:39–57
Mosse, C (1984/1987) La Grèce archaique d' Homère à Eschyle VIIIe- VIe siècles av. J. C. Editions du Seuil (Greek transl by S. Paschalis, Kardamitsa, Athens)
Newman WL (1887/2000) The politics of Aristotle. With an Introduction, two prefatory essays and notes critical and explanatory by W. L. Newman, vol II. Clarendon, Oxford (reprinted Oxford University Press)
Oikonomou E (1973) «Αι πιστωτικαί και δανειοδοτικαί αντιλήψεις της Παλαιάς Διαθήκης», εν Μελέται προς τιμήν Στρατή Γ. Ανδρεάδη, vol III. Athens, pp 453–464
Oikonomou Chr K (1980) Αυτάρκης και Αυτάρκεια στους Στωικούς και στον Απόστολο Παύλο. Δελτίον Βιβλικών Μελετών 9: 17–34
Oikonomou Chr K (2003) Καινή Διαθήκη και Πολιτισμός. Pournaras, Thessalonike
Oikonomou Chr K (2006) «Η συμβολη της Αγίας Γραφής στην ανθρωπιστική αντιμετώπιση των φτωχών και των καταφρονημένων του κόσμου», *Διακονία-Λειτουργία-Χάρισμα. Πατερική και σύγχρονη ερμηνεία της Καινής Διαθήκης*. Τιμητικός Τόμος *προς του Ομότιμο Καθηγητή του Πανεπιστημίου Αθηνών Γεώργιο Αντ. Γαλίτη*. Επιμ. Εκδόσεως Ι. Γαλάνης et al., Athens: εν πλώ, pp 443–456
Oikonomou Chr K (2010) «Η κοινωνική δυναμική της Θεολογίας από την Καινή Διαθήκη στους Τρεις Ιεράρχες» in Idem, Καινή Διαθήκη και Ερμηνευτές Πατέρες. Thessalonike: Pournaras, pp 17–43
Patras L (2007) Αρχέτυπα της κοινωνικής πολιτικής στη Βίβλο (Παλαιά Διαθήκη). Χρονικά Κεντρικού Ισραηλιτικού Συμβουλίου Ελλάδος 30(209):3–11
Philippidis L (1958) Ιστορία της Εποχής της Καινής Διαθήκης εξ απόψεως παγκοσμίου και πανθρησκειακής. Athens, Apostoliki Diakonia
Pohlenz M (1949) Paulus und die Stoa. Zeitschrift für die Neutestamentliche Wissenschaft und verwandte Gebiete 42:69–104
Repschinski B (2009) Warum mussten Hananias und Sapphira sterben? Protokolle zur Bibel 18(1)
Robbins L (1998) A history of economic thought. The LSE Lectures. Edit. By Steven G. Medema and Warren G. Samuels. Foreword by W. Baumol. Princeton University Press, Princeton, NJ
Ruef S-J (1960) Ananias and Sapphira. A study of the community-disciplinary practices underlying Acts 5,11. Dissertation, Harvard University Press
Schoinas F (2006) Οι πολιτικές αντιλήψεις του Μεγάλου Βασιλείου. Ελληνική Φιλοσοφική Επιθεώρηση 23:263–279
Schütrumpf E (1991) Aristoteles Politik Buch II. Buch III. Übersetzt und erläutert von Eckart Schütrumpf. Akademie Verlag, Berlin (Aristoteles Werke in deutscher Übersetzung 9/II)
Schütrumpf E (2005) Aristoteles Politik Buch VII/VIII. Über die beste Verfassung. Übersetzt und erläutert von Eckart Schütrumpf. Akademie Verlag, Berlin (Aristoteles Werke in deutscher Übersetzung 9/IV)
Stephanidis D (1948/2003) Η Κοινωνική Οικονομική εν τη ιστορική της εξελίξει. Athens (reprinted Athens: Eleftheri Skepsis)

Strack H, Billerbeck P (1992–1998) Kommentar zum Neuen Testament aus Talmud und Midrash, vol III. Munchen, Beck

Talamo S (1987) Il Sissizio a Creta. Miscellanea Greca e Romana 2:9–26

Taylor JE (1998) The so-called Therapeutae of De vita contemplativa: identity and character. In: http:www.findarticles.com/cf-O/m2399/n1-v91/20512260/p1-19/article.jhtml (Harvard Divinity School 1998)

Theodorakopoulos I (1974) Ο φιλοσοφικός ορισμόςς της εννοίας της ιδιοκτησίας. Πρακτικά της Ακαδημίας Αθηνών 49:354–360

Theodorou E (2009) *Εκκλησιολογικές διαστάσεις της Ευχαριστιακής Θεολογίας*. Θεολογία 80:45–75

Tsitsigkos S (1993) Ποιο ήταν το έργο των επτά διακόνων; Εκκλησία 70:450–454

van Effénterre H, Ruzé F (1994) Nomima. Recueil d' inscriptions politiques et juridiques de l' archaisme grec, I. Rome (Collection d' École Francaise de Rome 188, I)

Vasileiadis P (2002) Χάρις-Διακονία-Κοινωνία (Β' Κορ. 8-9). *Ο κοινωνικός χαρακτηρας του παύλειου προγράμματος της λογείας*. Pournaras, Thessalonike

Vasileiadis P (2006) Παύλος. *Τομές στη θεολογία του*. Pournaras, Thessalonike

Vasileiadis P (2009) *Συνοδικότητα και* Πρωτείο *στην* Καινή Διαθήκη. Η παύλεια «περιεκτική» *Ευχαριστιακή* θεολογία αίτιο και προϋπόθεση *της συνοδικότητας*. Θεολογία 80(2):43–65

Voulgaris Chr S (2012) Ιστορία *της* Αρχεγόνου Αποστολικής Εκκλησίας 33–70 AD. Apostolike Diakonia, Athens

Weiss J (1974) Soziale Schichtung in der korinthischen Gemeinde. Ein Beitrag zur Soziologie des hellenistischen Urchristentums. Zeitschrift für die Neutestamentliche Wissenschaft und verwandte Gebiete 59:232–272

Weiss J (2001) Das Urchristentum. Die Geschichte der Periode 30-150 n.Chr. Greek transl. by Savvas Agouridis et al. Artos Zoes, Athens

Zizioulas I (1965/2009) Η *ενότης της* Εκκλησίας *εν* τῇ θείᾳ *Ευχαριστίᾳ* και τῷ Επισκόπῳ κατά *τους τρεις πρώτους αιώνας*. Dissertation, Athens (reprinted Athens: Grigori)

Author Index

A
Agapios (Leonardos), 208
Agouridis, S., 206, 209
A'Hearn, B., 128
Alesina, A., 170
Allen, L., 138
Altman, D., 161
Amemiya, T., 163, 186
Anderson, A.R., 53
Anderson, B.M., 37
Angelou, A., 123
Antonopoulos, A., 199
Aoki, M., 106
Aristophanes, 162, 166, 192, 194, 195
Arrow, K., 50
Arvanitidis, A.P., 161–171
Asteriou, D., 10
Austin, M.M., 202

B
Baccini, B., 34
Backhouse, R., 39
Bacon, F., 58, 59
Baloglou, Chr. P., 199–216
Basu, K., 170
Baumann, Z., 84
Baumol, W., 46
Beed, C., 39
Bendix, R., 68, 69
Beraud, A., 47
Bernardello, A., 128, 134, 145
Betz, H.D., 210
Bhaduri, A., 137
Billerbeck, P., 208
Binder, A., 122
Bitros, G.C., 3–21, 45, 161, 163, 165, 182, 186
Blaug, M., 45
Blume, L.E., 24, 161
Boson, M., 95
Bovykin, V.I., 129
Boylaud, O., 12
Bradford, A.S., 177
Braun, N., 161
Breslau, D., 35, 36
Bright, J., 70
Brogan, H., 95
Brown, B., 207
Bruni, L., 40
Brusegan, M., 148
Buchanan, J., 167, 170
Buck, R.J., 201
Buijs, B., 17
Bunyan, J., 57
Burke, E.M., 163
Burn, A.R., 183

C
Cafagna, L., 128
Cairnes, J., 31
Caldwell, B., 39
Cartledge, P., 163, 180, 181
Chang, H.J., 82
Chatziioannou, M.C., 132
Christensen, P., 168
Cipolla, C.M., 128
Clark, M., 70, 71, 136
Coase, R.H., 45–47, 108
Coates, J., 183

G.C. Bitros, N.C. Kyriazis (eds.), *Essays in Contemporary Economics*,
DOI 10.1007/978-3-319-10043-2

Cohen, E.E., 163, 169, 186
Coleman, D.C., 62, 63
Conca Messina, S.A., 138
Corazzol, G., 148
Cordeiro, C., 103
Cowen, T., 118
Cowherd, R.G., 70
Creedy, J., 33

D
Davenport, H., 37
Davies, J.K., 106
de Jasay, A., 97
de Mandeville, B., 65
de Tocqueville, A., 95
de Voltaire, (Arouet, Franqois-Marie), 66
Defoe, D., 82
Della V.S., 104
Descartes, R., 58, 59
Despotopoulos, A., 177
Diamandis, P., 123
Diderot, D., 47
Dockès, P., 91, 94, 98, 99
Dolega, M., 123
Dow, S., 35, 36
Drakopoulos, S.A., 31–41, 60
Drakopoulou Dodd, D., 53–73
Durlauf, S.N., 24

E
Economou, E.M.L., 175–187
Edgeworth, F.Y., 31–41
Efféntere, H., 201
Eggertsson, T., 103
Eichengreen, B., 5
Elsby, M., 118
Ely, R.T., 37
European Commission, 7, 10, 13, 20

F
Farenga, V., 168
Feld, L.P., 161
Ferguson, N., 148
Figueira, T.J., 163
Finley, M.I., 163
Fiorakis, S.I., 202
Fisher, I., 31–41
Fontaine, P., 49
Foxhall, L., 163
Fratianni, M., 135
Freeman, R., 78, 119, 122
French, A., 163
Frey, B., 161
Friedman, M., 39–41
Fullbrook, E., 85
Furubotn, E., 46, 47, 51
Fussfeld, D., 65, 67

G
Gabrielsen, V., 183
Galli, A.M., 138
Gallino, L., 85
Gassendi, P., 60
Genovesi, A., 79
Georgakopoulos, T., 5, 6
Georgi, D., 209, 210
Gide, C., 94
Gilmour, D., 129
Ginsborg, P., 128, 129
Glete, J., 187
Goetzmann, W.N., 144
Gordon, B., 199, 216
Gotsis, G., 53
Grant, Fr., 209
Greenfield, K.R., 128, 129, 146
Greif, A., 170
Gritsopoulos, T.A., 129
Grossman, M., 120–122
Guala, F., 40
Gualerzi, D., 82
Gustavus, A., 105
Gwartney, J.D., 4

H
Hacker, J.S., 117, 118
Hadjimichalis, N., 206
Hale, J.R., 183
Halkos, G., 184, 186
Hamilton, W., 37
Hampson, N., 58–62, 64, 66, 67
Hansen, M.H., 106, 162, 163, 175, 179, 187
Hanson, V.D., 176, 178, 180
Harris, E.M., 163
Hatzis, A.N., 165, 168, 169
Hayek, F.A., 97, 98
Healy, M., 178
Heckscher, E., 105
Henderson, H.M., 46
Hill, C., 56, 57
Hirsch, F., 84
Hobbes, T., 54, 58, 60, 61, 64, 67

Hobijn, B., 118
Hodgson, G.M., 46, 51
Honeyman, K., 69
Hoover, K., 39
Hudson, W., 55, 57

I
Ioannidis, B., 214
Ioannidis, T., 209, 210

J
Jacoby, F,
Jeremias, J., 209
Jevons, W.S., 31, 32
Jones, A.H.M., 162, 165

K
Kagan, D., 196
Kaiser, B.A., 163, 183
Kane, O., 39
Karavidopoulos, I., 212
Karayiannis, A.D., 7, 18, 31, 47, 54, 161, 163, 165, 168, 169, 193
Karl IX, 104, 105, 115
Katsiardi-Hering, O., 131
Katsimi, M., 14
Katsoulis, I., 117–125
Kaufmann, B., 161
Keynes, J.M., 75, 77–78, 88
Karras, H.,
Kindleberger, C.P., 128, 132
Klausner, J., 209
Kliemt, H., 99
Knight, F., 24
Koerner, R., 201
Kolm, S-C., 97
Konow, J., 97
Korres, G.M., 13
Kotler, S., 123
Krentz, P., 180
Krugman, P., 84
Kyriazis, N.C., 161–171, 176, 177, 181–184, 186, 187

L
Lane, F.C., 132
Lane, P., 62–64
Lanni, A., 168
Latouche, S., 84
Latte, K., 201, 205
Lawson, R.A., 4
Lawson, T., 39
Lehmeier, K., 199
Leibniz, G.W., 58, 64–66, 68
Leijonhufvud, A., 78
Leroy, M., 95
Levi, M., 105
Lewin, S., 41
Link, S., 201–203
Locke, J., 56, 58, 60, 61, 64
Lyttkens, C.H., 103–115, 163, 167–169

M
Macpherson, C.B., 60, 61
Maloney, R., 199
Maltezou, C., 127
Mandalakis, A., 201, 203
Manning, J.G., 163
Marx, K., 75–80, 86–88
Marxer, W., 161
Matsusaka, J., 161
McIntosh, M.K., 136
McLure M., 40
Ménard, C., 51
Merton, R.C., 24
Mertzios, K.D., 131
Metaxas, T., 176, 181, 187
Meyer, E., 208
Microyannakis, E., 200
Mill, J.S., 31, 45–51, 75, 76, 78, 88, 92 97
Millar, J., 79
Miller, D., 187
Millett, P., 163
Mirowski, P., 31, 33, 38
Morris, I., 163, 169, 183
Morrison, J., 183
Mosler, K., 120
Mosse, C., 202
Moutos, T., 14
Muldrew, C., 138, 149
Müller, J., 161
Mylonas, P., 5

N
Nevett, L.C., 163
Newman, P., 34
Newman, W.L., 205
Newton, I., 58–60
Nicoletti, G., 12
Nikodemos, 208

Nordhaus, W.D., 170
North, D.C., 51, 103–106

O
Ober, J., 162–169, 179, 185
O'Connor, J., 80
Oikonomou, Chr. K., 214, 216
Oikonomou, E., 199
Oman, C.W., 187
Oxenstierna, A., 105

P
Pagoulatos, G., 13
Pallinger, Z.T., 161
Papaconstantinou, G., 5
Papaioannou, A.P., 131, 138
Papandreou, A.G., 5–8, 11, 16, 191
Paparrigopoulos, X., 175–187
Pareto, V., 40, 95
Patras, L., 199
Pecchi, L., 78
Pelt, M, 3, 15
Pepelasis-Minoglou, I., 132
Perrotta, C., 75–88
Petrakos, G., 10
Pezzolo, L., 128
Phelps, E.S., 78, 97
Philippidis, L., 206
Pierson, P., 117, 118
Piga, G., 78
Piluso, G., 135, 138, 148
Pinheiro, J., 103
Pitelis, C., 48
Pluche, M.A., 64
Pohlenz, M., 214
Pollin, R., 80
Polsi, A., 135, 138
Pope, A., 65–68
Porter, P.A., 10
Prahalad, C.K., 123
Psycharis, Y., 10

Q
Quandt, R.E., 46

R
Raauflaub, K.A., 175, 183
Rabbin, M., 1
Rankov, N.B., 183
Rawls, J., 93, 97–99
Reinert, E., 82
Rhodes, P.J., 162, 176, 182
Ricardo, D., 49, 75, 81, 84
Richter, R., 46, 47, 51
Rist, C., 94
Robbins, L. ., 207
Robertson, H., 56
Robinson, E.W., 175, 176
Rodger, N.A.M., 187
Rodriguez-Pose, A., 10
Rossi-Hansberg, E., 120–122
Rouwenhorst, K.G., 144
Ruef, S-J., 207
Ruzé, F., 201

S
Sahin, A., 118
Sakellariou, M.B., 177
Samuelson, P., 38, 40, 41
Savioz, M.R., 161
Say, J.B., 31, 49
Scarpetta, S., 12
Schaps, D.M., 163
Schiller, T., 161
Schultze, C.L., 170
Schumpeter, J.A., 47–49, 75, 91
Schütrumpf, E., 202, 205
Scott, M.G., 53
Sekunda, N., 177, 178
Seligman, B., 40
Sen, A., 47, 48
Shipley, N.R., 127, 134, 136
Shipton, K.M.W., 163
Shrivastava, M., 161
Sievers, H., 17
Simon, H.A., 168, 182
Siriopoulos, C., 10
Smile, S., 54, 69, 72
Smith, A., 31, 33, 45–51, 54, 67, 70, 72, 76, 84, 86
Smith, P., 56–59
Solow, R., 78, 88
Sombart, W., 55
Soros, G., 85
Spence, M., 117, 118, 122, 123
Spinelli, F., 135
Stanton, G.R., 181
Stapleton, J., 98
Stephanidis, D., 201
Stiglitz, J., 84, 121, 122
Strack, H., 208

T
Talamo, S., 203
Tawney, R.H., 54, 55, 57, 60
Taylor, J.E., 206
Terezis Chr, 199
Theodorakopoulos, I., 182, 206
Theodorou, E., 210
Thompson, W.E., 163
Thomson, A., 56
Tittler, R., 127, 148
Tobin, J., 35, 36, 38
Trainer, T., 88
Triantafyllou, K.N., 129, 131, 133
Tridimas, G., 163
Tsatsos, T., 181
Tsitsigkos, S., 208
Tullock, G., 167, 170
Turk, M., 32, 38

V
Vasileiadis, P., 210–212, 214
Veblen, T., 166
Vereker, C., 64–67
Vidal-Naquet, P., 202
Vieira, D.N., 103
Vincent, A.L., 148
Voigt, S., 161
von Reden, S., 163
Voulgaris, Chr. S., 206, 208

W
Walker, D., 92, 93
Wallace, W.R., 175
Walras, L., 31, 32, 91–99
Weber, M., 34, 55
Weiss, J., 211, 212
West, E.G., 47
Wicksell, K., 24, 25
Williamson, O.E., 46, 51, 108, 169
Wilson, P., 163
Wong, S., 38, 40

X
Xanthopoulou-Kyriakou, A., 129, 131, 132

Z
Zilibotti, F., 77
Zizioulas, I., 215
Zorzi, A., 128, 131, 132, 135, 148
Zouboulakis, M., 35, 45–51, 168, 183

Subject Index

A

Accountability, 20, 162, 196
Accumulation. *See also* Capital accumulation
  of knowledge, 164, 195
  of rights, 70
  of wealth, 77, 216
Adjustment costs, 10
Advantages
  comparative, 122–124
  of democracy and free market, 7, 18, 192
  of direct democracy, 161, 163, 164, 166–169, 171
  in the division of labour, 45, 47, 50, 51
  geopolitical, 8, 15, 16, 20
  of joint stock companies, 48, 50
  in the large scale production, 50
  of offshoring, 123
  relative, 103
Agency
  government, 104–106, 108, 113, 114
  impartial, 112
  regulating, 113
Anglicanism, 63
Athenian democracy
  durability, 176, 182, 185
  in the Lycurgyan age, 185
  principles and structure
    election by lot, 196–197
    isigoria, 186, 192
    isonomia, 181, 186, 192
    patriotism, 186

B

Balance of payments, 3, 5, 12, 193
  explosive deficits in the, 3
Banking system, 135
Bank of Greece, 11
Bankruptcy
  bailing Greece from, 17
  open, 14, 19, 20
Banks
  in ancient Athens, 186, 191
  nationalization of, 6
  too big-to-fail, 19
Barriers to entry, 5–7. *See also* Competition
Behaviour, 9, 21, 35, 37, 41, 60, 63, 66, 85, 104, 108, 165, 166, 171
  opportunistic, 108
Beliefs
  erroneous, 106
  incorrect, 104, 106
  system of, 61, 106
Bullion, 35
Bureaucracy, 86, 105

C

Capital accumulation
  process of, 45
  and technological unemployment, 81
Capitalism. *See also* Consumerism
  break down of, 79
  family, 147
  institutions of, 215
  the spirit of, 53
  steady growth of, 54
Classical Athens. *See also* Direct democracy
  accountability in, 20
  growth and prosperity in, 169
  public education in, 166
  seapower of, 176, 182–184

G.C. Bitros, N.C. Kyriazis (eds.), *Essays in Contemporary Economics*,
DOI 10.1007/978-3-319-10043-2

Classical Athens. (*cont.*)
taxation in, 162
warfare in, 182, 185, 186
Collective services. *See* Social services
Comparative advantage. *See* Advantages
Competition
capture theory of, 113
from European countries, 20
free, 55, 80, 93
international, 3
and market failures, 84
Competitiveness, 3, 12, 121
Complexity, 33, 67, 72, 86, 103
of the economy, 67, 86
Concepts of
anti-psychologism, 32, 40
classical mechanics, 36, 38
classical physics, 31, 37, 40, 41
economic calculus, 34
economic man, 40
formalism, 32
marginal utility, 36
non-profit (production), 86
psychophysics, 34, 40
saturation, 79
stationary state, 75
Consumerism, 86. *See also* Capitalism; Preferences
Contracting
collective, 7
individual, 7, 93, 108
rational, 93, 98
theory of, 32, 98, 181
Contracts. *See also* Contracting
in the case of concessions, 108
oral, 144
private, 194
Convergence
financial assistance and, 8–10
regional, 9
Cost of
Greece's bail out, 19, 20
living, 209
production, 81, 83, 87, 120, 121, 123
syssitia, 202, 203
Credibility, 169
Currency
in ancient Greece, 192, 193
floating of the, 124
in relation to bullion, 35

D

Deficit
in the balance of payments, 3, 12, 193
spending, 79, 80, 84
in the state budget, 80, 205
Delocalization of industry, 82
Direct democracy
optimal properties of, 95, 96
as practiced in classical Greece, 162
Distribution
of income, 78, 108
of wealth, 78, 92, 199–216
Disturbances, 19, 37

E

EC. *See* European Commission (EC)
ECB. *See* European central bank (ECB)
Economic growth
in ancient Greece, 168
in emerging countries, 5, 124
export led, 5, 124
impacts of tax policy on, 4, 124
peace and, 64
role of credit in, 3, 150
role of institutions in, 168
Economic integration. *See* Integration
Economic policies
credit, 6
employment-unemployment, 85
industrial, 6
interventionist, 86
macroeconomic, 16, 51
monetary, 4
welfare, 79, 87, 167
Economics
behavioural, 104
heterodox, 41
household, 199
institutional, 163
mainstream, 32, 35, 38–41, 106
methodology of, 32, 35–41
new institutional, 51, 106–107
orthodox, 32, 37
positive, 39
of public choice, 170
EEC. *See* European Economic Community (EEC)
Efficiency
economic, 63, 164, 169, 183, 209
material, 94
relative, 104
technical, 77
EMS. *See* European monetary system (EMS)
EMU. *See* European Monetary Union (EMU)
Energy. *See* Principles of Maximum Energy
Enforcement. *See* Sanctions
Enlightenment, 61–68, 71, 78, 79
Enterprise culture, 53, 57
Equality. *See also* Opportunities

of conditions, 95, 97
Equilibrium, 35, 36, 38, 46, 91, 92, 95, 124
Ethical norms, 166
in ancient Athens, 166
Ethics. *See also* Principles of, ethics
contractarian foundation of, 94
entrepreneurial, 53
foundations of, 62, 94
medical, 40, 93, 94, 181
professional, 85
European central bank (ECB), 25
European Commission (EC)
actions on Greece, 7, 10, 20
views on Greece's accession, 8
European Economic Community (EEC). *See also* Treaty of Rome
Greece's association with, 4, 7, 15
European integration. *See also* Integration
Greece and, 13
European monetary system (EMS), 19
European Monetary Union (EMU)
Greece's entry to, 5
European Union (EU), 3–21
Externalities, 166, 167

F
Fairness
business ethics and, 135
justice as, 95
Financial assistance
the debacle of, 9–10
from the European Union, 9, 10, 16
growth promoting investments and, 10
Truman Doctrine and, 15
Financial system, 19, 135–143, 149
Fiscal cliff, 17
Forces of dissent, 70
Free market economy
and democracy, 7, 18
Free trade, 69–71, 73

G
Game(s)
athletic, 176
in ancient Greece, 176
continuous, 169, 170
cooperative, 169, 170
dynamic, 169
period of the, 169
rules of the, 169
German Agency for Reconstruction (GAR), 26
German Central Bank, 25
Globalization
causes of, 118, 122
consequences of, 82, 120
Goods. *See also* Public goods
bulk, 186
essential, 66, 79
luxury, 79
material, 83, 211
repetitive, 80, 83–85
traditional, 79
Greek economy
and investment opportunities, 24, 26
nearly closed, 3
structurally unprepared, 6, 7
Greek governments and
EU authorities, 4, 8, 10–13, 19
financial assistance, 8, 10
structural reforms, 4, 5, 10–13, 17, 20

H
Human capital
and education, 79, 82, 122
investment in, 80, 87
and productivity, 79, 81, 87, 122
role in development, 81, 87, 88
Human needs, 81. *See also* Concepts of, saturation
Human rights, 93, 124, 165

I
Income
convergence in per capita, 8, 9, 117
distribution of national, 9, 117
Individualism
and democracy, 179
economic, 56, 60
independent, 56
possessive, 64
religious, 56, 59–61, 64–66
Individual rights, 179
Industrial revolution
business leadership in, 69
theology during, 63, 64, 69, 72, 73
Inequality, 76, 88, 95–98, 165, 202
regional, 9
Information
extant, 162, 178
imperfect, 103
new technologies of, 81, 82
perfect, 104
public, 50
symmetric, 169, 171
Institutions
defined, 106

Institutions (*cont.*)
democratic, 18, 171, 202
efficient, 103
failure, 6, 10, 19–20
feeble, 10
and financial assistance, 10
and the free market, 7, 18
performance in ancient Greece, 6
structure of, 6, 51
surprising, 103–115
Integration
economic, 13
European, 13
of knowledge, 164, 171
regional, 213, 215
Interest rate
natural, 24
nominal, 26
policies, 24–26
real, 24

J
Judicial system, 136, 162
county courts, 108–114
Justice. *See also* fairness
distributive, 92, 94–97

L
Laws
called corn, 72
called poor, 57, 70
in economics, 37
empirical, 37
of the mind, 61
of physics, 37
precise, 59
rational, 37, 60
Loans
mortgage, 134–139, 143, 145–147
open-ended, 138
promissory notes, 135, 136, 138–140, 144

M
Management
ideologies of, 68
joint stock or associated, 48, 50
principles of
by hired servants, 50
by the individual, 50
Market failures, 86. *See also* Competition
Marshall Plan, 15, 87, 88
Merchant house, 148
Middle class(es)
in advanced societies, 118
emerging, 117–120, 124
in emerging countries, 118, 119, 122–124
and the market, 117–125
Moral values. *See* Values

N
National bank of Greece, 11
Natural rights, 71, 181
Networks
entrepreneurial, 86
infrastructural, 86
social, 167
New technologies
implications of, 81–82, 87
ladder of, 122

O
Offshoring. *See also* Globalization
advantages in manufacturing, 123, 124
effects of, 120, 121
evolutionary practice known as, 120, 122, 123
process of, 122, 123, 125
Opportunities
equal for all, 26, 95
for investment, 24, 26
for social mobility, 69
Options
policy, 167, 169
trading of real, 24
Outsourcing, 119, 124, 125
Ownership
common, 203, 206
joint, 206, 207
land, 62, 207
private, 63
public, 203, 204

P
Political parties, 7, 162, 191
Preferences
consumer, 46, 84
individual, 84, 171
over public policies, 164, 169, 171
Principles of
ethics, 32, 93
governance in ancient Athens, 18, 192
human behavior

greatest happiness, 32, 34
utilitarian or egotistic, 32, 94
justice in democracy, 18, 93, 98
maximization, 33
optimization, 33, 36, 38
political economy, 32, 49
social justice, 95, 98
Principles of Maximum Energy, 32
Problem of principal-agent, 48–50
Property
land, 107, 108, 111–114, 146, 148, 192
landowners, 108
Property rights, 4, 6, 103, 104, 107–114, 165, 167–169, 171
Protestantism
entrepreneurial, 73
and individualism, 56
puritan, 56, 72
radical, 68
Public goods, 163, 166. *See also* Goods
Public interest, 162
Puritanism, 54, 55, 57, 61

R
Regulation. *See also* Competition
capture theory of, 113
Religion
and entrepreneurship, 53, 54
freedom in, 56, 67, 70, 72
as a source of moral values, 60
Resourcing, 124, 125
Rights. *See* Human rights; Natural rights; Property rights; Social, rights; Voting rights; Individual rights

S
Sanctions
legal, 166
social, 149
Shocks
domestic, 20
from entering into EU, 19, 20
External, 20
Slavery, 70, 205
Social. *See also* Values; Voting rights
cohesion, 181, 186
contract, 93, 98, 181
integration, 213
norms, 51, 106
rights, 124
values, 163, 166
Social services
education, 54, 79
environment, 68, 86, 168
health, 79, 86
transportation, 62
Solidarity, 16, 80, 86, 88, 99, 180, 181, 186, 210
Specialization
of labour, 47, 48
in production, 48
Speculation, 80, 83–85, 129
Stationary state, 75–88
Statism, 12

T
Technological change, 121
Thrift, 53, 55, 59, 61, 66, 69, 70
Trade unions, 191
Treaty of Maastricht, 12
Treaty of Rome, 4, 5, 7–9, 11, 14, 16, 20
Truman doctrine, 15
Trust, 48, 66, 105, 108–110, 147, 149, 169, 180, 181, 184–187, 192, 194
Types of social organization. *See also* Capitalism
communism, 203
socialism, 216

U
Uncertainty, 24, 46, 49, 103, 107, 115, 168
Unemployment. *See also* Economic policies
causes of
delocalization of industry, 82
lack of investment, 81
structural, 17
technological, 77
welfare policies, 82
Utilitarianism. *See* Principles of

V
Values
in classical Greece, 175–187
in Victorian times, 53
Venice
Greek community of, 130–133, 148, 149
Voting rights, 176

W
Welfare state, 80

MIX
Papier aus verantwortungsvollen Quellen
Paper from responsible sources
FSC® C105338

If you have any concerns about our products,
you can contact us on
ProductSafety@springernature.com

In case Publisher is established outside the EU,
the EU authorized representative is:
Springer Nature Customer Service Center GmbH
Europaplatz 3, 69115 Heidelberg, Germany

Printed by Libri Plureos GmbH
in Hamburg, Germany